How to Win You

How to Win Your Case

Sandy Kemp

Bloomsbury Professional

LONDON · DUBLIN · EDINBURGH · NEW YORK · NEW DELHI · SYDNEY

BLOOMSBURY PROFESSIONAL

Bloomsbury Publishing Plc

50 Bedford Square, London, WC1B 3DP

BLOOMSBURY and the Diana logo are trademarks of Bloomsbury Publishing Plc

© Bloomsbury Professional 2020

British Library Cataloguing-in-Publication Data

A catalogue record for this book is available from the British Library.

ISBN:	PB:	978 1 52651 678 7
	Epdf:	978 1 52651 676 3
	Epub:	978 1 52651 677 0

Typeset by Compuscript Ltd, Shannon
Printed and bound by CPI Group (UK) Ltd, Croydon, CR0 4YY

To find out more about our authors and books visit
www.bloomsburyprofessional.com. Here you will find extracts, author information,
details of forthcoming events and the option to sign up for our newsletters

To my children Valerie, Sylvia, Robert and Andrew.

Preface

When I started as a trainee solicitor in 1982 the world was a very different place. Copies were taken by carbon paper. Corrections were made by a white fluid called Tippex. The law was found in books. Messages were sent by letter or telephone. As a court solicitor I dealt with all kinds of issues, including personal injury claims, family law, commercial disputes, insolvency issues, criminal law, and employment cases. Employment law had not yet had the explosion of new rights and duties and European laws had yet to make much of an impact.

I would go to court, or to a tribunal, most days. Almost everything was done in person. When changes to pleadings were made, you used scissors and a stapler to add them physically to what was there, leading to a document that looked a bit like origami. When attending court, much time was spent waiting, but that meant that you could watch and listen to others, most very good, some less so, and learn from them. More experienced practitioners would give you tips, occasionally even whispered to you in the middle of your presentation to the court. They were also the days when legal aid was available to large numbers of people, and the cost of litigation was more moderate.

That way of learning is far removed from what happens currently, and is beyond the realms of possibility for those who are not lawyers. Those who do have a legal career specialise very early, and appearances in courts or tribunals are far less frequent than I enjoyed, as so much now is done electronically. Huge amounts of information are now accessible online. Legal aid coverage has been successively reduced, and the rates at which it is paid cut so that fewer lawyers now offer that. The cost of instructing a lawyer has increased. Far more people therefore decide, or are required, to act for themselves, or ask family, friends or others to do that for them. That is all before the effects of the Covid-19 pandemic are considered, with hearings taking place remotely.

When I left private practice and became an Employment judge, I found that I was on trains many days a week, or staying at some hotel somewhere. That provided me with the time to start writing down my experiences and thoughts about how a case in a court or tribunal could be conducted, by either party, from start to finish. I used my long experience of making mistakes, things that I had tried which worked, the experience of conducting cases in courts and tribunals, including at appeals up to the Supreme Court, what I had learned from watching others, and the teaching of advocacy that I had undertaken. I have tried to make the book one that someone with no legal experience of any kind would be able to read in a day, understand, and put into practice. I also wished to make it helpful for lawyers starting out their career, or in the middle of it. The attempt to keep it to a reasonable length means that it is not comprehensive, and I have left out areas that others may think I should have covered. These are not easy balances to strike, but I hope that I have mostly succeeded.

There are almost no references to the law, either substantive law on rights and obligations, or matters of procedure or evidence. The book concentrates on practicality, and gives examples of the points being made both as a demonstration of that and so that it might be a basis for drafting by someone who has no idea of where to start. This has limitations, as there are no right and wrong ways to do that, and what is presented is only my own style. There are many other styles, which some will think can be more effective, but I hope that this is a useful start for those who need it, and food for thought for those who do not.

I would like to acknowledge the assistance I have had over my career from certain people in particular. When I was a trainee solicitor Denis Yule gave me a great deal of time, and guidance, on how litigation should be conducted. Later I worked extensively with three Queen's Counsel and learned many techniques and tips from doing so. The first is Ian Truscott QC, one of the UK's leading employment lawyers who has recently retired from the bar but still sits as an Employment Judge, who achieved the most remarkable win against all odds that I saw in my career, the second Mike Jones QC, later Lord Jones, a Court of Session Judge who has very sadly passed away, who inspired me to become a solicitor advocate, and to teach advocacy, and the third John Cavanagh QC who is now a High Court judge who I was lucky enough to have been led by at a case that ended with success for our clients in the Supreme Court.

I have been fortunate to work with a large number of excellent practitioners both as partners and colleagues who are too numerous to name individually, but I might mention two former partners, David Burnside and Peter Anderson whose styles were entirely different but endlessly effective. I gained many insights into effective negotiation and ways to resolve disputes during mediation sessions with John Sturrock.

I would like to thank Andy Hill, Jane Bradford and Jenny Lank of Bloomsbury Publishing for their help and support in completing the book, with Jane in particular saving me from grammatical and other infelicities. Any that remain are my responsibility.

Finally I wish to thank my partner, Fiona, for her many helpful comments in revising the drafts, and the happy times spent during the writing of the book.

Sandy Kemp
September 2020

Contents

Source materials

General	ACAS website (acas.org.uk)
	HM Government website (gov.uk)
	Citizens Advice Bureau website (citizensadvice.org.uk)
Unfair Dismissal	Employment Rights Act 1996, Part X
	ACAS Code of Practice: Disciplinary and Grievance Procedures
	ACAS Guide: Discipline and Grievances at Work
Discrimination	Equality Act 2010
	Equality and Human Rights Commission: Code of Practice on Employment
	Equality and Human Rights Commission: Code of Practice on Equal Pay
	Secretary of State – Guidance on matters to be taken into account in determining questions relating to the definition of disability
Redundancy	Employment Rights Act 1996, Part XI
	Trade Union and Labour Relations (Consolidation) Act 1992, Part IV, Chapter II
	Department of Business, Energy and Industrial Strategy website gov.uk/government/organisations/department-for-business-energy-and-industrial-strategy
Whistleblowing	Employment Rights Act 1996, s 43A–43L and 103A
	Public Concern at Work (now Protect) website (protect-advice.org.uk/)
Health and safety at work	Employment Rights Act 1996, ss 44 and 100
Holidays	Working Time Regulations 1998, SI 1998/1833
	HM Government website

Breach of Contract	Employment Tribunals Extension of Jurisdiction (England and Wales) Order 1994, SI 1994/1623
	Employment Tribunals Extension of Jurisdiction (Scotland) Order 1994, SI 1994/1624
Data Protection	General Data Protection Regulation (GDPR) (Regulation EU 2016/679)
	Data Protection Act 2018
	HM Government guide to GDPR
	Information Commissioner – Data Protection Code: Employment Practices
	Subject Access Code of Practice
Procedure	
(i) Employment Tribunals	Employment Tribunals (Constitution and Rules of Procedure) Regulations 2013, SI 2013/1237, Sch 1
	Employment Tribunals Practice Directions (Joint, or for England and Wales, or Scotland)
	Employment Tribunals Presidential Guidance (Joint, or for England and Wales, or Scotland)
(ii) Court	Civil Procedure Rules 1998, SI 1998/3132 (England and Wales)
	Act of Sederunt (Sheriff Court Ordinary Cause Rules 1993, SI 1993/1956 (Scotland)
	(There are also Simple Procedure Rules and Small Claims Rules)

Chapter 1

Introduction

Litigation is the word used for a process by which disputes, which people or organisations have not been able to resolve themselves, are determined by the decision of someone independent who acts as a judge. It can cover a very wide range of subject matters and contexts in different courts or tribunals but the main ways of resolving the matter are generally the same.

Fewer people have access to legal aid than before, and the cost of instructing lawyers is for many simply too high. Those who do not have access to legal help can and do conduct the case themselves, ask friends or family to do so, or ask for help from various voluntary organisations such as the Citizens Advice Bureaux (CAB), Law Clinics, or campaign groups. Lawyers who are fairly early in their careers, or not used to dealing with litigation, find that conducting a case is not easy. For all involved in the process who have limited or no experience it can be quite daunting. This book provides some help.

The conduct of litigation is far more an art than a science, and there are many ways of conducting it. There is no right and wrong way to do so. The aim of this book is to give some guidance based on my own long experience both pursing and defending cases, some of it bitter; from my simply watching others and learning from those who were highly skilled at it; and from my teaching of litigation techniques for both lawyers and non-lawyers. This book has been kept reasonably short, which means that it does not purport to cover everything.

Fighting a case in a court or tribunal can be very difficult. The process is complex, there is a great deal to think about, and learning how to do it well is something even the most experienced and best advocates may never fully achieve. It is though possible to learn how to do it adequately, or to do it more effectively, and the intention is that all who read this book will be able to prepare for and present a case with a better chance of success.

The book takes the reader through the various stages in the process, whether making or defending a claim, has some basic source materials that might help start research in employment disputes, and then an Appendix with examples of documents in a case, including questions, submissions, and an outline of what a decision could look like.

This means that book is a form of toolbox. Whether the tools are the right ones, and how exactly to use them, will be a matter for the person conducting the case. Having a good paintbrush, paints and canvas do not make a good painter. What really matters is the skill of the person using them. The hope is that the advice about what some of the tools are and how best to use them will help the reader to do so more effectively, increasing the chances of success.

Chapter 2

The Basics

Terminology

The words used in litigation, whether in a court or tribunal, can be confusing. They become second nature to lawyers who are there regularly, and are used almost automatically. If during any hearing you are not aware of what a term means, then (unless you are a lawyer when you really ought to know) it is best to ask. But some preparation in advance can help.

The person making the decision is usually called a **judge**, but the terminology differs across jurisdictions, and sometimes it is made by a panel of three including a judge. The terminology of the litigants, and those advising and representing them, can also vary. The person making the claim can be called **claimant,** plaintiff, pursuer or similar terms. The claimant is usually an individual but can also be a company or organisation. The claim is made against another person, or organisation, usually called the **respondent,** defendant, defender or similar terms.

Parties can represent themselves, and if say a claimant is representing herself she is often called a **litigant-in-person**, or party litigant. Representatives for the party can be lawyers, known as counsel or barristers or advocates, including Queens Counsel (these are all lawyers who specialise in appearing in courts or tribunals) or solicitors and solicitor advocates (who are lawyers who both appear in some or all courts or tribunals but also are involved more directly in preparing a case or defence), or non-lawyers such as trade union officials, paid or unpaid unqualified representatives, representatives from professional bodies, unpaid volunteers such as from the CAB and other volunteers from third sector organisations, or they can be family members or friends. In some cases there can be more than one respondent; they are then called first respondent, second respondent and so on. There can also be more than one claimant where the circumstances allow that, but that is more rare.

For simplicity I shall refer to the person who makes the decision as the judge, the person making the claim as the claimant, the organisation defending it as the respondent, and the representative as **advocate** (whether as a lawyer or paid or unpaid adviser).

The place where the dispute is litigated might be a **court**, or a **tribunal**, or similar term. They are much the same, but not exactly so. They have different rules of procedure, and a different basis in law. Courts tend to be more formal, with more formal rules about appearing there (sometimes only parties or lawyers can attend), and conduct their proceedings more formally (for example the judge and lawyers may wear gowns, those who appear may require to stand up when addressing the court, and there may be use of more formal language). Tribunals can be Employment Tribunals and a series of other tribunals covering areas such as benefits, immigration and tax.

A list of some of some of the issues that are dealt with in courts, and some of the main issues dealt with in tribunals, is in the Source Materials section of the book. It is important to check that the court or tribunal you take your case in is the correct one. Tribunals are established by Act of Parliament or Statutory Instrument, and only have the ability to hear a case they are given responsibility for, called their jurisdiction. Sometimes the claim can only be made in one court or tribunal. For example a claim for damages from a car accident can only be made in court and a claim for unfair dismissal can only be made in an Employment Tribunal. Sometimes there is a choice, such as a claim for breach of a contract of employment by an employee, which can be either taken in court, or a tribunal (subject to various rules and limits). At other times which court can hear the case depends on how much is sought, or what the issue in dispute is.

What may in practice be the most significant difference between a court and tribunal is over the **cost** of litigation. In the tribunal, most often costs, or legal expenses, are not awarded to the party who wins. Each side generally pays its own costs, if they have them. In court it is different. The general rule is that the side who wins recovers all, or a proportion, of its costs or legal expenses from the losing side, and that applies even if the losing side is not legally represented. If therefore you are conducting your own case and lose, you might end up liable for thousands, or tens of thousands, or more, pounds in those legal expenses.

Related to that difference are provisions on representation. In most tribunals anyone can appear to represent a party, and that allows friends, relatives, unqualified advisers, or paid or unpaid advisers to do so, as well as lawyers. In court however the rules are different, and are different depending on which court hears the case. Generally representation is by lawyers, but it is possible for a person to act for him or herself, and it can be possible for a non-lawyer to appear in at least some cases in some courts. It can help to check that with the clerk of the court involved.

Documents in a case can mean what are normally thought of as documents such as contracts and letters, but also emails, social media posts, photographs, audio files, video recordings, models, items used in an incident, spreadsheets, maps, drawings, and anything else that is in a physical form They are normally collated into a single volume, with an index at the front and page numbers, called a Bundle of Documents, but in some courts each side prepares its own set, either called a Bundle or something like an Inventory of Productions, and there may be a number of these inventories for each party (labelled as First Inventory, Second Inventory and so on).

Some other terms are explained as they arise later.

Aim

The aim in litigation, whether it is being pursued or defended, is summed up by this quotation:

> 'You ask, what is our aim? I can answer in one word. It is victory' – Winston Churchill

The aim of litigation can be misunderstood. Quite often people describe litigation as a search for the truth. Truth is a slippery concept. It can change dependent on factors that include the point of view, the pleadings, the nature of evidence given or not allowed to be given, and details of the questions asked. In litigation the judge might try to find out, as best one can, what happened, and to that extent litigation does involve a search for truth, but it goes far beyond that.

There is also sometimes a view that litigation is about obtaining justice. Justice can however be a rather subjective concept. Almost by definition the result one side thinks just, because it has succeeded, the other may well feel unjust, because it has failed. What in essence happens is that the judge gives an opinion on both issues of fact, and the law, and gives what is believed to be a just decision. There is therefore a search for justice by the judge who has applied the law as it then stands. The law changes, and sometimes it does so as a result of the outcome of a case where the view is that that result is not appropriate.

In some situations the case can be about entitlement, such as the entitlement to holiday pay in an employment tribunal, or to benefits or to remain in the country in other forms of tribunal, and the party conducting the case on the other side can be the government, either as employer or not, with all the resources of the state, rather than another private individual or organisation.

Ultimately, litigation is usually about winning (and losing) a particular legal dispute within the rules of the process. The aim is to try to win that dispute, whatever that means in the context of the case. In some cases being defended it may be not so much about winning, but not losing too badly. For some it is all about how much is awarded, as the amount is indicative of the degree of success. For others it is not at all about money but establishing a principle. In some cases, there is not necessarily a winner and loser – for example in inquiries into deaths where the purpose is to ascertain what happened and try and ensure that it does not happen again. The majority of litigation however is conducted in the currency of money, with some form of financial award made or not made. It is very rare indeed where it can be said that there are two winners, more often one wins and one loses, and sometimes the result means that both lose. A large number of cases are not taken to a final stage because of an agreement to resolve it, when the parties themselves choose the outcome.

The exercise is not directly one to search for the truth, but to try to secure a successful outcome within the rules that apply. That essential aim affects how the case is conducted.

The basic structure of a case

Cases almost always have three parts – fact, law and analysis. The **facts** are what is found by the judge to have happened. That can be a combination of what the parties agree did happen, the terms of written documents such as contracts or letters, and what the judge decides is likely to have happened. What the judge decides happened is most often what is more important.

The judge then decides on the relevant **law**. Often there is little dispute on that, but on other occasions that is all that the dispute is about. Frequently the dispute is a mix of issues – deciding issues of fact which are disputed and determining the relevant law to be applied to those facts.

There is then an **analysis** applying the law to the facts, and a decision reached which can include a remedy if the claimant succeeds. Litigation is not a simple process, but, stripped to its basic essentials, that is its structure.

The facts and the law are different concepts and are treated differently, but the law has an influence on the facts. The law can direct what facts are, or are not, relevant, and what can or cannot be taken into account. The law can limit some evidence, or shape it or exclude it altogether. The law can also prevent a case from being heard at all, so that the facts are never established, for example if the claim is made too late. What law applies varies according to the case, and cannot be covered in a book of this size and kind, but some source materials for employment cases are provided as a starting point, and some guidance is given in **Chapter 8** on how to find out about the law that applies to the case you are dealing with.

As a very basic example of the three-stage process if someone's contract of employment has been terminated, without giving any notice (which is normally called a summary dismissal), that will be a breach of contract unless doing so was justified. Justification is where the employee has acted in a way which breaches the contract to a significant extent, in what is called a repudiatory way, and if that happens the employer is allowed to terminate the contract without notice. That is the law that applies. It is the facts of what happened that will lead to the decision whether or not there has been that significant breach or not. If the employee did breach the contract to a sufficient extent, there will not have been a breach of contract by the employer ending it immediately, but otherwise there will be, the employer will be in breach of contract, and the employee will be entitled to damages. The judge must establish the facts, determine the law, and then apply the law to the facts to reach a decision, including what the remedy should be if the claimant succeeds. What the remedy will be is another area where there will be fact, law and analysis. Depending on the analysis the award may be a large sum, nothing or somewhere in between.

I have used the example of a case of breach of contract as that is a claim encountered frequently, and the basic principles are not unduly complex. They are found widely across the world. I will use the example of an employment dispute, as that is an area where litigants themselves, or unqualified representatives, very often appear. It is also part of the case in the Appendix.

Let us assume that Linda was employed by VHS Ltd. Her contract said that she was entitled to notice unless she was guilty of gross misconduct. She was then suspected of being involved in dishonesty. It was investigated. A manager heard the internal disciplinary hearing and decided to dismiss without notice. She appealed, and that was heard by another manager, who refused the appeal. Linda then made a claim for the notice she did not receive (she had a choice of whether to do so in a court or employment tribunal in the UK).

Whether you are Linda and starting the claim, or VHS Ltd and about to defend it, the same basic information is needed. What is the claim for and why? These can involve questions which are pure facts, or a mix of fact and law. The addressing of these questions has various phases:

1   The first is to find out what happened, and gather evidence of that. That is all part of the investigation. What is also required is the context in which the events happened, and the law that applies. That guides what is relevant and what may not be. So the first phase is investigation both of the facts and the law. It can also involve negotiation of the claim, which can continue, or start, at any point from the first to last phases. Cases have been negotiated just before an appeal was due to be heard.

2   The second is putting the claim, or defence, into writing, which is usually called pleading. That gives the other side advance notice of what is being claimed, and why, or why the claim is being defended. The importance of it is that if something is not pled, it may not be possible to lead evidence about it, or seek the remedy you wish.

3   The third is moving towards the hearing of evidence, and is usually called case management. It can be very important, for example if there is a preliminary matter raised that may end the claim before it has begun, such as if it has been started too late.

4   The fourth is the preparation for the hearing of evidence. Preparation is something that lies underneath all well-conducted litigation, and is the foundation for all that follows.

5   The fifth is the conduct of that hearing of evidence, and is usually called the advocacy.

6   The sixth and last phase is the result, and reacting to that, and may be called the outcome. It can include an appeal.

The book shall consider each of these six phases in turn. They are naturally inter-related. One theme that runs through them all is the importance of good preparation. Putting it another way, the foundation for each stage, and what is hoped to be a good outcome, is how well the case is investigated, managed, and then prepared for in advance of the hearing before the judge. All that preparation is less exciting, if that is the right word, than the advocacy, but it is the basis of the advocacy. If there is some gap in preparation, something missed or not appreciated or followed up, that can lead to the old adage that of 'for a h'aporth of tar the ship was lost' applying, which means that a small hole left because of skimping on one point of detail in the hull eventually sinks the whole ship. Something seemingly small can cost you the case.

The reason why cases go to the stage of a hearing is very often because both sides think that they will win. One will not and sometimes neither really does. The margin between success and failure being narrow, at least potentially, often what makes the difference is not apparent until towards the very end. So the better prepared side has an advantage, and that may in some cases at least be determinative. Hard work can win the case. Do not assume that the better prepared side is the one with lawyers acting, or the one that you are on. The truth is that it is very difficult indeed to know how well the other side are prepared, or will be by the time the hearing commences or concludes. It is best to proceed on the assumption that the other side have prepared as well as they possibly could. You should do the same.

Chapter 3

Investigation

Introduction

The first stage of any potential claim or case is finding out what happened, and the basic law applicable. It has the effect of providing a frame for the case. That is not just an exercise in gathering evidence, although that is a very important part of it. It is also an exercise in finding out what the law is. That can be difficult for those not legally qualified, or not experienced.

It is very easy to jump to conclusions, or make assumptions. Things can seem very straightforward at first glance. But rarely is the first glance the best one. Usually, with investigation, the details uncovered mean that the impression can change substantially. I have always liked the following comments of Mr Justice Megarry in an old case called *John v Rees* [1970] Ch 345:

> ''As everybody who has anything to do with the law well knows, the path of the law is strewn with examples of open and shut cases which, somehow, were not; of unanswerable charges which, in the event, were completely answered; of inexplicable conduct which was fully explained; of fixed and unalterable determination that, by discussion, suffered a change'.

Normally however the first part of the investigation is the factual one, but that is more than simply what happened. There are some important aspects that are frequently overlooked. I suggest that the order should follow this basic structure:

(i) **Which parties are involved?** It is essential to identify the correct legal entities. Is the claimant an individual? Is the respondent an individual, or limited company, a limited liability partnership or a more general partnership, or an association of some kind such as a social club, or some other legal entity? If so, which one? If there is a trading name used, which legal entity is involved? That may be difficult to discover if only a trading name is used, as that trading name may be used by a number of different companies, or used by different entities at different times. If there is a public register to check that, such as Companies House in the UK, a register of properties kept for rates, the electoral roll, a telephone directory, websites and social media, do that. Much of the information is available online. If the entity is a limited company, or limited liability partnership, it should have a number issued by Companies House, and some form of registered office as well as having a trading office address. It is helpful to check these details, and use them to advantage.

If Linda does not check, and sues VHS Ltd, where the company is called VHS (Stores) Ltd, that may be seized on by the company's lawyers.

(ii) **Why is there a claim?** This means what law is involved – is it breach of contract which is a common law concept, meaning that it does not come from Parliament but the law developed over centuries and from a variety of sources. Is it from legislation, such as, in the UK, an Act of Parliament, or Statutory Instrument? Does it derive from a European Union Directive, or an international treaty or instrument? What cases are important?

For example if there is a claim of breach of contract there may also be a claim for unfair dismissal from the Employment Rights Act 1996, or a claim for discrimination which is normally from the Equality Act 2010, but can also have come from a European Union Directive (although this might increasingly be less important after Brexit). Knowing the legal basis to take the claim is fundamentally important. There may be a large number of cases which explain how the law is applied. Guidance can be found from various organisations and online, and there are some source materials set out at p ix to provide a start for that.

(iii) **When must it be commenced?** The concept of the timebar is critical in litigation. It means that there is a period of time for making the claim, and if it is made outside that time period then it may be too late. It doesn't necessarily matter that the claim is a very good one, a very important one, or a very valuable one, if it is late you may not be able to make it at all. The period of time can be measured in years – and in the case of breach of contract it may be five years (in Scotland) or six (in England and Wales). It can also be measured in months – for example most but not all claims in the Employment Tribunal must be commenced by starting Early Conciliation with ACAS within three months. It can also be measured in days – for example a claim for interim relief in an Employment Tribunal if the dismissal relates to trade union activities, health and safety or whistleblowing, in which case the time limit is seven days and Early Conciliation is not required so the Claim can be presented to the Tribunal (sent in) immediately.

(iv) **What are the basic relevant facts?** This means what happened, but focusing on what is important for the claim being made. In the example of the breach of contract claim by Linda, the key facts are what the contract is, whether or not items were dishonestly obtained, how it occurred, how much was involved, when and how important that is. Linda may also tell you that she found the work challenging, that she had time off work for stress two years before, or that her partner had been promoted, and they had spent the night before out celebrating until late into the night. Are those facts, which may be true, of any importance to the case? Are they relevant to the dispute?

(v)   **What documents exist that relate to the relevant facts?** In the example these will be the contract of employment, if one exists in writing, correspondence such as the letter confirming the termination of the contract without notice, written notes of meetings, payslips and other evidence of what has been lost financially. The term 'documents' can include any evidence, such as audio or video recordings and is discussed later.

(vi)   **Who might be a witness?** That includes someone present at a meeting, or who saw what happened, or heard it, or was involved immediately after it, as well as those who investigated the allegations, and heard the disciplinary hearing or appeal. Some witnesses are not witnesses of fact, but experts who provide opinions where that is required.

It is usually a good idea to start writing things down. The human memory is notoriously fallible. People forget detail. They try their best to remember accurately what happened, but the memory is filtered by factors such as upset, stress, self-interest, partiality, and many others. If you are Linda, as soon as you can, write a detailed account of what happened somewhere – in a diary, or on a computer, or on a scrap of paper. Most decision makers like to make decisions based on more than just an impression of how someone performs when giving evidence. Some of those who are very honest are not good witnesses. Some of those who lie do so, at least superficially, very convincingly. The power of the document is something to remember, and even documents created after the event can be helpful.

If you are representing Linda, ask her if she has done that, get that document if she has, and if not get her to start writing things down now. Documents as close in time to the event are helpful evidence, but there is nothing to be lost by doing one later, even quite a bit later. It will be more current than waiting until just before the final hearing, which is likely to be months or more away yet.

In addition to writing the events down, it helps to write down answers to each of the issues set out above, and start having both a plan to move forward, and a record of what was thought. That record can change, be added to, parts removed and replaced, or started again later, but it helps to keep details both available, and able to be worked with.

The differential diagnosis

Doctors have a process for considering at a first meeting what condition the patient might have. It is sometimes called a differential diagnosis. It is a kind of working guess as to what the condition is. What do they do then? They never proceed on that diagnosis alone, but carry out tests, checks, investigations and assessments to establish if it is the correct one, or not. That is a good guide for litigation too. Do not just proceed on the basis of your first assessment, or initial thoughts. Check it as thoroughly as time, cost, opportunity and common sense allows.

Where there may be witnesses, try to speak to them as quickly as possible. Sometimes getting to do that is not easy. If you have left the employment, and the witness is still at the employer, it may be necessary to ask permission to do that at the workplace, or try to find contact details and ask to see them outside work. If you are not sure if someone might help, ask anyway or try and get a message passed to them by someone else, such as a mutual friend or colleague, or just using social media. If they might be useful, find out if they are or not.

When you meet the witness, you are trying to find out what they know. That is not as easy as it might appear. It is possible to ask them if they agree with you that what happened was as you describe it. That involves asking a leading question, and that is called leading as the question leads to the answer, which is usually either yes or no. It is a limiting type of question. It is better not to ask that, but to ask an open question. Open questions are very different, and do not have as an answer yes or no.

How do you ask open questions? You don't start them with words like 'Did'. You start them with words like 'who', 'what', 'when', 'why' and 'how', or start with words like 'explain', or 'describe'. Those types of questions require a description of some kind, a narrative, not just a yes. Ask therefore questions like: 'What did you see?' Not: 'Did you see me take the money?' How to ask questions is dealt with more fully under 'Advocacy' at **Chapter 7**.

How do you investigate?

In days of old, some police forces taught new recruits this ABC when investigating crimes. I have always thought it very helpful for investigations generally. I understand that it is not used by the police any more, but I suggest that it is still a useful guide to how to investigate facts.

A   stands for **Accept** nothing. You may be told lots of things by people, but they may not be right. Do not make assumptions.

B   stands for **Believe** no one. For the same reason, do not believe what one person says. That may be because they are not telling you the truth, or they are trying to but are mistaken.

C   stands for **Confirm** everything. Try and find another source for the same fact. That may be a document, another witness or something you manage to find by research elsewhere, such as by using online resources.

Why take this trouble? There can be many reasons why what people say may not be right, and if you are the litigant you must include yourself in that. We can all be mistaken. Particularly if the incident was unexpected, stressful, harmful or detrimental in some way, our memory of that might be affected. If the issue was some time ago, the passing days, months or years affect the ability to recall correctly. So try and find evidence that helps to establish that what you, or a witness, believes happened, did happen exactly as described.

That includes searching for supporting documents. They can be very informal such as handwritten notes of meetings or telephone calls, emails, texts or other social media posts. In one case I remember, the witness had written on a letter a mark, which looked like a form of hieroglyphic, or putting it another way, was a squiggle. It was his own shorthand, he said, for making a call to someone and them agreeing with what he suggested. That tiny mark, made in under a second, was ultimately what led to success in defending a claim.

It also includes getting photographs where they exist, or considering taking them if not. A picture can explain things very clearly and convincingly. Try to ensure that it is taken at the right time, showing the right thing, and can be easily seen. If necessary, have it enlarged, or professionally printed, to make it as good as possible. It may in Linda's case show where she worked, how close or far away another part of the store where she worked was, and so on.

Similarly if the place where the event happened is not clear, consider obtaining a plan of it, or having one made up, or just drawing a sketch of it yourself. For example, an office layout showing the location of the desks people worked at, who sat where, where the door was and so on.

Evidence may exist from sources that you do not have control over, such as CCTV or an audio recording of a meeting someone else made. You may need to ask for it. When you have evidence like that, you also need to check how you are going to use it. If there is CCTV footage that lasts four hours, how is that going to be used in any hearing? Can you find out which parts of it are the key ones, and make extracts of those sections, with timings?

How is the CCTV evidence to be presented, on a laptop, or by use of a projector? If you do either, does that change how it is viewed, with colours for example fading and resolution lost if a projector is used? Can you use slow motion to demonstrate something? Should you have still shots taken to show an event more clearly, or have those enlarged for the same purpose? Is there a transcript of the audio recording? If not, can that be prepared, then agreed with the other side? Is there something on the recording that is important and that a transcript alone does not reveal, such as tone of voice, the sound of distress or anger, or faint external noises such as someone saying something, thinking that they were not heard?

The important thing to do is start to consider at this early stage what the evidence is that you can work with, and then if you need to present it in some way, such as to the other side at a meeting.

13

The other aspect of this stage is looking at it from the point of view of the opposition, and thinking what they might argue. That includes issues of evidence (fact) and submission (law).

The gross error check

When pilots are being taught how to fly, they are told to make a gross error check soon after taking off. Putting it at its simplest, it means making sure that you are flying in the right direction – say west over the land, rather than east out over the sea where you will eventually run out of fuel, crash and not survive. Similar techniques are used by doctors, to make sure that they operate on the left leg which needs the operation, not the right that doesn't. It sounds so obvious that it should not be needed, but it is needed because human beings make mistakes, sometimes catastrophic ones.

What kind of gross errors might be made when thinking of a claim? Some examples are – status, terms, and exclusions.

- Status is quite often raised in defences. For example, to make a claim of breach of contract in a tribunal you have to be an employee. For that claim there has to be a contract of employment. If you are self-employed, or the document says that you are not an employee, you may not be able to make the claim in a tribunal.

- Similarly if the document says it is a Heads of Terms and is not intended to have contractual effect, there is an immediate problem which might be insurmountable.

- If you are well outside any applicable time limit, you need to check whether or not that can be overcome. Sometimes it can be, but the test for doing so can be high in some cases. You need to understand what it is, and find out if you can meet it.

- For a claim of unfair dismissal, or for a redundancy payment, you need to have two years' continuous employment. If not, the claims cannot be made however unfair the dismissal might appear to you to be.

- If the event occurred outside the country, that can mean fewer or no remedies. So for example if you worked outside the UK, whether you can make a claim for unfair dismissal needs to be investigated.

- If to make the claim you must be a disabled person, ie for a discrimination claim, you need to investigate what the test is and whether you can meet it.

- Other exclusions or limitations may arise either under contract or by law. Examples include the need to make a claim within a particular period or in a set way, or liability being inapplicable in certain situations, or the amount of liability restricted in some way. A breach of contract claim is limited to £25,000 in the Employment Tribunal, and an unfair dismissal claim to one year's pay or a little over £80,000 whichever is lower.

Is it worth litigating?

Once you have carried out these investigations, it is best to draw breath, stop, and have a think. Is there enough? Do you have sufficient confidence in being able to take the claim further, or defend the claim being made?

I suggest that the following issues should be considered in most cases:

(i) *Importance* – why is the claim being made? Is it about money or more than that, such as reputation? Might what happened have an effect more generally, such as on your career or lead to action taken by a professional body?

(ii) *Prospects* – how likely is it, given what you know, that you will win?

(iii) *Cost* – how much is this going to cost, financially, but also in time spent, emotionally with the stress involved, and from any publicity of the case and a decision (which may be online and searched by future employers and others)?

(iv) *Remedy* – what is likely to be the outcome? Let's say that Linda has a claim for damages for breach of contract, for three months' lost earnings for her entitlement to notice, and that is worth £6,000. That decision may be affected by whether she can also seek unfair dismissal where her claim may be worth about a further £25,000 so that together they may be worth around £30,000. She is more likely to pursue these two claims if she has not found new work, and has not reduced the loss, which remains at that level. If, however, she obtained a new job paying the same wage within a few days, her claims may be worth less than £2,000. Is that value of claim worth pursuing?

Alternatives

It may be that litigation is not the only route to resolve matters. There are a number of other ways to do so. They include direct negotiation, mediation and using other channels such as regulators.

Negotiation

Some people fear that indicating a willingness to negotiate is a sign of weakness. It is not. It was well expressed in this quotation:

> 'Let us never negotiate out of fear. But let us never fear to negotiate' – John F Kennedy

Direct negotiation is usually worth attempting first, before a claim is commenced. To do this, the claimant writes a letter, setting out what the claim is for, why and seeking redress. That letter may or may not be sent on a 'without prejudice' basis, but it is almost always better to do that. The words 'without prejudice' are used to try and give the letter some protection, so that it is not used against the person who wrote it later. Sometimes those words work but not always. They are a form of shorthand which means that the letter is written in an effort at agreeing a resolution of the claim, but if that fails the proposal made, and what was said about it, cannot be used against that party in the hearing of the case. The law on what is protected, and what is not, is complicated, and it is important to be aware that using those words, either in a letter or during discussions, does not mean that they will always work. If for example you say something important in the case, such as admitting that there was discrimination against someone because of their disability, that can be admitted as part of the evidence, and your words can be used against you.

It can be worth writing a letter simply asking if the other side are prepared to have settlement discussions, and see what the answer is. If the answer is yes, it is worth then responding to say that all discussions are to be held on the basis of their being without prejudice to the position either side may take in court or tribunal should the discussions fail, and that nothing said during the discussions may be used in evidence by either party. If both sides agree to that, it allows the discussions to be more open, subject to the qualification that those words do not always work.

What the approach can do therefore is open the door to discussion before any formal action is taken. In some cases, that step must be taken first, and in others, if it is not taken, that may affect any awards of costs or expenses. For almost all employment tribunal cases, the discussion must take place through ACAS first in Early Conciliation, which is a form of negotiation, but that does not prevent separate discussions directly between parties or their representatives.

Making an approach also alerts the other side to the possibility of settlement. Sometimes that gives rise to a solution that one side had not expected. There may be a fear that the claimant is seeking a huge sum when really all that is sought is a reference for the future, or an apology. For the respondent, it is an opportunity to find out what happened, and try and resolve it without the cost of a litigation. Any settlement can also be with agreed conditions, such as that there is no acceptance of liability, and that the terms of settlement are confidential. It can include other issues such as an agreement not to repeat allegations made, or an offer of help with finding new employment, normally called outplacement, or otherwise. There is almost no limit to what parties may agree between them, but there is a limit to what a court or tribunal can do with a case before it.

Putting it another way, there is very often little to be lost by seeking to negotiate, and doing so is not indicative of weakness, but of strength. There are, however, times when that is not appropriate. For example, if a company is convinced that a member of staff has been involved in dishonesty, it may not wish to enter into any negotiations at all, lest discussing negotiation may give a message to other staff that it does not wish to convey.

When thinking of whether to make an offer to settle the case, bear in mind two key facts. The first is that if you do not, the other side have an easier decision – go ahead or cave in. If you make an offer, the decision becomes far more difficult for them, and they have something to lose by rejecting it. The second is that nothing is certain, and litigation is inherently risky. So a settlement (which is just any agreement to resolve the claim) removes the risk for both sides.

Some cases are ones that either cannot be settled, or are very difficult to settle. But even very difficult, high value, and important cases can settle, and that can happen at any stage, from before the claim starts, to just before the decision is given at the very last stage of appeal.

Negotiation is a skill of its own. When making an offer, it tends to be most effective not just to put forward a figure, but to do so in a context. That can either be quite sophisticated, setting out a review of the law, or of the facts, or prospects, or just by referring to risk factors that both sides have, or the cost of the litigation, or the time it will take, or the publicity that it might involve, or the effect on the longer term career of having the facts litigated publicly, or some combination of those, and other factors.

If the figure is too much at one end of the spectrum of potential awards by the judge, it will not be the best one to use. If you are the claimant, and you offer to settle for a figure that represents the very best you could hope for if you won, that does not make the decision for the opponent difficult – it will very likely be rejected as there is no incentive for them. It tends only to be made if you are likely to be right that you are pretty much guaranteed to win.

That is rather rare. In almost all cases, there is risk. So if Linda offers to settle her case, which she thought was worth £30,000 if she won every point, at £29,500 that puts little pressure on VHS Ltd, who are very likely to say no.

If on the other hand she offers to settle for a small fraction of the sum she expects to receive, it may very quickly be accepted, but she gets only that amount, and may well have been better off litigating, even with the risks involved. It may also give such a signal of weakness that no offer is made at all. There can even be a degree of satisfaction in trying and failing, rather than not going through that and having only a small sum which quickly vanishes, so too low an offer is very rarely the right tactic. If Linda were to offer to accept £1,000, VHS Ltd may quickly say yes, but she will have got very little money back for what happened, and may regret her decision later on.

The trick therefore is to pitch it at a level that is realistic. Give the opposition a difficult decision to make, which they will have to think carefully about. If you are advising Linda and think she has a good chance of winning, you might suggest that she offers a settlement with VHS Ltd paying £25,000. That then gives them a potential saving both of say £5,000 for the claim, and the cost of defending it for them, and gives them something serious to think about. It puts more pressure on them. If they then offer £5,000 that gives her a decision to make, as it is a more serious sum of money. The discussions can then continue, or not, depending on how each side feels about their case.

How do you know what to settle at?

There is no simple equation that works for all cases, but a basic one that is useful for the cases with a smaller potential award is this:

$$A \times B = C$$

A is the estimate of remedy on success,

B is 100 less a figure for the percentage estimate for risk, cost, and other factors (explained in more detail below), and

C is the resulting figure that might be proposed for settlement.

For example, if the estimate of how much might be awarded is set more realistically at £20,000 (one of the problems with claims of both unfair dismissal and breach of contract is that there can be double counting of loss for the same period, but not always does that happen and it is possible to have awards made separately for each) and the risks and other factors are estimated to be 40%, the discount on that to take account of risk and cost is the figure produced is worked out as:.

£20,000 (A) × (100 − 40 (B) = 60)%) = £12,000 (C).

This is not to say that the offer should be that amount. Each side may wish to start at a different point and move towards it in discussion, but it does at least give a figure to have to aim at, and helps frame the discussion. If Linda started at £25,000, and VHS Ltd started at £5,000, each has a measure of flexibility for the future discussions.

It can be tempting to work out what the difference is, and just split it. In the example, the mid-point of the two positions is £15,000. But that is very often too simplistic. It does not of itself reflect the strengths of the two cases, or the positions and reasons for that each side may take. For VHS Ltd they may simply say that if the offer of £5,000 is not accepted it will be withdrawn and they will fight the case. For Linda, she may say that her bottom line, the minimum sum she would accept, is £20,000 and in addition she would require a full reference. Unless one side changes its position very substantially no deal is done. But positions can sometimes change, particularly right before a hearing is to take place, and even when parties start very far apart doing a deal of some kind is not impossible.

Where the claim is more complex, and where the award may be higher, I have used a more complex formula when discussing the possibility of settlement, which is the following:

A = (B × C) – (D) –/+ (E) –/+ (F).

A is the settlement amount that the formula produces.

B Is the best estimate that there is of the award that a judge is likely to make if the claim wholly succeeds. That figure is then multiplied by C.

C is the prospect of success, measured as a percentage (for example 75/25 would be 75%). From the figure that results from B × C you then deduct (or add if applicable) each of D, E and F where they apply.

D is the likely level of any deduction for contribution, as a percentage, where that may apply.

E is the cost that the further conduct of the case is likely to cause, which cannot be recovered from the other side. It may be little, or nothing, if you are acting for yourself or you have free representation from someone, but if there are solicitors involved the cost can be significant. There is a deduction from the claimant side, as that reduces the net recovery, but an addition for the respondent side as it is a cost that is incurred, hence the -/+.

F is benefit of the management of risk, avoidance of publicity, and the saving in time (which can mean for respondents time spent on other work which generates income), expressed as a percentage normally but can be a single figure. My default position was to have that at 10%, but it may be higher than that in some cases. However, it could be nothing if that is the assessment. Again it may be a minus or a plus.

Again this does not give the starting point, but what might be an indication of the figure to aim to achieve. It is also important to keep in mind that other aspects of settlement can also be important, have value even if not monetary, and the formula is only an aid to the discussions.

Two examples of this formula being worked out may help to illustrate how it works, the first by the respondent defending the claim and the second by the claimant with her own one. The respondent will have a different view of some of the figures, but the process is the same.

Element	Respondent	Claimant
B (value of claim) × C (prospects for C)	£100,000 × 40% = £40,000	£120,000 × 75% = £90,000
D (contribution by C)	− 25% (£10,000) = £30,000	− £0 = £90,000
E (cost)	+ £20,000 = £50,000	− £25,000 = £65,000
F (benefits of settlement)	+ 10% (£5,000)	− £5,000
A (amount of settlement)	= £55,000	= £60,000

The respondent's assessment is as follows:

1 Start with how much the case is likely to be worth if it succeeds. Let us assume that the respondent thinks that it is £100,000. That is B.

2 Then assess the prospects of success, which is C. The respondent thinks that the claimant's prospects of succeeding are 40% (and that their own chances of winning are 60%). The first part therefore is B × C − (£100,000) × 40%) = £40,000.

3 Then make deductions from that. Work out D, the likely level of any deduction for contribution. Assume that that is assessed by the respondent at 25%, the calculation is (£40,000 × 25% = £10,000). That contribution is then deducted from C which is £40,000 − £10,000 = £30,000.

4 Then work out what E is. The respondent estimates its legal expenses, which it will not be able to get back even if it wins the case (which may be different depending on what is claimed and where that is) at £20,000. That is then added to the running total, and becomes £30,000 + £20,000 = £50,000.

5 Then work out what F is. It can either be a percentage or a fixed amount. Again for a respondent it is an addition, on the basis that there is value in the saving of time by not having to fight the case further. Let's say it is valued at 10% of E, which is £50,000 × 10% = £5,000. That is added to E, £50,000 + £5,000 leading to a total possible settlement value of £55,000.

The view of the claimant is naturally quite different. Going through the same steps, for the same case, they might look like this:

1 The figure for B is thought to be £120,000, and the prospects of success for the claimant are put at 75%, which is C. That leads to £120,000 × 75% = £90,000.

2   The claimant may believe that he or she did not contribute to the issue at all, and so there should be no value given for D. The running total remains therefore £90,000.

3   The claimant has legal representation, and will save on cost if there is a settlement without going to a full hearing. Let's say it is likely to be a saving of £25,000 for those costs. The running total is £90,000 – £25,000 = £65,000.

4   F is something that does have a value but putting a figure on that for a claimant is not easy. The claimant may not wish to have the details in a public document which future employers can search against. There can be other benefits, such as for example, if there is a settlement, state benefits received during the time from dismissal may not need to be repaid, but they will be if there is a formal decision. The claimant may put a value on this element at £5,000, which is deducted from £65,000 leading to a net £60,000.

Although the process is looked at from different perspectives and uses many different figures the outcome is remarkably similar. That is because factors such as risk, cost and benefit can cut both ways. The formula is only a tool and only as good as the figures used for it, but it gives the discussions a context and framework. Unfortunately the process does not lead so neatly to such similar outcomes in most cases.

This process nevertheless has flaws. It is not right for all cases. There may be other factors that are important, or require consideration. There can be a double counting in many cases for the prospects of success, and what the contribution by the claimant may be, and sometimes over the benefits of settlement. So the parties might privately do these figures, but for presentation purposes when discussions take place start with a higher level for prospects of success – if the claimant – or lower – if the respondent – and other figures to start from a better opening position, then negotiate after that down towards the figure shown above. It is important also to be flexible – there are times when the other side may say something that you are not aware of, refer to new evidence, or a new argument, and that does then need to be taken into account.

Whether the calculation made using the formula is something to do and then disclose to the other side to show the thinking is up to you. Sometimes it is worth doing, but not always, and tends to be most effective only as a last resort. You may wish to keep some, and perhaps all, of your thought processes private, particularly if you are not that optimistic about your own side's chances. On other occasions it may help to bring an issue into the discussions, such as what the legal costs of the case will be, and who is paying what for them for each side. That can also include arguments on what is called cost risk, which means that the side which wins might either seek, or normally be entitled to, the cost of the litigation, or part of it, from the losing side which is the rule in most (but not all) court actions. These issues have the benefit of being rather objective, and less emotional, than questions of prospects of success, or whether there was contribution. It means that these individual elements can be fed into the discussions one by one, as they develop.

Even if no detailed discussions are held, the very figure that is proposed by one side can in a sense be reverse engineered to find out, very roughly, what the views about prospects are. For example, if you think that a case is worth about £20,000 and after discussion the respondent offers £2,500 that gives a message that they are very confident of success. If the offer is £10,000 the message is different – they can be taken to base the offer on an assessment of about 50% chance of success.

That is why both sides tend not to make their best offer first, but start at an extreme, and then move on in baby steps, small increases at a time. There are differences between negotiating positions, which are fluid and liable to change, and final positions which are a form of bottom line, the maximum compromise that that party is going to propose for the settlement. One of the keys to these discussions is to keep them going until you get to the stage where you believe that you have wrung out of the other side as much as they are prepared to offer, if you are the claimant, or as low a sum as they are prepared to accept, if you are the respondent. It can be difficult to know when that is, but the more information you have on that the better, so discussing each of the aspects in detail can help. For the claimant that tends to focus on where they are strong, and for the respondent on either where they are strong, or where the claimant is weak, particularly on matters of risk or contribution.

Non-financial elements

Although money is the main 'currency' for settlements, it is far from the only one. Sometimes issues other than money are as, or more, significant. There are cases where an acknowledgement by one side, or more powerfully an apology, can either be sufficient, or act as oil to make the engine of settlement discussions run more smoothly. Consider this line from a song:

'Sorry seems to be the hardest word' – Elton John

It happens rarely that people are prepared to admit that they were wrong, and apologise, but when it does happen the effect can be far greater than the person saying it realises. People tend not to say sorry partly as they fear it will be taken as an admission of liability. The word sorry can therefore have a number of different contexts or meanings. It can be simple, straightforward, and an acceptance that what was done should not have been done. It can be more nuanced, not saying that what was done was wrong, but acknowledging the upset that it caused. It can be the equivalent of crocodile tears, not meant at all, but said in an ironic way, and really meaning that the speaker is very far from sorry.

For the claimant, if there has been a decision to end employment because of an incident which is said to be gross misconduct, or gross negligence, saying sorry may be too late. It may be more effective if there is recognition of not having done something properly before the decision was taken if an attempt is being made to keep the job. Sometimes it is because the employee does not acknowledge having done anything wrong that the decision is taken to dismiss. Even after dismissal however, acknowledging in private discussions some form of mistake or not having handled matters well or similar can open the door to discussions towards resolution.

For the respondent making some form of apology costs nothing financially, but may have a real emotional impact on the claimant. Even words that are guarded, such as 'I am sorry that things have come to this', which mean very little, can help.

Quite apart from apologies or acknowledgements, or explanations, there can be a degree of creativity in a result that is negotiated. The parties in that negotiation can be more flexible than a judge could be when determining a dispute. There can be a binary element to litigation, ie it is either win or lose. There can be cases where that is less so, with for example reductions in compensation if there is fault on both sides, or a failure to mitigate which is where the claimant has not taken reasonable steps to reduce loss to the minimum. There is no end to what parties can agree, and in some cases that flexibility will be far better than litigation, and benefit both sides.

Reasons to settle

It is always important to remember that there are benefits to a settlement, and it is something worth at least trying to achieve. The benefits include certainty, and that the decision on the outcome of the case is made by the parties themselves, not a third party. That produces an element of control, and also means that the settlement can include something that the court or tribunal cannot do – such as agreed apologies, announcements, a reference, an agreement about confidentiality, agreements not to work in competition for a period, and others.

The benefits also include the lack of a public record of what happened, and of the decision. That can be particularly important where there are sensitive allegations, or ones that might affect either party in future, for example issues affecting reputation. Having nothing public can therefore help both parties.

Another benefit is the simple avoidance of having to go to a hearing, which is a stressful exercise. Even those with great experience and self-confidence can find giving evidence a difficult process. There are examples of witnesses being so upset by what happened that they needed a long time off work afterwards to recover, or whose reputation either as someone who was straightforward or good at their job was seriously tarnished. One person involved in a case said that it was worth going to court just to see the hand of the witness for the other side, who had been a manager with a very direct style, shaking so visibly when pouring a drink of water during a long cross-examination.

The discussion – have an agenda

It can help to agree on what order to discuss issues before the discussion starts. The reason for that is that it is a very commonly used tactic in negotiation for the respondent defending the claim to discuss how much might be awarded on success first of all, and try to reach agreement on that, before then putting in issue what the changes of success are, and what might be a reduction for the contribution of the claimant. It can be an effective tactic. If the discussion starts on the how much question, with the claimant asking for £30,000 and the respondent suggesting that £25,000 is how much is likely to be awarded, the claimant may agree to the figure of £25,000 thinking that that would be an acceptable compromise.

There is then a suggestion that there are risks for the claimant, and that that is properly quantified at 40%, ie a 40% chance of losing and getting nothing at all. That would reduce the figure by £10,000 to £15,000. The respondent then suggests that the claimant was partly at fault, and the contribution should be recognised by a reduction of a third. That then produces an offer reduced by £5,000 to the sum of £10,000, a long way away from the £25,000 figure that a few minutes ago the claimant thought was on offer.

In any negotiation therefore it is important to create an agenda of the items for discussion first of all, and the order in which they are to be discussed. In many cases the basics are money, risk and contribution but there are others depending on the circumstances, including cost, time, the impact of publicity, and non-financial effects.

Generally speaking it is best for respondents to deal with money first, then risk, then contribution, then everything else. For claimants the order is most often risk, contribution, money and everything else last. Obviously one side has to concede on that, so before finalising the agenda and order of topics it is possible to ask for an outline of the position for each item – for example the claimant might say £30,000, no risk, and at worst 10% contribution, therefore £27,000 and the respondent might say £25,000, 50% risk and 80% contribution, therefore £2,500. That is a simplified version of the formula set out above. The two sides are very far apart, but it does at least start the process. The discussions can then focus on where the differences lie and why that is.

These figures are the opening shots of the battle. They are not ending positions, and are therefore treated with caution. Do not run away at the first sight and sound of battle. If you are the claimant and offered about 10% of what you want to achieve, hold your ground and explain why you are right and they are wrong. If you are the respondent and think that the claimant does not have a grasp of reality hold your ground, and explain why you make the assessment you do, what your evidence will be, and why he or she needs to reduce their expectations.

A golden rule in negotiations is not to bid against yourself. If you have made an offer of some kind, do not move from that until the other side have made a counter-offer. If you are the respondent and have offered, say, £2,000 to settle a claim you think has no real chance of success, and the claimant says something like 'that is really low, can you give me your best offer and I will think about it' you may be tempted to do so. But they may have accepted the offer made, so don't. If you are the claimant, and offered to settle the same case which you think is worth £10,000 for £8,000, and the respondent says 'that it is far too much, do you have something more realistic to propose', just say that you have a strong case, that it is realistic, and ask them for their response. Bidding against yourself only helps the other side.

But if the other side are being completely unrealistic, in your view, then threatening to walk away is one tactic to consider seriously. There is no real chance of a deal if the other side argue for a completely different outcome, and quick mathematics indicates that their opening salvo leads to a sum that would be completely unacceptable to you.

Walking away is a tactic to use with care. There are times when it is not a tactic, but the end of any negotiations, the case proceeds, and the risk of failure (for either side) becomes very real. A better way is to ask about the basis for the view being expressed, whether that is about key aspects of evidence, or a particular legal line of argument. If there is something in it, it will have to be considered. If not, or if there is a simple answer to it, that can be stated.

Experience suggests that the order in which issues are discussed in any negotiation has an effect of some kind on the outcome. This is not therefore a matter of convenience, as one of having some control over the end result. It can create a measure of momentum to have even a provisional agreement on one or more issues of a set, which one side wishes to discuss first, before considering the remaining issues which the other side is most keen on.

For the claimant, it is frequently an issue of how much money is offered, but that is not the only one, and sometimes is not even the most important. There are some cases where the principle is what matters, or reputational harm, or a sense of dignity, or a sense of simple fairness. These non-financial matters can be forgotten about in a litigation as the end result decided by the judge is usually expressed in financial terms. So the judge may look at the matter essentially as one about money, but the parties, particularly the claimant, may have a far wider field of vision. In any negotiation, the issues which have little or no cost can be the easier ones to discuss, and reach agreement on.

That is why it can be helpful to consider the "everything else" part of the agenda carefully, and work out what if anything falls within it, either what you wish to seek from the other side, or what you feel the other side may seek, or at least have an interest in if it were offered.

The end result of a negotiation usually is heavily influenced by two key factors: (i) the strength of the arguments; and (ii) the preparation undertaken by the negotiator. If you have never negotiated before, or not done so in this context, you may feel at a disadvantage if the other side are represented by experienced lawyers.

The truth is that if the other side is very experienced you are at something of a disadvantage. But the way to overcome that is to be as well prepared as you can be. You need to be as well prepared as if you were heading that day into the final hearing. You need to have a clear idea of what you want to achieve, but also why, and how you are to do that. There is no real strength in an assertion that you are 100% certain to win if nothing is said to back that up. If however you can point to evidence, such as CCTV footage showing exactly what happened, or statements from a busload of clergy who were watching what happened and all confirm that you were blameless, that creates an effect on the opposition. You are not just ranting. You are making an argument based on evidence, and what the judge is likely to decide based on that evidence. That is a powerful argument. It is not based on emotion. It is likely to have an effect on the most experienced and skilful of negotiators.

Amount

When it comes to the 'how much' part, be very clear as to how the sum is made up, and have supporting written evidence where available, such as pay slips, the attempts to find new employment, pay slips from the new employer, a written calculation of the loss of income, a report from your GP or consultant, statements from family members about the effect on you (if that is relevant to the issues). In any negotiation aspects can be included which a tribunal or court would not consider, and in some cases you may want to suggest a contribution to pension, a concession over shares held, or options for shares, or a gift to charity.

Be aware also of any tax issues that arise, and whether state benefits may need to be repaid if there is a decision in tribunal or court, but which may not need to be repaid if there is a private settlement.

A single document with the headings for the parts of the claim, usually called a Schedule of Loss, is very helpful in negotiations, and it is often a part of the preparations in a case (an example is in the Appendix). It can be prepared and given to the other side at any stage, even before a claim is formally made to the court or tribunal. It creates the impression of someone organised, prepared, and ready for the battle. If you wish to preserve the confidentiality of its terms, write on it also 'Without prejudice', which means that there is a good chance of being able to change the figures for the final hearing if negotiations fail. It also can give the impression to the other side that these are the figures today, but they might be higher tomorrow.

It can help to confirm specifically that if terms are not agreed the case will be litigated, and to do as much of the negotiation as you can in person or by phone. Negotiations by email do not work quite so well.

Documenting settlement

An offer is not binding until accepted fully. An offer not accepted can be withdrawn, and if accepted subject to conditions is not fully accepted and can be withdrawn. If an offer is made and withdrawn, it may not be made again, though often it does remain on the table. It is important therefore not to assume that an offer once made will always be there, and if you reject it do so with that in mind.

If terms are agreed, it is a good idea to confirm them in writing, and have both sides sign and date them. People can sometimes have second thoughts, and if you do have a deal, you will normally want that to be the end of the story, not the beginning of a new one. The settlement can be agreed through ACAS, in which case a form called a COT3 will be completed, and that gives both sides a good level of protection. It is also possible to confirm the settlement by what is called a settlement agreement. For that the claimant must have legal advice or advice from a qualified trade union representative. For employment disputes one of those routes should be followed, as without it there are times when the settlement you thought had been reached does not prevent another claim being made.

The settlement can include anything that the parties wish it to, such as a reference, or an announcement to staff, or outplacement facilities to help with finding new work, or an apology. These are outcomes that a tribunal or court would not generally be able to provide.

Mediation and other steps

Mediation is similar to direct negotiation, but involves a person in the centre who does not decide the dispute, rather it helps the two sides come to an agreement. The advantages of that are first that it is private, and secondly it can again be more creative in outcome than a litigation. Some services are provided free of charge, at other times the mediator must be paid. The mediator may be someone agreed between the parties, or appointed by the court or tribunal, such as a Judicial Mediator. It helps to prepare for a mediation just as you would for a final hearing, but there is no evidence heard, the mediator does not decide the dispute like a judge, but helps the parties to reach agreement. About three quarters of mediations succeed. One great advantage of them is that each side can tell the mediator what they want to achieve, in confidence. The mediator will respect that, and use the information given to help the parties move towards an outcome both can accept. If the mediation fails, generally nothing that is said during it can be used in the later dispute before a judge. There is therefore very little to lose by attempting it where that is possible. It is worth considering very carefully because of that.

It may be possible to refer the issue to a regulator, an ombudsman, or a government agency of some kind to investigate and adjudicate on. That is often free of charge, and less stressful than litigating. ACAS performs that function for employment disputes. There are a series of regulators, ombudsmen or similar organisations in other areas who can be contacted.

These options are all worth considering carefully before taking the matter to a court, tribunal or similar forum. Once a litigation is started, to at least some extent the control of that moves from the party, or parties, to the judge. The outcome is dependent on persuading that judge that you are right, or at least more right than the other side, and you may not be able to do so. You therefore must keep in mind at all times that there is the risk of failure, however strongly you believe in the merit of your claim, or the claim of whoever you are representing.

Considering risk

Litigation is inherently risky. People often say that they have a cast iron case. There is no such thing, as the quotation from Lord Justice Megarry mentioned before confirms. There is an old adage, not accurate but illustrative of this, that if you have a cast iron case it is in reality 50/50. The very best odds that you can normally hope for are, I think, 80/20. There are a few cases where they are higher, for example where there is a particularly strong issue of law that applies such as time bar, or jurisdiction, or where the other side simply has got things hopelessly wrong and cannot win, but they are very rare. On the other side of that coin, cases can be won where the odds of success are thought to be 20%, or less. Even what was thought to be a fairly hopeless defence to a case can sometimes succeed.

When assessing risk you are doing so with incomplete information. It is based on what you know at that time. You do not know all that the judge will know by the time the evidence is heard. You do not know what you, or your witnesses, will say when being asked questions, or what those questions will be. Under pressure the witness (or you) may say something entirely different from what was expected, or what was said before. You do not know precisely what questions the other side may ask you, or what the judge may ask, or what the judge may make of you or your witnesses when giving evidence. Other factors come into play. There may be some document found by the other side that you were not aware of that changes the impression of the facts. There may be a decision in another case, from a court possibly far removed from where you are litigating, that changes the legal landscape your case is based on. Your opponent may suddenly disappear, or go into liquidation, leaving you with a large level of cost built up.

Start any litigation with eyes wide open as to its risk, and cost. That cost can be in up front expense, or hidden expense if the claim is lost and there is then an award of the cost of the litigation against you. Not all cases carry that risk, but in some it is inherent in the process, and requires to be carefully taken into account.

Unforeseen consequences

Every time you make a claim, or decide to defend it, you send a message to the other side, which they may or may not react to in a way you expect. It is similar to this principle of physics you may remember from school days:

'For every action there is an equal and opposite reaction' – Newton's third law

The principle in any form of possible litigation is not exactly the same but it is always important to think, both when considering whether to start a claim and throughout the process, what the other side will do in response to what you do. If you do go to the stage of starting a claim, what might their reaction be? You may hope that they will cave in, and pay you. That may possibly happen, but it tends to happen less frequently that you might expect. What else might they do?

They might consider making their own claim against you. If your claim in the tribunal includes one for breach of contract because they did not pay you notice or some other sum or element that you were entitled to such as a bonus, they might pursue a counterclaim against you for what they think are losses you caused by your gross negligence. They might do that in the same proceedings, or they might go to court for that, as that involves you in higher cost, and may postpone your own case to allow the court action to proceed first.

They might make a formal report to some form of professional body to try and have you struck off, ending your career. They might contact your new employer, or a charity you work for as a volunteer, and say why you were dismissed. They might refer to matters more publicly with your former colleagues, who might also go on to social media to spread that allegation about you.

A claim in tribunal or court is a public act, and the media can (and sometimes do) report it, both when the claim starts, and during its process. That may be damaging to your reputation or embarrassing, or just something that you do not wish to happen.

These are all matters to at least consider. It does not mean that it stops you dead in your tracks. Sometimes the threats of these things happening are used to try and intimidate someone with a perfectly good case into dropping it. It is your decision on what to do, or it is your responsibility to advise the person involved on what are both the advantages and potential disadvantages of taking the claim. It needs careful thought first.

Interim orders

There are some occasions where you both want and need to get an initial remedy almost immediately. They are usually called interim orders or a similar term.

Very often there is a strict, and very short, time limit to do this. As has been explained, interim relief can be sought in the Employment Tribunal if there is a dismissal said to be for reasons such as health and safety, trade union issues, or whistleblowing. Then the need is to get a Claim Form commenced within seven days of the dismissal, or other incident.

Similarly you may wish to seek an interim order, such as an interdict or injunction, from a court and the longer that is left the less likely it is to be granted. It may be for example that an employee was dismissed for setting up in competition, and had emailed himself a list of all of his employer's customers to do that. Apart from the possible Tribunal claim by that employee, the employer may want to go to court to try and prevent the use of that customer information.

There are times therefore where speed is vital. It takes precedence over perfect pleading. It does not remove the need to take care, but the basics will suffice. Get something in, check that it seeks what you need, and sets out the fundamental requirements for doing so. Check the rules on what you need to do (for example some provisions require advance notice to the other side, such as if seeking an order about a strike against a union). At the same time consider whether you should give advance notice anyway, as a matter of courtesy or good form, or to help in seeking expenses or costs later.

Consider what documents you might need, whether you need something else to support the claim such as an affidavit, and what authorities you need to have with you for the purpose of the hearing before the Judge, which may or may not be disputed by the other side.

If there is a disputed hearing and you either win or lose, do not take that as determinative. It may or may not be. Consider what the decision is and why, and whether it is best to carry on, negotiate, or give up. Interim orders can be very powerful weapons, but can also be weapons in the hands of the opposition.

Dealing with inexperience

There may be a vast gap in experience between you and the other side. Gaps have dangers, as illustrated by this:

'Mind the gap' – announcer, Temple Underground station, London (and others)

It can be quite intimidating to take on a case where the opponent is a very experienced lawyer, whether as a solicitor in a firm, which may be very large and with huge resources, or with an advocate. The other side may also seem very confident, or appear to have an easy relationship with the judge who they obviously know well. This may be your first case, and may become your only case. The opponent may be at the height of a glittering legal career. How do you deal with that?

There is an adage – 'Old age and cunning beat youth and experience every time'. That is not always true. The person conducting their own case can succeed against a team of experienced lawyers. The representative from a voluntary organisation, or young solicitor, or trainee, can succeed against a solicitor with decades of experience. Advocacy matters. But it does not necessarily win the case. What it does is to increase the prospects of success. The underlying strength or weakness of a case can be just as important, and in many ways should be more so. In fact it often is.

The way to overcome that deficit in experience is hard work. Preparation is the foundation for every great advocate I ever worked with. They may seem to do it off the cuff, but it is the result of years of very hard work. It is a little like Roger Federer hitting an effortless backhand. Of course he has the basic tools to do that, but he worked at the skill for countless hours. The Beatles went to Hamburg and played cover songs twice a day every day before making a record. The guitarist Jimi Hendrix used to wear his guitar rather like a piece of jewellery, and play it all day every day before he found fame. When Churchill gave his most famous speeches as Prime Minister after 40 years as an MP and a lifetime learning how to use words, but he practised for hours in advance, sometimes learning the speech off by heart. You get the idea. Hard work pays off.

The second tip is to have confidence in your case. If you have done the work on it, and believe it to be right, do not be put off by suggestions that you are wrong, misguided, naïve, inexperienced, ignorant or otherwise. It is an old trick to try and put the other side off their stroke, or to try and get them to give up. It is part of the game of advocacy, to try and persuade the opposition that they have it wrong. Stick to your guns, unless they say something that you later, after reflection and checking, decide is correct.

The third tip is to remember that advocates of any kind are human beings. They can be prone to making mistakes, being complacent, skimping on hard work, or just being disadvantaged because they only got the papers the night before. There is an old Latin maxim (not that Latin is encouraged currently, but it has the benefit of saying succinctly what takes longer to say in English) 'aliquando Homerus dormitat'. It translates as even the great Homer makes mistakes. Ask any experienced lawyer and they are pretty much bound to admit that they have made mistakes throughout their career. I certainly did.

Dealing with those who refuse to settle

There are some cases that cannot be settled, or could only be settled by accepting too small a sum (from the point of view of the claimant) or paying too high a sum (from the point of view of the respondent). You may be very keen indeed to settle, and try everything to achieve it, but for whatever reason it proves impossible. You may then need to fight the case, whether as claimant or respondent, knowing that you face difficulties, some of which may seem insurmountable.

When you are at that stage, paradoxically, there can be less pressure. There is a sense of inevitability of the process, and that the reason for it taking place is not of your making. The first thing to do therefore is not to worry too greatly about the prospect of it not going well. You may even just accept that you are going to lose one battle, say that there was an unfair dismissal as there was no procedure followed. You can in that situation choose to admit that there was an unfair dismissal, and fight the case on other points. As it was put rather well in a film:

'That isn't flying, it's falling, with style' – Woody, Toy Story

The second is to work out what your strategy should be. As is covered elsewhere, try and choose your battles. Fight on issues where you have something sensible to say, even if it is only how much should be awarded. The how much question is never a simple one, and if nothing else you have the impossibility of predicting the future. So when the claimant seeks losses for a date in the future, you can make arguments about that, the possibility of the claimant having new income at some stage, or that the income from the respondent may have ended at some point for different reasons. You can argue that there might be reductions in the award, usually on the basis that the claimant was partly responsible for what happened, but in unfair dismissal cases it can also be on the basis that had the procedures been different, there could have been a fair dismissal. There can be arguments that the claimant could have taken different steps to seek alternative employment.

These issues arise less often for claimants, but they do arise. There can be the thought that the dismissal should be challenged because it has had such a devastating effect on the individual. There can be issues of the effect on a career, particularly in roles where there is a regulator. There can simply be the benefit of having someone who was previously in a superior position, in line management, subjected to the process of cross-examination where they are not the one in a position of power or authority. There is the possibility that, even if the case is lost, being able to challenge the decision, and the process by which it was reached, means that it was worth taking the case on. Sometimes the ability to get closer to the truth of what happened can have merit by itself.

In these cases therefore you embrace the difficulties that there are, and you try to fall with style. Sometimes by doing that you can do better than you might have expected. From the respondent's side, you can have a result that may be bad from one perspective, but you can know that it is less bad than it might have been.

Advising others

There is a unique responsibility in acting for someone else, whether paid or unpaid, and it comes with its own difficulties. Part of the role is to give advice, and be clear and candid when doing so. That different perspective, from not being the party, is important, and the two perspectives were well expressed in this quotation

'We give advice by the bucket, but take it by the grain' – Tom Stoppard

If you are acting as the adviser to someone else, whether as a lawyer, paid adviser, or unpaid one, you are likely to be either required, or asked, to give advice. That is in fact one of the main advantages of not acting for yourself, in that you have someone else who is not directly involved in the case, who does not directly benefit from the outcome, who can give an independent opinion.

Giving that opinion is not easy. It can be affected by personal relationships, particularly if you are acting for a family member or friend. You will naturally wish to believe the person you are acting for, who is close to you. But it is better if you can keep a certain distance, and then be candid. If all of the evidence points towards your family member being wrong in some way, or if it shows that your friend has a case that is pretty hopeless, it is not doing them much good if you pretend that they are bound to win.

When giving advice to the person who is making, or defending, the claim there are some very basic rules:

(i)   Be honest, and direct, about what you think.

(ii)   Try to give your own estimate of the chances of success. There can be a temptation to say something like 'it all depends on how the evidence goes, so I can't tell you whether you will win or not'. That is not right if you have done the preparations. You should be able to give at least a basic opinion on chances.

(iii)   When doing that, it can be best to do so using percentages. Unless the other side are certainly entirely wrong on both fact and law, it is my personal view that the chances are very rarely higher than 80%. As a corollary of that, they may be rarely less than 20% if there is at least a basic case with a chance of success.

(iv)   Give an opinion also on remedy, which means what may be awarded if the claim succeeds.

(v)   Cover the other aspects of the case, such as any risk of expenses or costs being awarded, the time it may take, publicity and anything else that may be relevant.

(vi)   Give the advice with a qualification. You are giving it from what you know at that stage, and not from what the judge will eventually hear. Things may well have changed by that stage.

(vii)   It can also be worth saying specifically that you are giving advice, not instructions, and that the choice rests with the person whose case it is.

(viii) Put the advice in writing in some way, as a report, or letter, or email.

(ix)   If circumstances change, such as when the hearing approaches and you may have much more information, check whether it is still valid and if not revise it.

(x)   For lawyers, it is important also to summarise both the facts as you understand them, and the law. It helps to explain why the analysis is as it is, applying the law to the facts as a judge would. Some lawyers give the advice in great detail, others far less so. It tends to depend on what the case is about, its complexity and value, and who is giving the advice.

If you are acting for yourself, then, if you can, do try and ask someone for a view, even if not formal advice. There is an adage that if a solicitor advises himself he has a fool for a client, and although that does not apply directly to people who are not lawyers, there is still a difficulty when acting for yourself. You are not independent. You can lose at least an element of perspective by being closely involved in the detail. That is why a perspective from someone else, even if a close family member or friend, can be important.

If and when you do get advice, whether that is formal from a representative, or informal from someone close to you, take account of it. They are trying their best to help you. They may say things that you would not like to hear, which can be anything from 'have you thought about' one point of detail, to 'you are entirely wrong and should give up'. It can be difficult to take advice, but at the least consider it very carefully.

Ultimately however the case is yours, and it is your decision, not that of anyone else, as to whether you proceed with the case or take any particular tactical decision in it.

Chapter 4

Pleading

Making a claim

Pleading a claim is a skill of its own. The format to use varies from one court or tribunal to the other. It is best to check whether there is a pro forma to complete, either online or by adding to a printed form. Very often there is. If not, there may be something that you can use as a basis for your own claim in a reported case which you might be able to find online. There are also books which provide guidance, or standard types of documents called 'precedents' or (in Scotland) 'styles'. The Appendix to this book has an element of that.

They are a starting point, but need to be used carefully. They may only help to a limited extent, and it is necessary to check whether the words used in that type of document are relevant to your own case.

There are some basics to follow:

1   Identify the parties as accurately as possible. For individuals use their first and last names at least, and an address. For limited companies or limited liability partnerships use the company number and refer to a registered office where you can. For partnerships, what you do depends on the law of the country you are litigating in. It may be necessary to refer to the firm name, or the names of all partners, or both. The rules for clubs and unincorporated associations are difficult, and need to be checked.

2   When stating the facts, keep sentences short and straightforward. Give dates where you can, as accurately as you can (if possible 8 March 2018, if not early March 2018, or March 2018, or the first quarter of 2018).

3   Do not copy and paste from a statement. Start again, and try to keep to key facts expressed succinctly. There is a balance to strike between two competing principles, of being succinct, and giving the other side fair notice of what your claim is. Too much brevity can be damaging. But too much detail can be a problem. There are some cases where the pleadings run to many pages, with some being not so short novels. In one case the long history set out was called 'a morass of sludge'. The longer the pleading, the more it seems that the person has not worked out what

the case is, and is just making a generalised complaint about everything. That is not what courts and tribunals deal with. They resolve particular issues raised on the basis of a legal framework. So be as clear and concise as you are able to. Mark Twain apologised for writing a long letter, saying that he had not had the time to write a short one. It does take time to set the required level of detail out succinctly. But that time can be repaid many times over later, and can help either to lead to a negotiated settlement, or success, later.

4   If there is a legal provision you rely on, particularly an Act or Statutory Instrument, or international instrument such as an EU Directive, quote that and the particular provision, eg section 1 of the ABC Act 2019.

5   If there are more than one of these provisions, set them out in separate paragraphs, and outline the facts relevant to each one. It is better to do that than have a long explanation of what happened, then a list of separate claims at the end, as each claim will be treated differently because it has a different legal test that applies.

6   Set out what remedy you are seeking – the rules on this again may change, but it is normally best to specify what it is you want and, if money, how much. You may also need to set out why that is.

7   Prepare a first draft, leave it for a while, then return and check it. Look at it from the point of view of the other side, and how they might attack it. Make any changes.

8   Send it to the court or tribunal, checking how to do so and that it gets there in time. If it is close to the time bar period, think about whether you need to deliver it in person, and if so to where. Be sure that it is received, and do not trust to post. Phone to check its receipt. Check that you have done all that you need to do, and in the right way. Clerks at tribunals and courts will often give some advice on this, and if that does not work do your best to find out.

Defence

In a sense pleading a defence is a little easier, as you have something to start with – the claim made against you. The same basic rules about being short, and succinct, and checking the draft, apply as above. In addition there are normally some ground rules to follow:

1   Check details like the parties, and whether the claim is in time or not, or taken in the right court or tribunal or not. If it hasn't been, say so.

2   Reply only to what is pled in the claim, at least initially.

3   If something stated in the claim is right, admit it. That makes it clear what is disputed, and what not.

4   Where there is a dispute, make that clear. That can be done after the admitted parts by saying something like 'The rest of the claim is denied'.

5   Then consider whether you can and should add more. You may wish to add a description to provide your version of what happened, or explain matters in more detail, or approach it from a different angle.

6   Consider whether to plead defences such as limitations of liability, contribution by the claimant, failure to mitigate loss (referred to below) or otherwise.

7   Consider whether you can make your own claim, usually called a counter claim. Sometimes you can in the same proceedings, and sometimes not. There can also be limits to what is awarded in a tribunal, and if the sum is large a separate action in court without that limit is better. There are different rules about the cost and expense of court actions.

8   Check when the defence is due to be lodged, and make sure that you do that on time and properly, just as if it was a new claim.

Why have pleadings?

It is sometimes thought that pleadings do not matter too much, and that as long as there is a basic outline that will be fine. That is not right. Pleadings are important, and can be decisive.

There are a number of things that pleadings do, which have been referred to above. They give fair notice to the other side what your case is. Their pleadings give fair notice to you. The rules about pleadings cut both ways. You can complain if you are taken by surprise over something that has not been pled, and so can the other side if you do that.

The pleadings tell the judge what the case is about, and what is at issue. Pleadings provide a framework for the case. On that framework the parties can then hang the evidence.

It is also the framework for assessing the claim made, and for remedy. So if you claim unfair dismissal, which has a limit to what may be awarded, and that is what is in your pleadings – that is the only claim that you can make. You have not made a claim of age discrimination, which has no limit to what may be awarded, and you or your witnesses may not be allowed to speak about what happened in a way that refers to age discrimination as either that may be objected to and that evidence not heard, or it may be heard but used only in the context of unfair dismissal. In turn, that means that the outcome could be a limited financial award, far less than might have been awarded had there been a claim of age discrimination set out in the pleadings.

That is why you should check what exactly it is you wish to claim for, and why that is. Check what remedy you are seeking, and whether you might have a better remedy that is not quite so obvious. Check whether there are limits to what you can sue for in the tribunal (for example in a breach of contract case, when this is made, there is a £25,000 limit in the tribunal but no limit in the court). Check that what you are seeking is what can be awarded – for example an unlawful deduction from wages claim in the tribunal may not include simple issues such as a claim for work expenses, or more difficult issues like share options.

On the other hand, do not just throw into the pleadings every single claim you have heard about. It is possible to claim discrimination for several protected characteristics, such as age, disability and religion or belief, and to sue for direct discrimination, indirect discrimination, discrimination arising out of disability, failure to make reasonable adjustments for a disabled person, harassment and victimisation. There can be claims similar to discrimination for issues such as whistleblowing, and dismissal for raising health and safety matters. But it is rare for so many and so varied claims all to succeed. By making a large number of them, you may camouflage the claims that are in fact strong ones. Too much claimed can reduce the chances of success.

You need to be an editor. Consider all of the claims, and think which ones you can seriously argue. If there are some that will not get off the ground, leave them out. It does no good putting in some claims that are bound to fail. If you think that it might possibly work, then do leave it in, but then check it again when you see the reply from the other side. If that makes it clear that there is no real claim there for one particular claim then drop it. Not only is that not a sign of weakness, but of strength, you will also be likely to have the approval of the judge who will see that you are acting responsibly and the respect of your opponent who will see the same.

It can be a difficult judgement to leave something out, or take a claim out of a case. You may not believe what the other side say in their pleadings. So you are entitled to leave a claim in where it is strenuously disputed, and you may be right to do that if what is left has at least a reasonable chance of success. You should however think carefully about the tactics of that decision, and whether the chances of success are good enough to take the risk that leaving a poorer claim in reduces the chance of success of the better claim that you really do think is your strongest point.

Changes to pleadings

Very often both sides will wish to change their initial pleadings. That can either be to respond to what the other side has pled, or to add information that has since come to light, or to expand on the initial pleadings as you understand the dispute better. This is normally permitted, but the details again depend on what process is being followed, as does the terminology to use.

Sometimes it is done in a new document and at other times by changing the initial Claim or Defence by tracked changes to it. Sometimes that needs the approval of the court or tribunal. It is best to check that with the staff there.

It is always important however to keep in mind two things. First if you do not plead what you are trying to get remedy for, you will most likely not be able to ask for it later. If you start with a case for unfair dismissal, and think after finding out more that there may also be a case for age discrimination, for example, do not leave the pleadings as they are. You need to add to them to bring in that new claim, and the facts that are relevant to it. You need to give the judge advance notice that that is your argument, as much as possible. You also need to give the other side the same advance notice, so that they can at the very least prepare their defence to it.

You may or may not be allowed to change your position in this way. It can often depend on how late in the day you make the change, and how big the change is. The closer to the final hearing it is, or the more significant the change, the greater the risk is of not being able to do that. So as soon as you are aware that this might be needed, start working on what you need to do, whether by a document such as an amendment, or by putting tracked changes to the existing pleadings. Make the application to do that in writing, or by email. In the tribunal it is something that is decided according to the judge's discretion, and is affected by the overriding objective in Rule 2 of the Rules of Procedure (which are in the Source Materials). It very often helps to refer to that, and explain why it is that the application is made at this stage, and why your application should be granted. Is it for example because of a document only recently sent to you? Is it because of something a new witness has just told you? In reality should you have been aware of it earlier, but you had not appreciated that because of your lack of legal training and experience? Whatever the circumstances, set them out. Also consider whether the change is liable to cause hardship to the other side. Will they have to investigate a new argument entirely, or is it something that is covered already by the facts set out, with a different legal argument made about it? Are they a large organisation with substantial resources who can look into the new facts easily?

The second point on pleading is that if you do not give fair notice to the other side, they will be likely to object to your evidence being led on the point at all, and that objection may very well succeed. So even though you have obtained what you think is strong evidence, it may not be heard and therefore not considered by the judge.

The third point is that if you are a litigant in person, it may be that you will wish to use the Claim you make as a basis for your evidence, and will want to have everything important in it for that reason too. It is addressed later on.

On the other hand if the other side try to do that, you need to think of your reaction. Should you just go along with it, or can you object? If so, should you? Can you use that as an opportunity to change your own pleadings? Might you need to do that, but not be able to at that particular point? You may for example be able to ask the other side for more time to consider what they are doing, and then respond to it. If you do wish to object to it, set out why that is, and what harm or hardship the proposed change may cause you. If it is very close to the hearing of evidence for example, does that mean that that hearing would have to be put off and a new one fixed leading to substantial delay? If so, you can refer to the overriding objective in Rule 2 which refers to avoiding undue delay.

Chapter 5

Case management

Introduction

Once the defence is produced, the extent of the dispute becomes at least a little clearer. What happens next can be vitally important. There is normally a very wide discretion given to the judge as to how a case is handled, and what happens to it when. There are again some ground rules that normally apply:

1   Use a diary, electronic or paper. Make absolutely sure that you know what is to be done when, and write that down somewhere so that you do not miss it. Missing deadlines can be fatal. That includes not just the final hearing (sometimes called a trial or proof) but earlier hearings, which can be in person or by telephone on occasion.

2   Very often it is helpful to write down what is called a list of issues. This is a list of the legal issues which the judge is to determine. In a breach of contract case, like the example involving Linda and VHS Ltd we looked at before, they might be:

    (i)   Was the respondent in breach of contract?

    (ii)   If so, was that repudiatory (meaning sufficiently serious)?

    (iii)   If so, what is the measure (amount) of the claimant's loss?

    (iv)   If not, was the claimant in breach of contract in terminating the contract without notice?

    (v)   If so, what is the measure of the respondent's loss?

3   Prepare a chronology. That is often very helpful, particularly in more complex cases. It is a list of key dates and events, starting with the oldest and ending with the most recent. Set out very simply who did what and when, which can be very useful when preparing questioning, and for the submission made at the end.

4   Start to prepare a list of all relevant documents, again starting with the oldest and ending with the most recent.

5   Think about what procedure is to be followed. That usually means considering whether there is to be a final hearing covering all issues together, or some form of preliminary hearing covering only one or more particular issues, such as whether the claimant had a particular status, or whether it is time-barred.

6   Another form of preliminary hearing is an argument over whether the claim is correct in law, or has sufficient prospects of success to warrant being taken further. There may also be applications about a deposit, security for any award made, and otherwise.

7   Sometimes there is a separation of hearings between the merits – who wins and loses overall – and the remedy – how much is awarded if the claimant succeeds. That tends to be sought by respondents who hope to avoid the cost of the enquiry into remedy, and just because it is asked for does not mean that it is necessarily appropriate or that the judge will agree to it.

8   Think about what evidence you have not got, but may need. That may be in the form of a document, real or electronic, or a witness who is not co-operating. Usually that can be sought by some form of order from the court or tribunal. For documents in the hands of the other side, the best course is to write to them or their representative, list the documents you want, explain their relevance if not clear, and ask for them. If they are not produced, then make a formal application for an order. For the witness, it may be necessary to ask for an order, saying who the witness is, what their address is, and why their evidence is relevant. In the Tribunal in each case the order is sought under Rule 31. Court rules vary according to which court you are in.

9   On the other hand, also think about what evidence you have, but may not need to use. There are two tests to consider. The first is whether it is relevant to what the court or tribunal is to decide. You may have gathered all your training records, or your full personnel file, but what is going to be relevant in the case? If nothing, do not use it. The second test is whether it is proportionate to have it. If you have gathered 100 photographs, do not just use all of them. That tends to mean that they have no real impact. Select the ones that best illustrate what you want. Similarly, if you have noted 200 incidents that you feel are evidence of discrimination, consider if they are all really going to help. Can you distil them into something like a top 20 or 30? Again doing that, making it clear that they are examples of a course of conduct more widely, may have greater impact.

10   Think about how you are going to show any particular evidence to the court. If it is CCTV footage will that be on a screen from a projector, or a laptop? Does the tribunal or court have the facility for that, or do you need

to provide it? If you do use a projector, does that make any difference to how the detail looks? How are you going to address many hours of footage, or many hours of audio recording?

11   Liaison with the other side is almost always helpful. It may be possible for example to agree part of the evidence. That can be done by a single document, called either a Statement of Agreed Facts, Joint Minute of Admissions, or similar. Where a fact is agreed, it does not need to be proved by other evidence. Sometimes all the evidence can be agreed this way, and that leaves only an argument over the law. The more that is agreed between the parties the better, both as it reduces the time needed for the hearing, is favourably received by the judge, and allows you to exercise a measure of control over how those facts are expressed.

12   Statements are sometimes used as evidence, and are sometimes just part of preparation. If in evidence, they are considered more fully later. If for preparation, which means that they are only seen by you, they can be a little less formalised, and are more a check to ensure that you know what the witness is likely to say, and can check that that is overall going to be more helpful than harmful. A statement is best taken in person, at a meeting face to face, but there may be occasions where that is not possible and it is taken over the telephone, or by Skype, or just by a series of emails. The statement should generally cover, in the person's own words, who they are, what they know of what happened, when that was, and what documents (electronic and actual) they either have, or are aware of. It is best practice to send the statement in draft form to the witness to check, and amend if they wish. It is also best practice to ask the witness to sign and date the statement once completed. That is useful for a number of reasons, first if the person happens to die, move abroad, or otherwise become unavailable when the statement might (not necessarily always) be something to submit to the judge as evidence, or secondly if the witness later changes his or her mind and says something very different, or thirdly as an aide memoire particularly if there is a long delay until the evidence is heard.

13   After taking the statements, consider who to call as a witness (which means who it is you are going to ask, or require by an order, to attend the hearing to give evidence for your side) and why that is. Will their evidence overall be sufficiently helpful? They might be clear on one aspect, but not for other parts of the case. They may help your argument partly, but if asked on another aspect may be damaging, and you need to assess overall whether they help or hinder. It is your decision who to call or not, and there can be risks in doing so. There have been many cases where a witness was called by one side, but then used by the opposition in their cross examination to their advantage. It is also however relevant to consider the reaction if a witness is not called, as the opposition can argue

that that leads to the inference that the evidence would not have assisted you. These can be difficult decisions, but you simply have to decide on balance whether there is more to be gained than lost.

Formal witness statements

There are some litigations that have evidence given partly by written witness statement, either as a standard process or following some form of order made in the course of that particular case. This then replaces the evidence given orally for the party calling the witness, known as evidence-in-chief. The witness statement is signed, and after the witness has been given the oath, that evidence is adopted as their own evidence, and the case moves normally to cross-examination by the other party. These witness statements are exchanged with the other side, and are seen by the judge. They can also be referred to when questions are being asked of other witnesses.

Witness statements used this way have some advantages. They save time for the witness in giving evidence, and for the judge in hearing it. They allow each side to control at least a part of the evidence. The statements being exchanged in advance helps each side to know the strength or weakness of the case the other side is putting forward, and that can assist in moving towards a settlement. They do however also have disadvantages. They take time to prepare, and where legally qualified advisers are engaged can add greatly to cost. There can also be something of a filtering process involved when the statement is being prepared, as it passes through the mind of the adviser who drafts it. The words used can be a mixture of those the witness used originally and those the framer of the statement has proposed. The statement can be the product not of purely open questions, such as 'what happened' but very leading questions such as 'the claimant tells me that the till was left open from time to time. I take it you agree with that?' That can then lead to the line in the statement 'Linda left the till open from time to time'. It may not be possible to know from the statement produced whether it was produced by predominantly one or more of this style of questioning.

There are some basic ground rules to consider however:

(i)   Try to ask open questions when framing the statement. The reason for that is that asking open questions is the best way of finding out what the witness is likely to say when questioned in the hearing. There is not much benefit of a statement that looks good on paper but falls apart when cross-examination starts. If you put words in the mouth of the witness by saying things like 'Did Linda then leave?' that risk is greater. How to ask open questions is considered in more detail later.

(ii)   Use the witness's own words when framing the statement wherever possible. A good trick in cross-examination is to ask the witness to explain what a particular word in their statement means, when the belief is that it comes from the adviser not the witness. That is so particularly for words that are legalistic, or unusual, or where they are not used in everyday speech. If the witness cannot say what a particular word means that tends to devalue the statement as a whole, as it gives the impression that the words are those of the framer of the statement more than those of the witness.

(iii) Keep sentences short.

(iv) If there is a reference to a document, email, note of meeting, etc, identify it clearly and where helpful quote in the statement the particular part that is helpful, such as 'In the meeting on 2 April 2018 this was accepted. It was confirmed in the note of the meeting, at page 125 of the bundle, where it records 'John accepted that he saw the till open from time to time, and sometimes closed it himself'.

(v) Stick to facts. Who did what, when? Who was present? What was seen, or heard?

(vi) Where opinions are provided, make that clear. Then check whether that is appropriate to include or not.

(vii) Go into as much detail as you can. Drill down into it. If it is said, for example, that a letter was found in a desk, ask things such as – where was the desk, where in it was the letter, if a drawer, which drawer, was it locked, where in the drawer, how was it found, was it on open display or hidden, or in an envelope, or otherwise?

(viii) Use paragraph numbers so that it is easy to navigate around the statement when evidence is heard.

(ix) Prepare a first draft and check it for accuracy. Check it against other documents you have, including other statements

(x) Send it to the witness to check, and say that it is a draft which they can change, take things out, or add more things.

(xi) Once finalised, have it signed and dated.

There are times when things go wrong. You may have needed to provide a document of some kind by a certain date, and you realise that you have missed the deadline. You may have tried to get evidence you need for something, such as medical records, but the surgery took far longer than you had expected to send them to you, and the time to produce them has passed. In short, you have made some kind of mistake. Everyone does.

'Anyone who has never made a mistake has never tried anything new' – Albert Einstein

What can you do?

The rules of procedure in tribunals and courts vary, but generally speaking more minor mistakes, delays or other similar failures do not mean the end of the case. In the tribunal for example there is an important Rule called the 'overriding objective' that includes dealing with cases justly and fairly. That tends to mean that if you were supposed to provide a schedule of loss by 5 April, and you do so on 12 April, the case is not likely to be struck out, which means that it is ended there and then. You may be given a bit of a telling off for being late, but usually that is all.

There are times however when that does not happen and being late can on occasion be disastrous. That is why having a diary is so important, and paying attention to dates is so important. If you simply fail to turn up for a hearing, the fault for that is entirely yours, and if the other side were there with all their witnesses some of whom had to travel from far away and take time off work, you may find that you have missed your chance.

Where mistakes arise, do not try to cover that up, or give a wrong explanation. As soon as you can, contact the tribunal or court, with a copy to the other side, set out what happened, why that was, what you now ask for (is it to receive the document late, or give you more time as you still do not have it?) and give an apology. Be candid, and then try to make sure the same problem does not happen again.

There are sometimes particular orders given to do something by a set time, and if that does not happen then either the case is struck out or the response is struck out. It is usually called an 'unless order'. It means that unless what is needed is done on time, and properly, your side loses. Pay special attention to those orders. They mean what they say.

Tactical admissions

As was mentioned earlier, it can be helpful not to fight a point that you are almost certain to lose. It can be better therefore to decide what to accept, admit that, and fight the other points. That tactical admission can shape the case, and move you from defence to attack. This applies mainly to respondents, but not exclusively.

There is a temptation for some respondents to fight everything, deny everything, and agree nothing. But that is not always the best tactic. There are times where it can be tactically very astute to admit the breach or failure. That means that there is no evidence heard on that point, and the focus can be on other areas, such as whether there was contribution by the claimant to a dismissal, or lack of mitigation.

Arlo Guthrie wrote a protest song for the Vietnam War called Alice's Restaurant. It is mainly a story he speaks, with a chorus he sings, with the words 'you can get everything you want, in Alice's restaurant'. The Alice of the song bought an old church, converted it to a restaurant, and he helped to remove the rubbish from that. He took the rubbish to a local dump and left it there. The local police found it and investigated, finding things like letters with addresses, and took lots of photographs and other pieces of evidence to prove what had happened. It went to court as a criminal prosecution. The police arrived with all the evidence, beautifully presented. The photographs were printed out, and enlarged, in colour, and there were charts and plans to show what had happened in great detail.

As Arlo pled guilty, however, all that evidence was not looked at. Although the point of the song was not that, but that because of the conviction for littering he was not drafted into the army, it is mentioned here for the principle that if the facts are not good on a point, it may be best to accept that, and admit it. Fight instead on the points where you have a realistic chance of winning them. It may be better not to dispute the part of the case you are very likely indeed to lose, in case doing so means you lose everything.

If therefore you are defending a case, and on some part of it there is a problem, think about embracing that, not fighting it. If there was a dismissal, but no procedures were followed at all, it can be best to accept that, and admit that there was an unfair dismissal. You can then argue that there would have been a fair dismissal had there been a different procedure, and separately that the employee contributed to the dismissal to the extent of 100%. That means that the tribunal does not hear evidence about how bad the procedures were, or that there were none, it hears evidence on other aspects where you can go on the attack. The opposition may be wrong footed by that, and not realise that they are the ones on the defence until it is too late.

If you are the claimant, and accept that you did something wrong but think that it was fairly minor and did not justify dismissal, you can either embrace that and accept a degree of fault, or argue that it was so minor as it should be disregarded entirely.

Preliminary hearings

There can be a variety of reasons for holding a preliminary hearing, but the three most often used are as follows: for case management issues; to determine a point or points that will have a real impact on the claim; or to consider applications for strike out or related matters.

Case management

In some situations, such as discrimination claims in the tribunal, a case management preliminary hearing will almost always be arranged. If not, and you think that it may be helpful, an application to hold that hearing can generally be made. A case management preliminary hearing is not a stage when evidence is heard, but will discuss the case as it has been pled, address how it is best handled, and what the next stage should be. Sometimes an agenda is sent to each party to try and find out more about the case before the hearing. If that is sent, it should be completed and returned to the tribunal within the time given. A case management preliminary hearing is referred to as a closed hearing, as it is just the parties or their representatives who attend, and it can be either in person or by telephone.

It is always best to prepare fully for one of these hearings. Do not treat it lightly as if it does not matter. You may be asked to explain what your case is about, and what legal provisions you rely on. There may be a discussion about whether there should be a preliminary hearing on one point, such as time bar or the other examples given below, and you may wish to argue that there should not be that, but that all points should be held over to be decided after all the evidence has been heard at a final hearing. The time bar rules are not simple, and you may wish to argue that the claim is not time-barred at all, for example because of there being a series of acts that continued up to the point of dismissal, or that there is a way to proceed with the case even if it is outside the normal time limit. The test for that can vary between claims. In general the two issues are whether it was reasonably practicable to have done so in time, or whether it is just and equitable to allow the claim to proceed. They are different tests and are looked at differently.

It can also help to discuss what happens next with the other party or their representative before the hearing takes place. That way you may gain some additional knowledge of what their position is, and have the chance to see what progress can be made.

Very often at the case management stage there will be discussion about practical matters such as documents, agreement on facts, and remedy. On documents there may be a discussion about how long it will take to be ready to exchange them. Be careful about agreeing too quick an exchange. It may take you longer than you expect to get what you need, particularly if that is from someone whose response is outside your control. Generally speaking there is a period to exchange, and then one party prepares the single Bundle of Documents, which is indexed and paginated. In court, the rules may be different.

There might be a discussion about having a Statement of Agreed Facts (other terms can be used in court) which records those facts that the parties agree and that do not need to be referred to in evidence because of that. In some cases all, or a very large part, of the facts can be agreed, and what is left is an argument over applying the law to them, but even in a heavily disputed case some of the basic facts can be agreed, and that helps to save time. It allows concentration on those parts of the evidence that are in dispute.

There can be a discussion about whether or not to have a preliminary hearing to determine one or more particular issues, such as a time-bar. Again be careful, and do not agree to that too readily. Very often it is better for a claimant to have a final hearing fixed, than have a preliminary hearing on one point that may well lead to a delay in the case being concluded, or the dismissal of the case before the evidence is heard. The discussion can be about practical issues for a final hearing such as whether or not to use witness statements in evidence.

More often there will be a discussion about the remedy sought, and the preparation of a Schedule of Loss. That is a document that sets out what financial claims are made. An example of that is in the Appendix. Think carefully about that. The remedy sought can be important. Is it just financial compensation, or is there also a claim for re-instatement or re-engagement?

The discussion may also be about the dates for the next hearing, whether preliminary or final, and you should check with your witnesses about whether there are any dates to avoid for holidays, hospital appointments or similar. You should do that for yourself as well. It can be useful to discuss that with the other party in advance as well, to find out how many witnesses each side has, and how long the case may take.

There are a large number of other issues that can arise, as provided for in the rules. They can include issues such as restricted reporting orders, or orders seeking to preserve confidentiality, holding hearings in private (or parts of them), lead cases if there are a large number of similar claims, and others. The rules should be checked as often there is a provision about the matter you wish to consider, or if not there is at least a general power for case management that can be referred to.

Determination of issues

A preliminary hearing can also be fixed to determine one or more points, and that involves the hearing of evidence. It is called an open hearing in tribunal proceedings. It tends to take place in the tribunal building, although sometimes, especially in light of the Covid-19 pandemic it takes place remotely. The hearing can address a large variety of matters, but they tend to be about ones that determine a large part of the case. They can include the following:

(i)   Issues about jurisdiction, such as whether the case is time-barred, or whether the claim is about circumstances outside the UK and the provision does not apply.

(ii)   Issues about status, such as whether the claimant was an employee or a worker or was neither of these. If the claim is for unfair dismissal, for example, the claimant must be an employee and if for holiday pay, they must be an employee or a worker.

(iii)   Whether the claimant has a protected characteristic such as a disability in order to claim discrimination.

(iv)   Whether there was a protected disclosure for the purposes of a whistleblowing claim.

(v)   Whether there was a transfer under the TUPE Regulations 2006.

(vi)   Whether there was a redundancy involving 20 or more people which triggered the need for collective consultation with a union or elected representatives of the workforce.

As these matters can either lead to the dismissal of the whole claim, or a substantial part of the claim, they should be treated as importantly as if it was a final hearing.

Strike out

The third category of preliminary hearing is where there is an application for strike out of all or part of the claims made. It is often made with an alternative application for a deposit order in tribunal claims. In court the process can be different depending on the rules that apply, but the principle of seeking the ending of the claim on the basis of what is pled is similar.

    Strike out may be considered if there are no reasonable prospects of the claim succeeding, or if there is some other reason to do so such as if a fair trial of the issues is not possible (in the Tribunal Rules it is provided for in Rule 37; in court there are separate provisions either in the Rules or from practice and authority in other cases). For the respondent it has the advantage of being able to argue that either all of the claim, or parts of it, should not proceed to the stage of hearing evidence, which saves much time and expense, as well as risk. The test is a high one, which means that it is not easy to achieve success. It may also lead to the claimant providing further details of the claim, which may be by amendment, to respond to the arguments made. Whether to seek strike out therefore is something to consider carefully.

    There are a number of tests that are generally considered when addressing the application, but in simple terms there are two tests – first is one of the provisions in the Rule made out, and secondly is strike out of the claim the proportionate approach in light of the overriding objective? In discrimination cases there is a particularly high test, as there is a public interest in having such cases heard, but it is possible to meet it. The same approach is taken in cases similar to discrimination such as whistleblowing.

    An alternative remedy is to seek a deposit order, provided for in Rule 39. That arises if there are few reasonable prospects of success. If so, the tribunal has the ability to order that a deposit must be paid by the claimant before the case continues. The amount of that deposit is fixed having regard to the claimant's means, and tends to be at a relatively low sum. It is also limited, at present, to £1,000. If a deposit order is granted, that is a strong hint that the claim is thought likely to fail, and that should be considered carefully for that reason. The real effect of the deposit order however is if the claim does proceed because the deposit is paid, and the claim fails. If that happens, there is a strong chance that the tribunal will find the respondent entitled to some, perhaps all, of the costs or expenses it incurred after that order was made. That can be a very significant sum.

If, therefore, the respondent does make such an application, it needs to be considered carefully. It can be tactically sensible to offer to withdraw what may be weaker claims, leaving stronger ones, rather than insist on pursuing everything. On the other hand there may be something that can be added to the pleading to make it clear that the claim does have some reasonable prospects of success.

Settlement

As the date of any hearing to conclude the case draws near, check again about the prospects of success, and whether an alternative resolution may be possible. It is sometimes thought that approaching the other side late on to ask about that is a sign of weakness. It is not. It is a sign of maturity. The risk of litigation cuts both ways. Sometimes the other side will hope that you make the first move. If you hope the same, nothing happens. The cost in money and time can affect both sides, as can the stress of it. Those issues are highlighted most acutely as the date of the hearing approaches. It is one reason why many cases settle so late in the day.

If that is not possible, or you are sure that you want to proceed and do not wish to try to settle, then the case moves towards the stage of hearing evidence. That is usually the final stage, subject to any appeal. It requires a great deal of time to prepare for properly. Of course it is possible to turn up and see how the case goes without that, but preparation is the key to winning.

Chapter 6

Preparation for the hearing

Preparation has been mentioned before, and I make no apology for its repetition. It is the single factor that is most likely to make the difference between success and failure. It was expressed very effectively in this line:

'The harder I practice the luckier I get' – Gary Player

The words of a golfer are entirely appropriate for litigation. Although luck plays a part both in sport and in litigation the basic rule in both is that the better the preparation, the higher the chance of success. There is no direct relationship between the two, but preparation is the area where you have the ability to control what you do. That is all very well, but how do you prepare? That in my experience is best done back to front.

At a hearing (whether a preliminary hearing for one or more points to be determined as discussed in **Chapter 5**, or a final hearing) there are two phases. The first is when the evidence is heard. The second is when there is an argument presented by each side as to why they should succeed, or the other side should fail. It is usually called a submission. When preparing for a hearing, it is best to start with the submission and work backwards from there. It is the document that sets out the facts you hope to prove, the law that applies, and the analysis as to why you win. It is like a map of your side of the case, which is why starting there tends to help.

The submission

How to set out a submission is considered in greater detail later, but at this stage what you are looking to do is create a very basic framework to help in your preparation. The basic structure of a submission is normally this:

(a)   Set out what you want the tribunal or court to do.

(b)   Set out the main facts.

(c)   Set out the law.

(d)   Explain why the law, applied to the facts, gives you the remedy you seek.

(e)   Confirm again what you want.

The Law

When preparing the submission the best place to start is the law, even though that goes after the facts in most submissions. Why is that? It is because the law directs what is relevant, what matters, and is the foundation for the decision on remedy. What law is relevant has been referred to above, but can be a mix of common law principles and statutes of a variety of kinds. You need to tease out from these sources the legal principles that are relevant. They can be deceptively simple such as: 'was there a breach of contract? If so, was it material (meaning sufficiently serious to be fundamental and a repudiation)?'.

These become the legal issues that the judge will decide. That list of issues is like a series of individual games that are played which in the end determine the result. They can differ between themselves, and the evidence for each issue may be very different, such that the outcome of each issue can itself vary widely.

Setting out the relevant law therefore establishes the framework that the case will be decided against. It directs you to what facts are likely to be the key ones, and those areas that may not be relevant at all. Without knowing the law, it is not possible to know not only where the goalposts are, but what game you are playing.

The Facts

The second stage is working out what the facts are. That includes not just the facts that you think you can establish, but also what the other side are trying to prove, and what you can do either to disprove what they allege, or reduce its impact in some way. That can be found in their pleadings, but also from correspondence and documentation. Although this also applies in a preliminary hearing it is particularly important at the stage of the final hearing.

It is easy to fall into the trap of expecting that all of your evidence will be accepted. Rarely if ever does everything go as expected, perfectly. It is a little like asking your horse at the Grand National to jump every fence without touching any part of any one of them. Theoretically it is possible, but in reality it is not what happens.

How then do you do this? One way is to sort out the evidence into those aspects that are 'good' facts and 'bad' facts. A good fact is one that helps you prove what you want to, or to disprove what the other side are arguing. A bad fact is the opposite – it helps the other side in some way.

There may be facts which are neither good nor bad. That may be because they do not really matter, or because they help neither side particularly. In the breach of contract case, there may be no dispute over the size of the company, its structure, what it does, and its policies and procedures. They are facts that are relevant to the decision as providing background and context, but do not inform the decision maker as to which side is to win. They are therefore relevant, but neutral.

There may be other facts that are simply not relevant. Witnesses may wish to tell you a great deal about what happened to them, or how they felt about things, or anything else that they feel important, but that may not be of any help whatsoever in deciding which side is to win this particular argument. Part of the process therefore is to distinguish between what is relevant, and what is not.

This can be done is a number of ways. One is to start with the chronology, add to that the information you have, then write next to each fact either words such as "good" "bad" or "irrelevant", or an initial such as 'G' 'B' and 'I'. If a fact is not relevant, it can be deleted either by a line with a pen, or by removing it electronically.

What is left is then a list of those facts which are good, and those which are bad. The good facts tend to speak for themselves, but not always. It can be important both to be sure you can prove them, and to highlight them. Proof can be from more than one source, such as a second witness, or a written document of some kind. If you don't have that, consider whether to obtain it, and where from. Use the ABC guide set out above.

The focus is also on the bad facts. They can lose you the case. Depending on how many they are, and how bad they are, they can be conclusive. They require great care and much thought. If there is a particularly bad fact, what are you going to do about it?

There are a number of ways of addressing them. The guidance can be broken down into Context, Consistency' and Contact.

Context is all about who knew what and when. There may be an email where something damning is said. What did the person know at that time? Was it knowledge, or pure suspicion? Did they have any involvement in the process, anything to gain, any personal stake in the issue?

Consistency is about the other evidence – were they alone in having this thought? Do others disagree? Who are they, what did they know. How long is their experience, how many qualifications do they have? Why might they be right?

Contact is about the person – who are they, why might they not be believed? Are they independent, or not – if not why not? Have there been issues as to the honesty of that witness before, either in a disciplinary context or criminal convictions for example? It is however not necessarily straightforward to attack a witness's credibility. Unless the grounds to do so are very clear, it can be a dangerous tactic that can backfire, particularly for witnesses who have nothing to gain from giving evidence.

Be careful therefore about trying to ignore evidence that is contrary to your position – hoping that it won't be believed by the judge, or won't come up, or believing that it can be easily disproved or discounted. In the battle between theories of conspiracy or cock-up, the latter almost always is proved to be the right one. Conspiracies do happen, but they are rare, and proving them is not at all easy.

It is helpful to do all this while keeping in mind a simple concept – what is the story that you are trying to tell? At the most basic level, for a claimant that story is very often: 'something happened which I think is wrong and which the other side is legally responsible for'. For a respondent it is something like: 'the claim made against me/us is not legally right'. The terms of the story around that, and how it is told, vary from case to case. Sometimes it is found purely in documents (for example what a contract says). But more often it is a mix of evidence from witnesses supported by the documents.

Analysis of prospects

After marshalling all of the facts, and considering how good or bad each one is, you need to stand back and consider how likely it is that you will win. The prospects may vary from one issue to the next. It is best to look at the evidence as a whole, and consider how likely it is each issue will be determined for or against you.

That is no easy task. It depends on an assessment of factors such as the weight of evidence, and the strength of that evidence. It is a mix of quantity and quality. It involves considering how likely it is that each witness may be regarded (not by you, but by the judge) as credible and reliable. There is an important difference between them. Credibility is about telling the truth. Most witnesses try to do that, although not all do. There are times where it can be demonstrable that a witness is lying, or very likely to be lying, but again that tends to be rare.

Reliability is a different concept entirely – it is whether the witness is more likely to be accurate.

There are a number of factors that usually come into play when considering these points. They include:

(i)   Documentation from the time of the event. Where documents are prepared at the time, often before any dispute has formed, they tend to be more reliable than recollections later which can be affected by the dispute.

(ii)   Statements that are inconsistent. If someone says A one day and B later, the more inconsistent A and B are the less reliable that person is, and depending on context that may also raise doubt as to credibility.

(iii)   Statements that are not challenged. If in a letter, email, minute or other document A says something that B later alleges was wrong, but did not challenge at the time, that tends to mean that B is less reliable on that point, on the basis that if it was wrong you would expect B to say so.

55

> There may of course be a reason for that, and if that is set out well the impression may be different.

(iv)   Evidence from a witness who has no particular interest in the matter, and no axe to grind, can be particularly powerful. A truly independent witness may not be easy to find. Sometimes people's very role in an organisation or event makes them not entirely independent, but where that is very minor their perspective can be as good a basis as any to get to the truth of what happened.

(v)   The more witnesses there are saying the same thing tends to indicate that they are being accurate. It is not simply a numbers game, but the more the numbers the greater usually is the strength.

(vi)   Common sense plays a part. If what is being suggested is in accordance with normal expectations, or normal practice, or just what you would feel would be expected, then that tends to be viewed more favourably than what would be unusual.

There are others, but these are often those that help in the assessment. Using the so what test, which is described below, is another helpful way of considering how good, or bad, the evidence on any point is.

Where you are both the party, and the person trying to make the assessment, objectivity is impossible. You will be bound to believe that your explanations are correct, and should be accepted. So wherever you can, ask someone else for their perspective. Put all the details on paper, so that they can read it alone and without having you looming over them and influencing their thoughts, and ask them for their view of it all.

It is important not just to concentrate on your own case. Think about what the other side are to argue, where their good and bad facts are for those points, and what you can do about them. They may have an issue that they wish to raise, that you do not (for example time bar). Address each issue directly.

It can then be a good discipline to try and work out prospects of success for each issue, and give reasons in writing for that. There are some points that may not be seriously disputed where the prospects can be very high, even 100%. But generally where there is a dispute, the prospects of success would not be likely to go much above 80/20. If you do not know how good or bad they are, the starting point is 50/50. If you feel that the prospects are less than that, be honest with yourself and say so. But remember that litigation is risky. Cases with what had been very low initial prospects of success have succeeded.

Analysis of facts

I mentioned earlier the ABC of preparation. It is important not to take a first impression of something, particularly something that is a bad fact from your own perspective. See if it can be presented in a way that is less bad. It was put this way:

> 'Facts are like cows. Stare at them long enough and they move' – Dorothy L Sayers

Dorothy L Sayers was a crime writer in the mould of Agatha Christie. Her point is a good one – if you consider the facts long enough, new ones or different ones can emerge.

Even though you have already started some of the preparations about the facts when starting the case, go back over each issue, and all the evidence, and see what can be done to improve the prospects, particularly for those aspects where the chances of success are not as high as you would like. Can you get any more evidence on the point? Is there another witness you might speak to? Check, and check again, until you feel you have done all you reasonably can. It is amazing what can sometimes be achieved if you dig deep enough. A fact that appears very unhelpful to you, perhaps something that may well lead to you losing, can be set in a different context entirely and then it is either not damaging at all, or not so seriously damaging. It happens in fictional crime dramas all the time, of course, and there are times when there is simply too much bad evidence against you. There is however a need to keep going, think, and check.

To take one example, there may have been a statement during an early stage of what happened. What exactly was said, what was known then, and why were the precise words used? What could the person actually see from where they were? What could be heard? When did events take place? Is the evidence inconsistent with some other aspect? Is there any incentive you are aware of for that witness not to be truthful? Is there anything that might lead to them being suspected of being inaccurate, such as being partial, or tired?

What lies at the heart of adversarial litigation is the concept that by each side doing what it can to find evidence, and put forward its case as best it can, there is the best chance of getting to the truth, and achieving a just result. Facts most often win cases. The trick is to find them. That means looking at all the evidence you have, and seeing what you can do to improve the part that t looks bad.

The OJ Simpson trial, where he was accused of the murder of two people, was televised, and illustrated the lengths to which it is possible to go to challenge each and every fact against a party, or put it in context, or consider it from a different angle. What at first glance may have seemed compelling evidence of guilt was made to appear less so, to an extent that influenced the jury. Simpson was acquitted of the criminal charges, but when a civil case was brought, where the standard of proof is not beyond reasonable doubt but the balance of probabilities, he was found to have murdered the two victims. Some of the trial footage is on the internet, and the trial was also the subject of a drama on TV.

You will not have the resources to do the same as in that case, but the principle is the same. You can challenge any item of evidence, examine it, put it into context or look at it from a different perspective, and that can change how it looks to the judge.

The importance of every word of every document

Emails tend to be rushed, sent off almost without thinking. In long meetings, people sometimes relax, and start saying things that they later regret. What is said in the pleadings at the start of the case may seem entirely wrong about half way through, when more is known.

It is important to be able to check therefore all words used in every document. Check for consistency, and for inconsistency, both for the opposition and for you. One of the techniques in cross-examination is to use someone's own words against them. It can be devastating if done well, and entirely disturb the serenity of a witness. To do that, it is essential to know the documents, and to study them. It is also essential to get all the documents that are relevant. That does not mean just getting every email someone has sent over the last five years. Too much documentation is a problem, not least for the judge hearing the case. But the right documentation is different.

Social media is increasingly a factor in this. That can be texts, but online posts and blogs from Facebook, Twitter, Instagram, Snapchat and others. Gaining access to that may not be straightforward. Having it in a form that you can work with is also not straightforward – it may be on a phone. So get it printed off, into the same style of page as other documents, and start looking through them.

The 'so what?' test

It is always important to be clear on why a particular fact is both relevant and helpful to your argument, or unhelpful to the other side's argument. So often evidence is just given, a long story about all that happened, and much of it is of no importance in the case at all. It is as if it is a kind of therapy, and the witness is using the opportunity to get a lot off his or her chest about, for example, how awful life at the employer was.

Litigation however is about winning the dispute within the rules. To do that, you need to be constantly asking yourself about whether the evidence you could present is relevant. If it is not, then do not do so. Concentrate ruthlessly on what is relevant. That will mean that your case is put far more powerfully and persuasively.

Inferences

An inference is a very useful way of filling gaps in the evidence. If you are trying to prove something, but do not have direct evidence of it, you may be able to do so by using an inference.

An inference is something that arises from the evidence heard, and is a form of natural consequence of those facts. It is almost like educated guesswork. You start with one set of facts that you can prove, which are normally called primary facts, and from those you can try to make the inference which is normally called a secondary fact.

In the case of Linda that we have looked at, VHS Ltd may not have direct evidence against her. There is no CCTV footage that shows her doing anything, and no admission from her. So instead they can try to set out a series of primary facts, from which it can be inferred that she was involved in dishonesty. That could be from the following:

(i)   The evidence of what other people said about her.

(ii)   Her own breach of procedures.

(iii)   What she said when questioned, which includes what she did not say but later alleged:

These facts do not directly prove that Linda was involved in dishonesty (fuller details are in the Appendix), but create a possibility that she was, and the stronger that possibility the more likely it is that the inference can be drawn that it was her.

If you are to try and rely on inference, it is important to be clear as to which primary facts you are using, and what evidence you have for each of them. You also need to think of whether there are more of these primary facts that you can use – the more you have that are relevant, the better the chances.

The difficulty of the use of inferences is the very absence of direct evidence. The other side may try to demolish each of them, or at least some of them. Linda may attack the evidence against her from others, minimise the effect of her own breach of procedure, show that she made no personal gain from that, and give strong reasons why others may not be telling the truth.

Inference is particularly important in those claims where the person is not likely to admit what is alleged, either because they are lying, but also because they do not see the point and do not admit that they have acted as alleged, even to themselves. That is particularly so in cases of discrimination. Someone may not appreciate that they have a discriminatory mind set, and believe, quite honestly, that they are above that. Others may not wish to be thought of as someone who has such a mind-set, and fight the allegation very strongly because of that. Discrimination can be conscious, or unconscious.

Tribunals do not therefore expect there to be direct evidence of discrimination – it can arise, but its absence is no bar to the case succeeding. But where there is no direct evidence, what matters is whether the inference can be drawn, and in turn that depends at least partly on what the primary facts are.

It can also be affected by whether or not there is a prima facie case, meaning one which can succeed in the absence of an explanation, when the onus may move from the claimant, to the respondent, with the respondent then required to prove that there was no discrimination.

In this situation, what tends to be used most often is evidence of events that are not what would normally happen, or are against normal practice or procedure, or which somehow look out of line, or simply 'odd'. The more of those that there are, the more they might arise because of some form of discrimination.

For example, if the case is one of sex discrimination, with a woman complaining that she was not selected for interview for a job for which she was qualified, and the short list was all male, the primary facts might be:

(i)   All of the senior managers were male.

(ii)   Her CV showed that she met all the qualifications requirements for the role.

(iii) The person appointed did not have all those qualifications.

(iv)   Her experience was far longer and at a higher level than the person appointed.

(v)   No woman had ever held a management role at the organisation.

(vi)   The organisation had had two other employment tribunal claims involving women who claimed discrimination on grounds of their pregnancy, each of which was settled on the morning of the hearing.

(vii) One funder organisation for them had publicly withdrawn support for them last year because of their lack of diversity.

(viii) They did not have any policy for equality or diversity, and no policy or procedure for selecting applicants for interview.

(ix)   No notes of the process to select for interview were kept, and the reasons given for not selecting the claimant were different between each of the three men on the panel.

These facts are sometimes described as 'red flags', which means that they give the impression that something might have been wrong in the process. They do not directly prove discrimination, but they show that that was at the very least possible, and raise the prima facie case which means that the organisation has to prove that it did not take place. They might be able to do so, despite these red flags. If for example they can say that the successful applicant had a particular set of skills and experience that was vital for the role, and only that one person did so, then they have at the least a fighting chance.

The elevator pitch

The story being told is not just what happened. It is also why that version should be believed. That 'why should I win' question is covered more fully later, but at this stage it is helpful to think of the story as being the answer to that question, in a single sentence that can explain in a minute or two what the case is about and why. That then forms the foundation for all the other preparations. For the case Linda is making, it might be something like:

> 'I was unfairly dismissed because the investigation was wholly inadequate, and had it been made properly that would have established that I was innocent of any dishonesty.'

For the respondent it might be:

> 'We carried out a reasonable investigation and had a reasonable belief that Linda was involved in a dishonest scheme, and we were fully justified in dismissing her summarily.'

An 'elevator pitch' is a proposal either for a business idea, or a product, or a service, which can be made in the time it takes a lift to go up a few floors. It means putting the proposal into very short and direct terms, which can be communicated in a minute or two, but effectively, so that by the time the lift reaches the floor the pitch can succeed. It is not easy to do, but very useful.

Winning a case requires more than just the evidence. There needs to be a reason why your evidence should be preferred to the evidence of the other side, and why that means that you win. That requires an explanation. The claimant and respondent are fighting the same case, but each comes at it from a different angle, and the answers to the same question of why should that party win will be very different. The stronger the arguments in your favour, the better the chances. So on top of the story of what happened, you need a second story which persuasively explains why the judge should find for you.

That means working out what is the best argument – or arguments – for you. Is it simply that something was not done that should have been? Is it that a document has a provision that you can use? Is it that the case was taken too late? Is it that a witness could have given vital evidence but was never approached? Is it that the story of the other side has changed over time, and the one prepared in writing at the time of the incident is the one most likely to be right?

Whatever it is, think at this fairly early stage how you are going to persuade the judge, and what are the key points for that. There may be one, or more. Sometimes a case in reality is resolved by the answer to one single question. At other times it is more a case of considering all of the evidence as a whole, and that needs to involve many individual points of evidence. This, though, is the time to start thinking of what are the point or points of which you need to persuade the judge.

Remedy

Whether you are making the claim or defending it, make sure that you include the remedy in the analysis. What are you seeking? Why is that? Is it only money or something else, such as re-instatement to your old job?

What evidence is there over the amount claimed? What needs to be proved? What documentation is there to do so? If there is an issue of loss of earnings for example, what evidence is there of the earnings before termination of employment, the attempts to get employment, including those that failed, and of the new level of earnings? What were the benefits before termination, and currently? How much should be attributed to factors such as pension, insured benefits, bonuses, allowances, overtime etc?

Mitigation of loss is a basic principle of the law. If you are claiming money as damages, you have a duty to take reasonable steps to keep your loss to a minimum. That can mean seeking a new job, or undergoing treatment to improve your medical condition in some situations. Whether or not your failure to get a new job is a failure to mitigate depends on a variety of factors, such as the attempts made, your health, the job market where you live, and others.

It is a good discipline to prepare a document for the sums claimed, often called a Schedule of Loss, which includes each element of the claim, and attaches documentation (often called vouching) to prove each one. If you are defending the clam, ask for it if it is not part of the process or seek an order from the judge. Then consider whether you are going to attack it, or accept it. If you do not agree with it, why is that, and do you have evidence to prove it? Could you get it? Where from? For example, if you think that the attempts to find new work were not sufficient, what do you say should have happened, what jobs were there, how could they have been secured, and what would they have paid? What evidence is there for that, such as advertisements online or in newspapers, or from a recruitment agency who can provide the detail?

Expert evidence

There are occasions where more than factual evidence is necessary. That is when you consider using an expert witness to provide their opinion in their area of expertise. They can cover particular areas of a case, such as evidence on whether a professional person was guilty of negligence, or remedies including calculations for pension loss. They can cover a wide range of problems, such as the law of a foreign country where that needs to be considered (which, although a legal matter, is a question of fact, counter-intuitively) or the circumstances of a claimant medically either as they are, or would be but for medication being given for example, but they should be used with care. They do not remove the judge from the case, and expert evidence is like any other evidence and needs to be relevant to the issues, and is then weighed in the balance with all other evidence. A judge is not bound to accept expert evidence either at all, or in any particular respect.

There is an almost infinite variety of experts, or those professing to be. The choice of which expert to use is therefore an important one. Many cases have foundered because the expert one side chose was either not the right one at all, or one who was less well suited to give evidence on that particular case. If the issue is a medical one, for example, there is a world of difference between using an expert who is a consultant in Accident and Emergency medicine, a consultation orthopaedic surgeon, or a consultant neurosurgeon. Each one may be the right expert for a particular case, depending on what exactly the issues are. But the other two may well not be, even though they may have a great deal of knowledge and experience.

Experts can, and increasingly are, appointed jointly by the parties. The parties then generally agree to be bound by the opinion given. Experts can also be instructed by each side, so that each one has its own opinion and those opinions can be, and not infrequently are, in conflict.

When instructing an expert the following is a basic list of the issues to consider:

1   Is it necessary? Expert evidence be not always be accepted by a court or tribunal, and if in doubt it is best to check.

2   Who will pay? The cost can be significant, and it is not an issue that normally can be left to the end of the case when you hope you will have won.

3   Who should be instructed? It is vital to get the right expert, someone with the necessary qualifications and experience to address the issues being referred. Check both their qualifications, not only on the issue, but also their experience in giving expert evidence in court or tribunal. Ask them for a CV. Check online for any comments about them – not all are as they seem, and if there has been critical comment about them in another case that can be damaging.

4   What should you give them? It is best to be clear on that, and if in doubt ask them what they may wish. Normally you provide: (i) all pleadings; (ii) statements; (iii) documents lodged by both parties relevant to the issue; and (iv) a letter of instruction setting out the questions you need their opinion on. In addition you may need to provide other materials such as medical records, a company's records of a matter, an HR file, or otherwise.

5   When you get the report, consider carefully what to do with it. Are you happy that it covers the issues as you wish? Do you wish to propose any changes? That is generally permissible, but should be done with great care.

It is the expert's opinion that is being given, and that is given, although initially to you, in reality to the court or tribunal. You should not be seen to influence it unduly. You may therefore ask them to consider changing an aspect, or correcting a point of detail or providing more information not previously given, but seeking wholescale changes to suit your case may well go too far. You may be better off getting another expert, or recognising that you now have greater problems than you had anticipated.

6   If both sides are getting reports, consider whether you send yours to the court or tribunal, or suggest swapping them with the other side first. Consider therefore whether you have an advantage in providing it sooner, or whether it is better to hold it back for as long as you can.

7   If there is a report from the other side, ask your own expert for his or her comments about it. Check their expert's credentials online. Check their qualifications, length of experience in the field, prior experience in providing expert opinions and, separately, in actually giving evidence and having that tested. Look at what they have seen – have they got all the documents your expert got, have they based their opinion on any facts that you challenge or on assumptions that you consider to be wrong? Have they carried out any investigations of their own, undertaken any research or testing or similar? Then consider whether to have a meeting with your expert to check all of these issues, see whether the opinion you have might need to change, or why it is that your expert says that he or she is satisfied that they remain right and the other opinion is wrong.

8   Recognise that when two experts disagree, the role of the judge is different from the assessment of facts. The judge can agree in part with both, side with one completely, or consider an alternative decision. Making an assessment of how expert evidence may be treated by the judge is particularly difficult because of that.

Technical evidence

Technical evidence is rather different from expert evidence. It is essentially not about opinion, but fact. It may be very complicated fact, and difficult for a judge who is not aware of the background to that, but it is factual evidence like any other. It does however require careful handling. The technical evidence may be for example about how a particular item of equipment should be operated when someone was dismissed for doing so wrongly. It is likely to be something that the judge does not have personal knowledge of, but understanding it will be important in deciding the case.

First it is often easiest to present it in written form if you can. That gives the judge time to consider it, re-reading it if that helps. Secondly, it is important to explain the context. Treat the judge as if they are a complete novice, assume no knowledge at all, and start from basic principles. Thirdly, explain all technical terms, acronyms or similar. They may be entirely familiar to you, and the witness, but mean absolutely nothing to the judge. Fourthly, be clear what the relevance of the evidence is. Quite often, it is little more than background information, where the issue that matters is not in truth the technical one at all. But there are times where the evidence is crucial to the main issue. If for example the case is one for unfair dismissal, and the employee was dismissed for what was claimed to be gross negligence, where the role being performed was a highly skilled one, some understanding of the role, why it was said to be negligently performed, and what the appropriate penalty for that could be, could be necessary. If the case is one of breach of contract also, the test is a different one, and there the expert evidence may be a benefit but not a need.

Finally, do not just use words. There are times when a photograph, plan, drawing, map, or something visual like that, can be very helpful in demonstrating to a judge what is meant.

Documentation for the hearing

Most often, documents must be provided to the court or tribunal a set number of days before the hearing starts, with a copy provided to the other side, and copies available for the judge, any others involved in the decision (such as lay members of a tribunal) and for the witnesses giving evidence.

Sometimes they must be provided in a single bundle, with sets of papers from both sides incorporated together. At other times each side provides its own documents. That can be in either one document or a series of documents. Usually there must be some form of front page with a list of the documents, which can be called an inventory, and the documents must be both indexed, and paginated. That makes it easy to find a particular page or passage when someone is later giving evidence, or when submissions are made.

This all takes time. If there is a single bundle, normally one side is told to prepare that. It should be a mechanical exercise of collating two sets of documents. Usually the bundle follows a basic format as follows:

1   Pleadings (such as a Claim Form and Response Form).

2   Founding documents (such as a contract of employment, policy documents etc).

3   Factual documents on the merits of the case in chronological order, starting with the oldest and ending with the most recent.

4   Documents on remedy, including financial matters.

The rules can be different depending on where the case is being litigated, and as referred to above, there may be separate inventories prepared by each party.

It is then necessary to check the bundle, or equivalent, to ensure that it is paginated properly, that double sided documents have not been single copied so that pages are missing, that the quality of the document is legible, and that the index properly lists all documents and their page numbers. Some documents may require special treatment:

(i)   If there is any form of recording, such as one from a mobile phone, usually it is best to provide that in some format, and a transcript of it. That way it can be checked before the hearing starts to identify any disagreement or issues as to its quality, or whether it is to be accepted into the evidence at all.

(ii)   Photographs should be clear, and preferably in colour if that is the original. It can be important to know who took the photograph, and when.

(iii)   If there is any form of moving image, such as CCTV, footage from a mobile phone or similar, consider how best to show that to the judge. It may be necessary to do so from a projector, and check on how that is to be achieved, and whether you need to provide whatever is needed to show the footage. Or can it be done by sending an electronic file to the judge for viewing on a laptop? How will that be viewed by a witness? Will the view from a projector be the same resolution and clarity as if on a mobile phone? What you want to do is present the evidence as effectively as practicable, and that may not be as simple as it first appears.

(iv)   Policies, procedures, etc should all be those in force at the time of the incident, or event. If there are changes afterwards, and that is relevant, produce both versions.

(v)   If some documents contain sensitive information, such as highly personal medical details, confidential business plans, commercially sensitive pricing information or similar, it may be possible to remove reference to that by a process called 'redacting'. That means hiding the sensitive detail, either by use of a thick black highlighting pen, or electronic removal, or similar. It should however be clear that there has been such a redaction, and if there is any dispute over that it is best dealt with earlier than at the hearing itself.

Other preparation

Some other matters may require attention, depending on where the case is being heard. Some witnesses will appear voluntarily, but some may not be at all keen to do so. You may therefore need to seek some form of order to compel their attendance. Once granted, that may be sent to the witness by the court or tribunal, or it may need to be something that you should attend to, either personally or through some form of officer of the court.

You may need to consider arrangements for vulnerable witnesses. That category can include children, those who are disabled, or a witness who is vulnerable because of the nature of the case (for example one about allegations of sexual harassment by a manager at work).

For children and disabled persons, including those with some form of mental health condition, special arrangements may need to be made. It is often helpful to discuss them initially with the other side, and then to raise them with the judge in advance of the hearing. The tribunal or court are unlikely to know if a witness is vulnerable, and what arrangements may be needed, so you need to tell them, and do that in advance so that the arrangements needed are there on the day.

What those arrangements are will depend on the circumstances of the witness. For some it might mean a more considerate approach to questioning, such as by ensuring that there are no raised voices, short and simple questions, and having a relative in the room for support for example. For others it might be having regular breaks. Some may need to use aids, such as notes, in advance. In more extreme cases there have been suggestions of the need to give advance notice of questions, or the ability to give answers other than orally (such as by using a laptop or similar).

Where there are allegations of harassment, intimidation, exploitation, victimisation or similar, the claimant may be very nervous of appearing in the same room as the person accused of the behaviour involved. That is particularly so in cases of sexual harassment. The mere presence of the person alleged to have harassed the claimant can be an issue, and that is made more difficult if the person is involved in the case as a party, and more difficult again if that person is acting for him or herself. Special arrangements may need to be considered if that happens.

That can include discussing whether the questioning can be by the alleged harasser at all, or whether that should be by the judge on questions prepared by that party, or whether there needs to be different hearings at which each of those two parties gives their evidence separately. That is very unusual indeed, but shows the extent to which the normal arrangements can be varied if there is a proper reason to do that.

Some courts require the evidence to be recorded by a shorthand writer, which the party pursuing the case has to organise. There may be a need to play some form of visual evidence, either from a DVD or some form of electronic file. You need to ensure that the facility to do so exists where the hearing is being held, and if not, consider whether you need to bring that with you.

You, your client or a witness may need a translator, or a signer, or someone else to assist in the giving of the evidence. You almost always do not need to arrange that yourself. You tell the court or tribunal what the position is, what kind of translator is required, and the clerk there will make the arrangements. Translators are selected from an approved list, and are independent of the parties.

The productions in the case may be more than just documents. There may be a model of the equipment, or a large plan of the premises, or the piece of equipment that was involved which may be quite large, or unusual in itself. You may have photographs, but wish to present them in a large format to show a particular point. You may wish to use any number of visual aids, diagrams, sketches or similar, which may not fit neatly into an A4 size for the bundle. It may not be possible to have copies of those, or clear colour copies in the same size.

Your witnesses may be abroad, and wish to appear by video conference. There may be a need to anonymise documents to preserve the confidentiality of witnesses, others involved, or even the parties. The nature of the issues in the case could be highly sensitive, such as allegations of sexual harassment, and require particular arrangements to be made.

It may therefore be best to discuss with the other side what you propose to do, and then check the requirements with the clerk of the court or tribunal to ensure that it is feasible. If there are any issues, it may be best to highlight them to the judge well in advance.

You should also liaise with the witnesses who are appearing voluntarily, which means without a witness order, to tell them when they are required to be there, where the tribunal or court is, and what to do when they get there. Generally they report to a clerk, and say that they are a witness in the case you are involved in, and it helps to give them the full name of that case, and its reference number. They will then generally be directed to a witness room, or a waiting room for your side of the case, whether claimant or respondent. You can say that you will meet them there, or outside the building or nearby.

Making arrangements with witnesses is not always easy. They may wish to be inconvenienced as little as possible, but you need to be sure that they are present when required. It is extremely difficult to estimate how long any particular phase of a case may take. So you should err on the side of caution and tell them to be there early, and to wait. If you wish to have someone appearing later, such as after lunch on the first day or on day two or three for example, it helps to discuss that with the other side first and to raise it with the judge at the start to ensure that that is not going to cause any concern.

Who goes first is also not always simple. Generally speaking it is whichever party has to prove facts to succeed, ie has the burden of proof, also called the onus of proof. Often that is the claimant, but not always. If the claim is for breach of contract and there is a summary dismissal, with no notice given, the burden shifts to the respondent to prove that they were entitled to do so. If the claim is for unfair dismissal, the burden is on the employer to prove the reason for dismissal and generally they go first. If the dismissal is called a constructive dismissal, when an employee feels forced to resign, the claimant must prove that first, and he or she goes first. If there is a claim of discrimination the claimant often goes first, but not always, particularly if there is also a claim of unfair dismissal. If there is a claim for an accident or similar, the claimant goes first.

In many claims it is not for the parties to decide, but for the court or tribunal to do so. The normal rules can also be changed either with agreement of all including the judge, or if the judge decides that that would be the proper way to proceed.

If therefore you are not sure who is to go first it makes sense to raise that with the other side first, and if there is no agreement to approach the court or tribunal to address that if possible. If it is not possible to arrange it in advance, just assume that you might have to go first and that one or more of your witnesses may need to be present at the start.

The arrangements for witnesses are different according to where the case is, what it is, and what the rules are. In England generally witnesses can be present in the room where the case is conducted, and hear evidence of other witnesses. In Scotland they tend not to be allowed to do so before giving their own evidence. But witnesses might be permitted to attend in some circumstances, or it may be preferable that they do not attend to hear the evidence before their own in particular circumstances even if that is generally permitted. Again, if it is not clear, raise it with either the clerk of the tribunal or court, or with the other side.

If one of your witnesses is not able to attend the hearing because of illness, you need more than their say so. Often you need a certificate from their GP stating that they are unfit to attend the hearing, giving a basic reason and it is helpful to state how long that may be for (and therefore when they might be able to attend later). In Scotland that certificate needs to be given 'on soul and conscience'. You should then approach the tribunal or court, and the other side, to request an adjournment as soon as possible. You may or may not be granted that, but the sooner you act the better.

You want to have as many potentials issues covered, resolved and clear before you head off to the tribunal or court.

What are the questions to ask witnesses at the hearing?

At the stage of the final hearing the judge is listening to evidence which will decide the case. Evidence is given by both question and answer. The witness provides the answer. The question can also provide a measure of evidence, and sometimes in reality all of it (for example when there is a leading question and the answer is yes). How that is done comes later, but it is fundamental to the process of providing evidence that it is obtained by someone asking questions.

There are many different types of question, and sometimes it can appear more as a statement of fact, or putting a proposition, than a true question. But however they are asked questions lie at the heart of litigation. It is the end product of all of the preparations.

Documents, photographs, emails, plans and the like do not prove anything by themselves. You cannot win a case by these productions alone, almost always. You need someone to give evidence about them, and that evidence comes from questions.

Questions can also be used to tell a particular story, so that it becomes clear what a sequence of events was that led to a particular end point. They can be used to guide the process, and keep it on track.

Questions can also be used to highlight certain aspects. They can emphasise important words in a document: 'can you read out the third paragraph of this letter?' They can explain emotion: 'When you heard that, how did it make you feel'. They can be used to frame an event 'How quickly did the police arrive?' or 'How long have you been waiting for the surgery to take place?'

It is vital to keep in mind that the judge will not necessarily know anything about the case at the start. Your job is to educate them. Take him or her through each step of what happened, each document or other item of evidence, explaining what it is and why it is relevant. You try and persuade.

Much of the time will now be spent in discussing how questions can be asked, what techniques can be used, how they can be very different depending on the phase involved, and why a good question can lead to success.

In many ways this can be the most important part of the preparation. If questions are prepared well, they can help to win the case. If the questions are not prepared well, the key point can be lost, or a vital part of the evidence is not put before the judge.

Presenting evidence by questions

When framing questions you are not just ensuring that you give the judge the evidence that matters, you try and do so in as effective a way as you can. Consider this quotation:

'Art is not what you see, but what you make others see' – Edgar Degas

It sums up the art of asking questions very well, I think. If there is any one quotation that sums up what you are trying to do when preparing the questions to ask a witness, this is it. I would advise you to remember it, and keep applying it throughout the case.

Advocacy is about presentation of evidence that you have chosen, in a way which you chose, that you hope will make the judge see what you want him or her to see. That involves all aspects of presenting evidence, the way a question is asked, the words used, the tone and pace of voice, what documents are referred to and how, and what other evidence is referred to such as photographs, plans, text messages, social media posts, and physical objects. It involves the order in which the evidence is presented, and also covers exactly what is said when submissions are made at the end. It is the painting of a picture in order to persuade.

I shall give two examples. In the first, the claim is that a manager at work sexually harassed a younger female employee. You act for the claimant, and have a report from the GP that confirms that she had a month off work, and was treated for anxiety and depression for six months. You could simply ask her in her evidence about that report. That would at least be a basis to argue for an award for injury to feelings. You could also however check if other evidence could be given from her partner, or a parent, or a friend, about how she changed after that experience. You could ask the claimant when she gives evidence not just what happened, but what the effect on her was, but in a way that emphasises the evidence you seek. Instead of asking: 'How did that make you feel?', you can ask: 'How upset were you immediately after it happened?', 'How long did that feeling of being distraught, crying and not sleeping last for?' 'How badly did it affect your relationships with your [partner or parents]', and so on, and only after that ask about going to the GP and the report. The two kinds of picture are very different.

The second example is from the respondent side. You act for a small shop which dismissed an assistant for speaking inappropriately to a customer, after which the customer complained. You can ask about why it is that the decision was taken to dismiss, and not to issue a lesser penalty such as a written warning. That would be adequate to argue that the penalty was within the range of reasonable responses to make it fair. Or you could ask about what the business of the shop is, what community locally it serves, who the customer was, what role they play in that community, why you believe that they were so annoyed at what happened as to complain, how small the profit margins are in such a shop, what would have happened to the business of the shop had you not dismissed the assistant, and how that would have affected its profitability or its ability to survive. Once again that paints a very different picture, and sets the decision that was made in a wider and more persuasive context. Whether it will be enough to lead to success will depend on how it is assessed by the judge, but in both cases the evidence gives a better chance of success.

To be able to carry out each of those processes well you need to understand fully all aspects of the case, both the parts for and against you, investigate them fully, consider them carefully, work out what questions to ask which witnesses, and prepare for the final hearing by covering all the points that might arise. Advocacy therefore covers a series of different aspects, but lying at the heart of everything you do is the preparation that is undertaken. The more you prepare, the better the picture that it is possible to paint.

There are limits to what you can choose to do. You should never mislead the judge or the other side by saying something you know to be untrue. If you wish to refer to a document such as an email, you must produce all of that email, not only the part you think helps. Where it is part of a sequence, you generally must produce all in that sequence.

There can be orders made to produce documents, and the practice about that changes between courts and tribunals. Sometimes you need only produce what you intend to rely on. At other times you have a duty to produce any document that might be relevant to the issues to be decided. It can therefore be important to make sure that when you are choosing how to present the evidence you do so in a way that is not misleading, and not improper. That can sometimes involve difficult decisions, and if that arises it is helpful to ask for advice wherever you can.

What you ask, of which witness, using which words in each question, and how they are asked, can make a major difference to the outcome.

Methods of preparation

The questions you ask at each stage of examination-in-chief, cross-examination and re-examination must be very different. The rules that apply change during the case.

There are a variety of methods of preparing the questions. There are some who do not have any notes, and simply do it all off the cuff, using their experience and intelligence, in effect doing it all in their heads. Very few can do that successfully. I do not recommend it for anyone.

The second way to try to ask questions is to have a list of key points, a form of checklist. That used to be the way many lawyers conducted cases. It at least meant that there was a note of the points that had to be covered, it was easy to use, quick to prepare, and had a certain benefit. It is what I used to do when I started as a trainee solicitor, but over the years I learned that it was not the best technique.

The third way is to use written statements for each witness as a basis to ask the questions, ticking each paragraph off as it is addressed. It is a commonly used technique now, and again has the benefit of being quick. The difficulty with that method is that forming the words for the questions must be done at the time of the hearing, and the opportunity to check the words of each question, revise it, improve it, change the order of questions and so on is lost. It can work out well enough in practice, especially for those who are experienced, but is not the best way to do so in my view.

The final way is the one taking the most time, but leads to the best outcome. It is to write down, in advance, every word of every question you want to ask, check it, change it, and then when finalised use it as a framework for the questions. Usually the questions can be asked as they have been prepared, but sometimes they are better changed during the hearing, and not slavishly followed.

Sometimes there is a need to react to a particular answer, go off on a tangent, and come back to where you had been. Sometimes the very act of writing them down and checking them means that they are well established in the mind, and can be spoken to without being looked at. But this form of preparation does in my experience lead to the best form of advocacy.

It tends to be more effective to prepare the questions in the quiet and peace of a time you choose, when you can prepare a draft, look at it, and check it. The English language has over 170,000 words in current usage. What you try to do is choose exactly the right words for each question. My own experience is that if you have prepared each word of each question in advance, you are far more likely to ask good questions, at the right time, in the right order. Order is important as we shall come to. For the present, let's concentrate on the words of the question.

The importance of control

Pilots in training or where there are two pilots flying a plane must know which pilot has control of the plane at all times. To do that, control is made clear and passed from one to the other specifically. The pilot who has that control passed to him or her says 'I have control'. That is the sense that you as the advocate need to have. Whilst the judge can direct you as to what happens, and intervene from time to time, it is you who decides what words to choose for each question, what order they are asked in, what tone of voice is used, what emphasis is placed on any word, and what pace the questions are asked at. You can see what the witness is doing, and what the judge is doing. You can choose to refer to a document, or a photograph or something similar. You can choose what to ask about it.

The witness may be nervous. He or she has sworn an oath, or given an affirmation, to tell the truth. The judge is watching. That all creates pressure on a witness to be scrupulously honest, in a way that may not have happened before.

As the person asking the questions you are in a position of great responsibility. You have in a sense a power over the witness. Well framed, and well asked, questions have reduced witnesses to tears, to change their evidence entirely, to admit to lying, or mistakes, or that they had just misunderstood things. But well framed and well asked questions also show that a witness has been consistent all along, and is obviously both telling the truth, and being accurate in recounting what happened.

Examination-in-chief

In most cases someone will need to ask questions of a witness called for his or her own side. If the only witness is the party, and that party is representing him or herself as a litigant in person, that does not happen. It is discussed later.

73

It is all very well saying that you must ask questions to get the evidence, but what questions, and how? Again, some very basic rules apply:

1   The task is to get all the evidence that helps you to be heard, (and normally written down in some way) by the judge.

2   That involves identifying the key points, and making sure that they are presented as best you can.

3   Organise the material that you have for each witness, which is essentially what their witness statement says (assuming that you have that) and the documents or other productions that they can comment on.

4   Have a structure that makes it easy for the judge to follow what is happening.

5   The simplest way to do that is to follow the chronology.

6   Before starting that however you need to establish who the witness is, and their background where that is relevant to the case.

7   Keep each question short.

8   Have one point to each question, never more than that.

9   If you use technical terms, get the witness to describe them.

10   If there are acronyms, get the witness to describe what they mean.

11   If there is a document that is relevant get the witness to describe it, describe their role in its preparation if applicable, and then take them to particular parts of it, either with them reading it or you doing so.

12   If there is a photograph, get the witness to confirm who took it, when, and what it shows.

13   All this must be done without asking leading questions.

What are leading questions?

Leading questions are used in conversation all the time. They are an easy way of speaking, and it can be extremely difficult to avoid using them. But avoid using them you must, unless: (a) the fact that they lead to is not in dispute; (b) the matter is within judicial knowledge (taken to be known by the judge because it is so obvious or widely understood); or (c) it doesn't matter, and you don't mind if anyone objects. Usually (c) does not apply, as if it doesn't matter you need to ask whether you should be pursuing that question in the first place.

Leading questions are those which lead to the answer, particularly the answer 'Yes'. They often start with the word 'Did'. So to give an example: 'Did you watch television last night?' is something we might say any time. It is a leading question, as it leads to an answer 'Yes' or 'No'. To turn that into a non-leading question, you can ask: 'What did you do last night' or: 'What did you watch on television last night?' Both are non-leading questions, as they cannot be answered sensibly with a yes or no.

The rule in examination-in-chief is that the evidence must come from the witness. If you ask a leading question it does not – it comes from the question you ask. The rule is that you cannot and should not do that. Putting it simply therefore you should not ask leading questions at the examination in chief stage.

If you do, there may be an objection from the other side, or the judge may intervene and tell you to rephrase it. But if neither happens, you may initially get away with it, and the witness may answer 'Yes'. The trouble is that when it comes to assessing that answer, the judge can entirely disregard it as it has come from a leading question. The evidence can be entirely ignored. It means that your case may fail because you asked the wrong question on a key point. That is why you are better not doing so, and should not do so.

Some tips on asking non-leading questions

How you start a question often determines if it is leading or not. Some words are very good ones to start with if you need to avoid asking a leading question. These are:

- What
- Who
- When
- Why
- Where
- How

There are other words that work well when asking non-leading questions. They include-

- Explain
- Describe
- Tell [me, or the judge]

What is difficult however is to ask a question that is not leading the witness, whilst also being in control of the witness. How to do that is discussed below.

Changing leading to open questions

It is possible to ask what seems may be a leading question, but is not, by adding the opposite later such as: ''Did you watch television last night, or did you not?' But that is rather artificial, the initial part is leading and can be objected to, and is better avoided.

A better way to convert a leading question into one that is not is by adding at the start the words 'what' or 'to what extent'

You can then ask something that starts with words like did or is. For example the leading question 'Did you watch television last night' can be turned into a non-leading question 'What did you watch on television last night'. Of course, if the person did not watch any television the question is less than perfect, but if you know that they did, the question can be a good one.

The initial phrase 'to what extent' is a useful way of asking a non-leading question where you would normally do that in a conversation. So you can ask: 'To what extent did you know the precise requirements of the procedure you should have followed?'

That can be expanded to: 'To what extent, if at all, did you know the precise requirements of the procedure you should have followed'. That question can be asked placing emphasis on the 'if at all'. That then gives you a greater level of control over the witness but in a permissible way.

Keeping control

The difficulty about non-leading questions is that the witness may not give you the answer you want. They lead to at least a partial loss of control. If you ask a leading question, you have more control, simply because the answer might naturally be a yes or a no. When the answer cannot be yes, you may end up with a very long answer none of which you want.

There are ways of trying to avoid that. The key is the use of language. It can be very general, or very specific. As a basic rule, the more general the language the less control you have, and the greater the risk of the witness straying off the line you want to keep on.

The classic non-leading question is: 'What happened next?' It is not a leading question, but the risk is that the witness does not really know what you mean by 'next'. So the answer you get may not be what you want. It is also a good example of what can happen if the preparation does not inform the words of each of the questions. During the hearing, when you can be nervous, under pressure by questions from the judge, or interventions from the other side, is probably the very worst time to be working out what words to use.

The use of context

A better way to ask the question: 'what happened next?' is to put it into a context 'After you arrived at the office, what did you do next?' gives the witness a little more context. But it is still rather vague, and can lead to the wrong answer. More specific is this: 'Immediately after you arrived at the office, what did you do next?' More specific still is: 'You said that you arrived at the office at 9 am. What was the first thing that you did immediately on arriving?' This all requires you to know the detail.

Taking the evidence step by step can also help to keep chronological order. If you just ask: 'What happened next' it is not clear whether you mean the next second, hour, day, or month, for example. So putting the question in a clear timeframe helps to achieve that.

Know the answer

Another basic rule of asking questions (particularly in cross examination as we shall come to, but in all questioning) is not to do so unless you know the answer. Why? The risk is that if you ask a question without knowing the answer, you get one that is not what you expected, and can lead to things going wrong. An example of this was an inquiry into a helicopter accident. The pilot, one of very few who survived it, was asked a question by one QC along the lines of: 'as you approached the airport to land, which gear were you in?' The answer was something like: 'Sir, we don't have gears in a helicopter'.

The question was asked without the questioner knowing what the answer was, or would be. Sometimes the question might seem a simple one, such as who prepared the letter that has the witness's signature. But if you do not know who prepared it, there is no need to ask that. You can just ask whose signature appears on it. If you ask who prepared it without knowing, you may be surprised to hear that it was the person who heard the appeal, or that it was prepared by HR and the signature was added under protest. That evidence can be very damaging, and was not necessary. Even very experienced senior counsel can make mistakes like that, but it is possible to avoid them by the work done in advance.

So to be able to use the right words you need to know what the person should say, and that means that you have gone through the detail with them, or by other enquiries so far as you can, beforehand.

Have a reason

Another rule flows from this, which is that there should be a reason for asking every single question. The reason should be that it gives you evidence that helps your case. It may be factually true that the witness arrived at 9am, but if nothing happened until 4.30pm asking a series of detailed questions about what was done, at what time, by whom, for issues that are of no relevance or assistance whatsoever will risk the judge either becoming bored and switching off, or the impression that you either do not know the case or are trying to lead the judge up the garden path.

There must therefore be a purpose behind each question, even if it is only a necessary step to get to the goal you are trying to reach. One way is to ask yourself this:

'Why am I asking this witness this question at this point?'

If you cannot answer it, you may need to take that question out of your preparation. If you have an answer, even if it seems a minor matter or only a step towards a bigger issue, then it is worth persevering with. Check that you are asking it at the right stage, and that it might not be more effective either earlier or later in the sequence.

But how you ask that question then becomes the key. There is an infinite number of ways of asking the most simple of questions. There is no particular right or wrong way to do so. But there are generally more effective ways, and less effective ways, and the trick is to find the very best way for each question you ask.

Choosing exactly the right words

The use of language is vitally important. Here are some examples of the different ways you can do so:

- 'After you arrived at the office, how quickly was it that you were shouted at?'

- 'After you arrived at the office, how long was it before you say that you were shouted at?'

They each get to the same basic point, but ask it in very different ways, and give a slightly different context. The use of the descriptive words of quickly or how long (it could have been slowly but how long may be better, as the word long can be emphasised) frames the question. In a sense it gives the witness a hint at what you are seeking by the use of the words you choose. If you say 'quickly' the hint is that you want the answer to be a short period of time, or a description of something that happened almost immediately. If you use a word like 'long' the hint is the opposite, that the last thing you want is the reply 'immediately'.

Adverbs are therefore a good way of framing questions. Words such as 'loudly' or 'softly', 'strongly' or 'weakly', 'happily' or 'sadly' and so on can be very useful.

Precision of language is so important. The perfect word can make all the difference. A good example is from the question asked by the comedy character Mrs Merton of a guest, Debbie McGhee, on her chat show: 'What first attracted you to the millionaire Paul Daniels?' Debbie was Paul's wife and assistant. He was a magician, not known for his good looks. The use of the, on one level unnecessary and on another level perfect, word 'millionaire' gave the question an entirely different comic flavour than if it had been missing, or replaced by 'magician' or 'TV personality'.

But an additional word can ruin an otherwise perfectly good question. An example of this might be from an investigation meeting when the allegation was of drinking before coming to work. If the question was: 'Had you been drinking?' and the person had consumed alcohol of some kind the answer might need to be: 'Yes', if being honest at least. If the questioner added the word 'alcohol' that would still lead to the answer yes. If the questioner added the word 'beer', the content of the question changes. If the person had been drinking vodka, the honest answer can be given as 'No'.

So be careful about the unnecessary extra word that might undo all the good work of the rest of the sentence.

Short words

There is a particular power in choosing short words, in short sentences, to frame questions. There is sometimes a temptation to use longer words, as if they sound better. Resist it, unless the longer word is exactly the right one (and it may be particularly if it is a technical one).

Churchill was a great fan of short words, which he used frequently. Think of 'I have nothing to offer but blood, toil, tears and sweat'. That was said when he became Prime Minister, in his first speech. The Reverend Martin Luther King Junior issued his rallying call for civil rights with the words 'I have a dream'. If you wish to have some guidance on how to choose the right words, and then separately how to deliver them, search for some of the speeches of those two great orators. They can be found on places such as YouTube. Even now, many decades later, they have a power and majesty that can still move.

I do not suggest that you try to emulate them. Making submissions in a court or tribunal is not the same setting as those kinds of speeches. Politics is not the same as law. But the basic techniques are similar, and the use of carefully chosen words, delivered well, is an important part of persuasion.

Another way to find out how it is done is either to visit a court or tribunal, and watch, or go online and see cases in the Supreme Court which can be viewed on its website (although the questions are asked there of the QCs, not of a witness). It will give at least a flavour of what can be done, and matters such as the pace of the words spoken, the tone of voice, the volume used, and the styles of advocacy, which can be very different between two people who are doing what is basically the same job.

Referring to documents

It is important to have witnesses comment on documents. That is so for a number of reasons. The context in which the document was written may be significant. Who took which notes may be relevant. When the notes were prepared can be important. What a document says can be important, and that can be highlighted by having the witness read out the words used and comment on them.

For example, the notes of a disciplinary hearing can say that there was a five-minute break, but not why. If that was because someone was upset, the witness can explain that, in what respect the person was upset, how that was manifested, and how they were after the break.

Most usually however the reason words from a document are referred to is because they help your case. You want the judge to be aware of them, and the best way to do that is have the witness read out the key words.

That means identifying in advance what are those key words. I often do that by a combination of a highlighting pen and initials on the side of the page. That meant that the words could be found quickly. You may then be able to say to the witness something like:

> 'Please turn to page 76. This is the third page of the minutes you have just told us about. Can you look at the third paragraph, just beside the upper hole punch. Do you see the sentence starting "JB said that he had seen AK take money from the drawer"? Could you read to the Judge that and the following sentence?'

The art of asking a question therefore includes making sure that each word you use is the right one, that no words used are going to devalue the question, and none are missed out that could be helpful. It is not easy to do, and that is why preparing your questions in advance is so helpful, if not essential.

Referring to other productions

Productions are other physical evidence that is in the Bundle of Documents (although they may not be documents as such). This can include photographs, CCTV footage, audio recordings, plans, drawings, social media posts, screenshots, models of equipment, and a wide range of other items. You and the witness will know what they are, but the judge may not have any idea at all. For a photograph, for example, it helps to set out who took it, what it shows, provide an orientation such as north/south, and relate it to other evidence. Get the witness to describe the important aspects of it for the case. The same general comments apply to CCTV footage, or to an audio recording, which you may need both to play, and provide a transcript for. It is then helpful to direct the witness, so that the judge understands, to the precise part of the transcript that is relevant for the case.

Working out what exactly to ask is not as easy as it might at first appear. Take your time to prepare these questions one by one, so that you can be sure that the point that you want to get across is made clearly and in a way that can be understood by someone with no prior knowledge at all.

Funnelling

Another way of asking questions is a process called funnelling. This is when you start with a general description and gradually work down to a point of detail. An example might be this:

• You have told us that you arrived at the office at 9am. Where did you go when you arrived? – My room.

• Where did you go in the room? – I sat at my desk.

• What was on the desk? – A pile of papers and a telephone, PC and keyboard.

• What were the papers made up of? – A series of invoices.

• Which invoice was on the top? – It was from ABC Limited.

• How can you recall that? – I remember it as it was for £100,000 and I had not seen it before.

By asking questions like this, rather than going straight to the issue of the invoice, you can help the witness walk through their own recollection of what happened. It also gives the description a bit of colour, and helps give it an air of authenticity. It would have been possible to have asked: 'When you arrived at the office what attracted your attention?' but the picture painted is rather less detailed. It misses out points of detail that can help give the impression of a witness whose memory is good, and reliable.

Loopback

As I said before, having a structure is important. Sometimes it is necessary to divert from the line you have started on for a particular reason. It may be that you want to discuss the process of invoicing, who does what in the company, before coming back to where you were. How do you do that? One way is to say: 'I now want to take you back to the evidence you gave earlier when you said that you were sitting at your desk and noticed the invoice from ABC Limited. What steps did you take at that time in relation to that invoice?' It is a technique called loopback, and is very useful. For it to work well you need good notes. You can then both put a marker on the point you want to come back to (I used to draw a kind of star) and then write the words that were used so that you can quote them again, both to refresh the memory of the witness and to let the judge know the context of the question.

Structure

One of the real skills in asking questions is using the order in which they are asked for effect. It helps to keep control of the witness, but also to put the evidence in context. It is important in cross examination as we shall come to, but no less so in examination in chief. To help remember it, keep in mind the following:

'Order, order, order' – Speaker John Bercow

There is a technique that can help a witness give the answer you want by the process of taking it in stages, slowly, leading up to the point that you want to make. It tends to be the opposite of what we do in everyday conversation. In life, we might well jump to the point by saying: 'Did you see the news last night about the election?' Where the point is one of reaction, emotion, response or similar, it is usually best not to go straight there, but to move slowly.

- You have said that your manager shouted at you. What did he say?
- How did he say it?
- How loudly did he shout?
- What was his facial expression at the time?
- What was he doing with his hands?
- How close to you was he standing?
- How tall is he?
- How large is he in comparison to you?
- When he shouted at you in this way how did you react?
- What did you feel at that precise time?
- What did you do immediately after that?
- Why did you make that immediate complaint to HR?
- What were you feeling when you did so?

and so on.

You can also use words that indicate where one part of the questions stops, and another begins. It is usually called signposting. You can say: 'That is all I wish to ask you about the work that you did. I now want to ask you about what happened after you left the company.' It tells both the judge and the witness where you are, and the context of the questions that follow.

When preparing the structure of the questioning, remember that you want to finish strongly. In examination-in-chief it is difficult to start strongly as you need to begin with basics like name, address, role in organisation and the like. So if you cannot start strongly, you need to finish strongly. That means working up to what you think is either the key issue in the case, or the strongest piece of evidence.

Addressing the other side's case

Remember too that as well as putting forward the case you wish to, you need to consider the case made by the other side, and how to respond to it. They will almost certainly raise that in cross-examination, but there are often benefits in you raising it first. The reasons for that are that you can frame the questions as you want to, that the evidence then comes first of all with that being done rather than in cross-examination, and you also get a second opportunity to address the issue if it is raised in cross-examination. That is not however always the case – sometimes it is better to leave it alone. If it is not clear exactly how the other side are to argue matters, or if there is a nervousness about addressing the issue yourself as you are not sure how the witness is going to handle it, it may be better to avoid it, and wait.

If however you are to raise the issue, it can be helpful to start with what is pled. You can refer the witness to the page of the documents with that pleading on, and read it out to them. Rather than then just say: 'What is your response to that?', as is sometimes done, it is better to break it down into individual propositions, and ask about each one. The formula: 'To what extent, if at all, is that accurate?' or similar can be a useful start. If there are documents that help you, you can refer to them, ask the witness to read out the key part, or do so yourself, and simply bring that evidence to the attention of the judge.

Once you have asked all that you require to, you can signal to the judge that you have finished. 'Those are all the questions I have, thank you' or similar. If you have been standing, sit down. The first phase is over.

Do not stop thinking. How has it gone? Has the witness said what you expected? If not, what damage has been done? Has it gone better than expected? What new points emerged, and what do you need to do with them either for other witnesses of your own, or in cross examination of the witnesses for the other side?

Bad questions in examination-in-chief

The first example of a bad question is a leading one. It runs the risk of being objected to, or the judge may largely or wholly discount the answer because it came from a leading question.

The second is the mixed question. It has more than one point. It is something we often do in conversation, but is not easy for a witness to follow or to answer clearly. Something like: 'Tell us about your career, what your qualifications are, who you have worked for and when, when you started with the respondent and what you did for them then' is not a leading question, but covers many individual matters. The witness who is not able to take written notes of the question needs to remember all of that, and try to answer each element separately. It is a near impossible task. So break each element down into one question, hence the one point per question advice given.

If you wish to have examples of how not to ask questions, watch television, and either news programmes or documentaries with some form of investigation. Whilst some journalists are very good at it, many are not. They tend to like the sound of their own voice, and either ask leading questions, or questions with more than one point, or ones that are vague and unclear. They can use language that is hyperbolic, overblown, unduly emotional or plain wrong. That may be fine in that context – although I am not so sure personally – but in litigation it tends not to work. For example, if someone's hours at work have been reduced, use of that word 'reduce' in a question about the reduction in hours is likely to play better with the judge than use of a word like 'slash'.

Be careful also of asking a question in a way that the individual described it to you, which may have been filtered through great emotion. Judges avoid emotion, for obvious reasons. More moderate and accurate language therefore is more likely to be persuasive.

Be careful similarly of guiding the witness into exaggeration by your use of language in the question. 'How distraught were you?' may give a misleading impression of the response to what in fact was a more minor issue. The danger of doing so is first that the judge may think that the witness has lost a sense of proportion, but also that the opponent in cross-examination can use that and exploit it, putting your witness on the back foot because of that. Keep the questions aligned to the context and factual basis of what exactly happened. Too much 'spin', massaging the facts to suit your own purposes, can seem tempting initially, but cause the case to fall apart later.

Another issue to be careful of is humour. In real life we use it all the time. It can be effective to deflate an argument we do not like, annoy an opponent, ridicule the effect of what is being said and so on. There can sometimes be a temptation to do that in this setting too. I would encourage you to resist that. It has gone wrong on many occasions, and whilst you may feel that something is side-splittingly humorous, the judge may feel the very opposite and that you are treating the proceedings without adequate respect. Unless therefore you are absolutely sure that humour will work and help your arguments, leave that for after the hearing is over.

The hostile witness you call

If you call a witness who is hostile to you, you may be allowed to ask leading questions in at least some circumstances. Whether you do wish to call a witness who is hostile is a different question. It is a risky strategy. You should think carefully whether that risk is worthwhile, or whether it is better not to call that person, and argue that the other side have not when they would be expected to. There are however times, particularly for those defending claims, when you must call a hostile witness. For example, the person who decided to dismiss the claimant may later have been dismissed him or herself, and is now very hostile towards the company, but their evidence is essential in defending a claim that the dismissal was unlawful discrimination.

A hostile witness usually requires some form of witness order to attend, as they may well not turn up otherwise. If you do wish to do that, and then to ask leading questions, it is usually helpful to tell the other side first, and then raise it with the judge before the witness is called in to the hearing to give evidence. That then allows the point to be addressed without the witness hearing it, and being even more against you.

When questioning a hostile witness, it is best to take the questions slowly. Rather like closing off escapes in cross-examination which is covered below, the structure of the questions is important. It can for example help to go through what the process was intended to be, if that is relevant, before addressing what happened. If the witness conducted an investigation or disciplinary hearing, and now is trying to distance him or herself from the decision reached, it can be useful to start with what the policy says about having a full and fair investigation, or words to that effect where they exist, then suggesting that the witness would not wish to breach that deliberately. One way to address the same point is with witnesses who are governed by professional standards. You can check online to see what those standards are – they apply to a wide range of medical professionals, care staff, architects, accountants, lawyers, dentists, surveyors, engineers, and many other similar roles. Where there is not such a role, a company handbook, or guide to acting for many public and third sector roles, sets out standards of conduct or behaviour that can be referred to in the questions. You should ensure that these documents are in the Bundle so that they are available for use when questioning. Refer the witness to them, and get them to confirm that they set out the standard of behaviour required of them in their role. Try then to get the witness to accept that they were aware of those standards at the time of the event, and that they would not knowingly act in breach of them.

You can then address what they did at the time, by referring to the notes of meetings, or emails, or records of decisions made whether that is in a report, or note of outcome, letter of decision or similar. Concentrate on what was done there and then, rather than what the witness may now say he or she believes the case to be.

Evidence by the litigant in person

A litigant in person obviously does not have someone else to ask questions. That changes the way that the evidence can be presented. It is not question and answer, but a form of speech. That poses some challenges for the person involved. How can they make sure that all of the evidence is given, and that it is done in the most effective way?

There are various ways in which that might be done. For some cases, formal witness statements might have been ordered. That means that all or most of the evidence-in-chief is given by that statement, and the litigant in person swears an oath or affirms to confirm that it is true and accurate. There may be a need to give a little further evidence to address something in the witness statements of the other party which has not been covered, and normally that will be permitted. It may however be necessary to ask for permission to do that at the very start.

However, witness statements will not always be used. If that is the case, it might still be possible to ask that your own evidence is given by that method, even though other witnesses will give their evidence orally. That may be possible particularly if because of some form of disability, either physical or mental, you would find difficulty in giving evidence just by speaking from memory. Again, however, that may not be possible, and it may be objected to by the other side especially in cases which are largely determined by an assessment of who is telling the truth.

The next possibility is to ask to use what is normally called an aide memoire – which is a list of points you wish to make as a means of ensuring that all points are covered. It is usually a short document, of a page or two, with bullet points. It might cover the order of points to make, the page number of documents to refer to and the paragraphs to highlight, and is not a script but a bit like a running order of what are the key aspects of your evidence. If you wish to do that, you might ask the other party if they object, and then before the evidence starts ask the judge if that can be permitted. It is also something that could be brought up during any preliminary hearing, or by application to the court or tribunal in advance, which may be possible to make more informally by email.

There is no guarantee that that will be permitted, but often it will, provided that a copy is given to the other party in advance so that they can see it is not being used improperly. It is generally not permitted to take your own notes when giving evidence, or your own copy of the Bundle of Documents on which you may have written various comments and reminders. You use the documents other witnesses also use, so that everyone has the same material to work from.

If there is no aid of any kind therefore you will be dependent on your memory. But there are some other ways that the documents can help. The most obvious is the Claim Form, or the document that starts the claim. You will have drafted that, and it should set out all that you are seeking and why that is. It can be used as a basis for your evidence. You do need to check whether it has been amended at any time, and if so that amendment document should also be in the papers. You can also use the reply by the other side, often called the Response Form, as that sets out their position, and again refer to any amendment to that. It is worth reading those documents very carefully in advance of the hearing to check what they do, or do not, say.

There are other documents that are important. In a dismissal case, there should either be a letter confirming reasons for dismissal, or if it is what is called a constructive dismissal case your letter of resignation. That can be a basis to set out the evidence of why what happened was a dismissal and was unfair, if that is what is being argued. If you are the employer, your letter of dismissal should outline the reasons, and you can use that to expand on what is said, and set out more fully your thinking process.

If there are notes of meetings or minutes, they can be useful as records of what happened, but you should check that they are accurate and comprehensive, and if not, check if there is a document to refer to explaining the errors or omissions. Also, the minutes or notes may not cover all that is relevant. It may be that at one point you, or someone else, became upset or angry or started to raise their voice. If that happened and is important, you will need to remember to explain that, and in your preparation think of ways both of remembering to do that, and how it may be explained.

Remember also to cover what it is that you are asking the judge to do. If you are the claimant, cover what remedy you seek, and where that is about financial compensation, what it is you seek and why. That may be outlined in a Schedule of Loss, which can be used as a basis for that evidence. If you are the respondent, and think that the sum sought is excessive, remember that you will need to explain why, and refer to documents where that is possible. The burden of proof is generally on you to show why the claimant has not taken reasonable steps to mitigate loss (ie reduce losses to the reasonable minimum), and the claimant may have said very little because they do not have to prove much. If you are arguing that make sure that you cover it.

Cross-examination

Cross-examination applies many of the same techniques, but some are different, and the context is different. First, this is not your witness, but the opposition one, and may be the person who is trying his or her best to beat you. Secondly, you both can, and in my view should, only ask leading questions. You do therefore have more control. Thirdly, you must ask the questions you need to ask – so you must put to the witness the key parts of your own case, where they are able to comment on the facts. Fourthly, you put factual questions, and never ones that involve conclusions about the facts. You ask about what a witness heard, or saw, or did, not whether they thought that what was done was inappropriate, the manager acted unreasonably or the car was being driven too quickly for example.

It is important to restate the basic rules, which are similar to those in examination-in-chief but with some differences:

1   Keep each question short.

2   Have one point to each question, never more than that.

3   If you use technical terms, describe them.

4   If there are acronyms, describe what they mean.

5   If there is a document that is relevant, describe it, describe the witness's role in its preparation if that is what happened and if relevant get them either to refer to their own signature, or to an email responding to it, or to the fact that they did not question it at the time

6   Then take them to particular parts of it, either with them reading it or you doing so.

7   Only ask a question if you have reasonable confidence that the answer will help you, or you need to put your case to them

8   If you know or think that they will dispute the matter, just put your case to them. Try not to give them a chance to explain why they think as they do

9   Do not argue. This is not a conversation in the pub. A good indicator that you are about to do so is when the question starts with 'But'.

10 Do not get angry. It can be easy to do so if you feel that the witness is simply lying, but if you become angry you lose control of your emotions, and that can affect how the case is conducted. Stay in control, and maintain your focus on what is happening.

As with examination-in-chief, keep your eyes open both for the witness and judge in particular, and note down all that is said. Go slowly and methodically.

When asking questions in cross-examination, you are often not really asking a question, but putting propositions, which are based on what your own case is. For example, you may ask the following: 'You came into work after drinking alcohol that day, didn't you?' That is a standard form of question and suggests an answer of yes or no. But it is also possible to ask it as a statement: 'You came into work after drinking alcohol that day'. That is a statement, but can be asked as a question in litigation using inflection in the voice, as you are trying to get the witness to agree with you. You are trying to push the witness into saying 'Yes'. Purists (and some judges are purists) may not like that style, but it is used very frequently in cross-examination and can be both more direct and effective. It is a style I used most all the time when cross-examining, and there are styles of question like that within the Appendix.

If there is an objection to that form of question by the judge, or by the opponent which the judge agrees with, you just convert the statement form back to a standard question by adding something like 'didn't you' or 'that's right isn't it' or similar. Some questioners just add the word 'Yes' at the end, to try and turn it into a question, although I have never liked that style and I am not sure it works grammatically. If you are told by the judge to ask standard style questions you do need to do so. It can be rather repetitive, so to vary it you can put the 'Didn't you' part at the start, for example.

How you ask the questions about what your own case is, which you must put to the main witness for the other party, or where a witness might know about the fact involved, depends partly on when the evidence on your side is given. It may be either before or after you cross-examine. If it is before, then how you ask it can depend on whether the witness was present at that time that evidence was given or not. If he or she was, you can say something like:

'1   You will recall the evidence by Ms Smith that she smelt alcohol on your breath when you attended work that morning?

2   She did so because you had drunk alcohol before coming into work that day.

3   She considered that you were not fit to work safely that day.

4   She was correct, wasn't she?'

If that evidence has not yet been given, the questions can be something like:

'1   We shall hear evidence later from your manager Ms Smith.

2   She will say that when you attended work that morning she smelt alcohol on your breath.

3   You met her in your office at about 9.15 that day.

4   You had drunk alcohol before coming into work that day.

5   She will say that she considered that you were not fit to work safely that day.

6   She was correct, wasn't she?'

Weak questions

There are some questions that are asked sometimes because they have been heard from films, TV shows or otherwise, or because the questioner thinks that they sound good. They are best avoided. They are ones like:

- I have to put it to you that …
- Isn't it the case that …
- Might I suggest that …
- The truth is, as you well know …
- My client's case is that …
- Would you be prepared to concede that …

These are bad questions as they are weak ones. They can give the impression that the questioner is going through the motions, and does not believe in their own case. The words that introduce the question add nothing to it.

Bad questions

Other bad questions in cross examination tend to be any that are not leading questions. Leading questions give you more control. If you do lapse into open questions, thinking that the person can only answer that in a helpful way, you risk unintentionally opening up a whole area. You cannot then complain if the witness answers the question in the way that they want to and you had not anticipated. So as a general rule of thumb it is best in cross-examination not to ask open questions – the very type of question that you must ask in examination-in-chief.

There are, however, times when asking an open question, not as a mistake but as a deliberate tactic, might help. That includes when you think that a witness is lying, and when they give a very vague answer to a question, or come up with something that has not been mentioned before and is a bit of a surprise to you. You may then wish to probe them either for more details, or to ask why it has not been mentioned before. That might be done using open questions, at least partly, and is discussed in more detail later.

Open to closed questions

There is a technique to change what starts as an open question into a closed, and leading one. It is by giving the answer at the end. An example is:

> 'When did you first see the investigation report – seven days before the hearing?'

If the question stopped after the word 'report' it is open, and gives the witness a lot of scope to answer. By adding the final words, it converts it into a leading question, and the witness can say 'Yes'. It is not however as strong a question as one such as:

'You first saw the investigation report at least seven days before the hearing'.

Know the answer

Do not ask a question unless you know the answer. There is a reason for that – if you do not know the answer the risk is that, when it comes, it harms you. That is the same rule of thumb as in examination-in-chief. There can be exceptions, such as when the answer does not matter. This can arise in evidence about mitigation of loss, when you may not know what the claimant did to try and find a new job, or why it took a year to get that new role, or why it paid only half of the former level of salary. But you do need to be aware of the higher level of risk involved when asking questions where you do not know what the answer will be.

Put your case

In cross-examination you may need to ask questions where you are unsure of what the answer is to put your side's case. It is necessary to suggest to the other side, where they are likely to be aware of the detail, what your witnesses are to say, or have said earlier, about relevant facts. A respondent may wish to argue that even if there was an unfair dismissal the employee contributed to that by what he or she did, and the evidence that its witnesses gave about that is something that should be raised with the claimant when he or she gives evidence.

Loose questions

Another style of question to avoid is the loose question – which does not give enough detail to the witness. The classic loose question is: 'what happened next?' It is far more effective to be specific as to time and place, and be very clear when doing so. That is so particularly in cross-examination. For example in the case of an alleged theft, the better question is something like: 'Immediately after you closed the drawer of the till, you left the shop didn't you?'

Other tips

Short questions are almost always better because they are less easy to avoid. Do not therefore drift off into long and rambling questions. Often the natural reply to a short question is either simply yes or no. If you ask a short question, and it is not answered candidly that way, that can be picked up when making submissions later. It can be a good indicator that the witness is not being either truthful, or accurate, and giving evidence that is partial in some way. The longer the question, the easier it is for the unclear reply to be explained.

Be careful of compound questions, which have a basis in one fact and then a second fact. 'When did you stop taking cocaine' implies that the witness did previously take cocaine. If that has already been accepted by the witness, or if you have clear evidence to support the allegation, that is fine but if not, it is dangerous. If the witness says that he has been teetotal throughout his life, never taken illicit drugs, and there is no real evidence to the contrary save suspicion, the answer to the question will be potentially harmful to you.

In general therefore compound questions are best avoided. It is more effective to break them down into constituent parts.

Ask about facts

Unless the witness is an expert, which is dealt with later, it is as has been mentioned best only to ask about facts, and not to ask about conclusions. The reason for that is that facts are far easier to control. Conclusions are more 'slippery', in that they can be argued over and debated as opinions. Facts are more objectively based. A fact is either proven, or not. An opinion can be held which may be agreed with or not, but two different opinions can be equally valid. For example, the interest rate from a particular bank on a given day is a fact. It is what it is. Whether the rate will then go up, or down, and when are not facts but opinions, and there could be two experts, each highly experienced, who have opinions that are diametrically opposite, but each of which are based on good arguments. Sometimes what happens later can be shown to be either correct or not, but often with expert evidence it is not so binary – it is less clear and simple than just which way interest rates might go.

There are two words that give a clue that the question is about to be about a conclusion. The first is 'So'. Again we use it in conversation all the time. But it tends to suggest that you are straying into conclusion, and that is best dealt with by submission later, when the evidence has been heard, locked down and can be commented on more safely.

The second word is 'Therefore'. The same rough rule applies. Whilst these words may not mean that there is about to be a conclusion put, be wary of them. What do they add to the question? Frankly, nothing.

Stopping the Great Escape

An important part of most cross-examinations is by the use of a structure, with questions in a particular order, closing off potential escape routes before putting the key question. Quite often someone who is not experienced will rush to ask the question about what happened, and the witness gives an unhelpful answer. So before asking that, the idea is to anticipate what they may say to get around it, close those possibilities off, and then ask it when the witness has nowhere to go.

For example, if the issue is whether someone made a mistake, there could be a number of potential excuses given for that. You try and predict them, and close them off one by one, such as:

- You started your shift that day at 9am didn't you?

- You were aware of the grievance procedure?

- You had not complained in writing at any stage of having an excessive workload?

- At the annual appraisal in June that year you had said that everything at work was going well, hadn't you?

- We see your signature on the form just below those words, on page 100?

- Page 150 is a list of the training you had undertaken?

- It is accurate isn't it?

- It shows that you completed a training course in using the HD machine in April that year, doesn't it?

- The company issued procedures for using that machine to you?

- They are at page 200?

- They set out clearly what to do when using the machine?

- That was covered in the training in April wasn't it?

- You signed the attendance sheet after that training to record that, didn't you?

- That is found on page 170 of the documents?

- On page 202 they say at paragraph 12 that you must check that the guard is in place before switching it on, don't they?

- You switched the machine on, when working on 12 September that year, without checking that the guard was in place, didn't you?

- The guard was not in place was it?

- You did not follow the procedure that applied?

- You did not follow the procedure which you had been trained to use?

- If you had followed the procedure you were trained on, the incident would not have happened, would it?

Inconsistent evidence

Quite often, there will be a difference in the evidence of a witness for the opponent between either what is said in evidence, or in the pleadings, or in a meeting, with what had been said earlier in their evidence, or their witness statement. Sometimes that is because memory fades over time. Sometimes it is because people who have a personal interest in an issue tend to remember facts in a way that helps them. Sometimes people lie to try and win, or help someone they feel should win. There can be other reasons, but the important matter for present purposes is that there can be a difference in two parts of the evidence. That is something that can be very important indeed in litigation, and very useful to focus on in cross-examination.

As a rough rule of thumb, the closer to an event the description is, the more accurate it is likely to be. If therefore there is a meeting shortly after an event and that is recorded in some way, either as a written statement, or an email, or a report, or the note of a meeting, and the detail in that is then not the same as the later evidence that the witness gave in examination-in-chief, whether that is before the judge in the case or the witness statement, the differences can be highlighted.

There is a technique to do so that is tried and trusted. It is used most effectively where the person has given the inconsistent evidence on oath in examination-in-chief, but can also be used where there are two separate pieces of evidence such as an email and the note of a later meeting, but I shall use the example of where there is both an earlier document, and evidence given in the examination-in-chief. It has three stages: **Repeat, Explain, Put** (**REP**):

1   **Repeat** what was said in the evidence. That way the judge is reminded about it, and the witness is committed to it. Something like: 'When you gave evidence this morning, you said that you had not been in your office on the morning of 3 June. You remember saying that?'

2   Then go to the inconsistent document or evidence (such as another witness saying that the person then giving evidence said something at the time, now denied), and **explain** what it is, set out the context for it, and why that other evidence is reliable, such as:

   Please turn to page 300. Is this the note of a meeting you held with your line manager on 4 June?

   That was the day after the incident wasn't it?

   The meeting was held at 10am and lasted about an hour according to the Note – that is right isn't it?

   Do we see that it was emailed to you that same day, on page 303?

Above that email do we see your reply, sent about an hour after the email to you was sent?

Does that reply say that 'Yes, this is an accurate record'.

You were not being untruthful when you said that, were you?

If we then go to the Note on page 301 and paragraph 23 does it say 'On 3 June I arrived in the office at about 9am, and went to my desk. I worked on a tender for about an hour, then had a conversation with Mrs Jones ....?

3   Then **Put** the evidence you wish to say is right, so as to contrast it with what had earlier been said. The word 'put' in the legal sense means that you make a particular suggestion to the witness and is what you say the true position is. It is where the phrase 'I put it to you ...' comes from. In this example the put phase may be:

You were in the office on 3 June [emphasising the word 'were'].

That was recorded in the note of the meeting we have looked at, wasn't it?

That is what you told your manager that day?

You later confirmed that the Note he had prepared was accurate.

You were wrong when you said in evidence this morning that you had not been in the office on the morning of 3 June.

It is easier to do this when you know in advance what the witness will say, and that there was something inconsistent in the documents from an earlier date. It is harder where it comes out of the blue. It does mean that you need to know what is in all of the documents. That is why having your own chronology can help, but also being aware of all of the details in them so that you can act on the inconsistency when it takes place.

The reason why you follow this process is two-fold – first it highlights to the judge that the witness is not reliable, and may not be credible (putting it simply they lied under oath), and secondly that the accurate version of events was the one given earlier, which is one that helps your side of the case.

The circumstances are not always of a prior statement that has a particular comment in it, but instead what matters is what is not there. In some cases this can be particularly powerful. It is not so much the inconsistency of two statements that you wish to highlight, but what was missing at the earlier stage. That earlier stage can be at many points – the first statement, report, meeting, complaint or similar, later on in the process when there is some kind of more formal internal procedure, including an appeal, or later still when the claim is made initially in the court or tribunal.

In that situation the process is the same but the questions are slightly different. The **Repeat** phase is as before. The explain phase then concentrates on the point in time when the person gave a description of some kind. Before going to that, it is helpful to set out the context, such as:

You gave Mr Smith an account of the incident that day.

You wished to tell him everything that had happened.

You were telling him the truth.

You knew that he was writing down what you said.

You knew that it was important to give him accurate details.

You knew that it was important to give him all the details.

The **Put** phase is then to highlight the omission. It is best to keep control by something like:

Nowhere in your statement to Mr Smith do you mention [what was said in evidence].

You made that up for the purposes of your claim [or the defence to the claim].

There are also some times when there are two statements, neither of which you accept, but which are inherently contradictory. That requires a similar process, but the explain part is worded rather differently, as you do not accept that it is accurate. What you want to do is highlight that there are two differing statements, and they cannot both be right. The **Repeat** phase is the same, but the **Explain** phase might be something like this:

Please turn to page 300. Is this the note of a meeting you held with your line manager on 4 June?

Do we see that it was emailed to you that same day, on page 303?

Above that email do we see your reply, sent about an hour after the email to you was sent?

Does that reply say that 'Yes, this is an accurate record'.

If we then go to the Note on page 301 and paragraph 23 does it say 'On 3 June I arrived in the office at about 9am, and went to my desk. I worked on a tender for about an hour, then had a conversation with Mrs Jones ....?

The **Put** phase may also need to be different, such as:

You told your manager you were in the office on 3 June.

You told the judge earlier today that you were not.

You were lying to one of them at least, weren't you?

Cover all you need to

The two fundamental purposes of cross-examination is both to challenge the facts you dispute from what the witness said in the examination-in-chief, and where the witness can do so, to respond to your case. Make sure that you have asked all the questions that you need to. If you wish to check for a few minutes, you can ask the judge for that time, either by adjourning the case for a few minutes, or just with silence for a short period while you check your notes.

When less is more

There is always a temptation to go the extra mile, and prove a point. Resist it. Ask the questions you have to, then stop. There is a well-known story of a trial of a large number of accused, where the allegation was that there was in effect a riot. The main police witness was giving his evidence. After he had done so for the prosecution, he was questioned by the advocates for each accused. One of them asked a question along the lines of: 'I see that you have not said anything about my client, Sergeant Smith.' The answer was: 'Yes, but in fact he was at the front of the group, waving a big stick.' If the question had not been asked, the absence of the evidence could have been addressed by the submission, very probably successfully.

Recognising when to stop may not be always simple, but is something that you should be prepared for.

Opening and closing

As with examination-in-chief, you want to finish strongly, but here it is also possible to start strongly too. That is so particularly if you are challenging the person, not just what they did. If therefore the person has some question over their honesty, or character, that you can make use of, you may wish to start with that. It could be a criminal conviction, or a decision from a regulatory body, or a warning at work given after a formal process, or any similar fact that you can establish, and use to attack the credibility or reliability, or both, of that person as a witness. So whilst it is normal in examination-in-chief to ask basic questions first about who the person is, what their experience is and so on, with cross-examination you can, if you wish to, go straight to a key point.

When preparing opening and closing questions, always think of how they will look to the judge. Will he or she like you going straight to that key point out of the blue? Think also of how the witness will react? Are they likely to crumble before your eyes, or fight back? A further point is whether you miss the opportunity to close off escape routes first.

The order of questions in cross-examination is therefore important, and can mean lots of chopping and changing when working out how best it is likely to work out.

Dealing with experts in cross-examination

Some cases need expert evidence, which is not about the facts of what happened, but an opinion assuming that the facts are either agreed or proved. They are not easy to cross-examine, as they are, by definition, expert in their field. You are unlikely to be. There are however a number of ways in which you can try to devalue what they say in evidence.

First, start with their CV, which is usually part of their report, or referred to in evidence. Check what their qualifications are, what they have done professionally, and whether their expertise is the right one for the present case. Not always is that so. Check whether they have given expert evidence before. Some may not have. Or others may have done so very regularly, but always for one side. Check the internet for comments about them, you may be able to find critical remarks about their evidence in other cases.

Secondly, consider what they knew, or more often what they did not know as they were not told of it. Did they have all the information that is now before the judge? Did they have an incomplete, or wrong, understanding of what happened? You can ask them both what they were told about, but also put to them what they did not know, or were not told, or were not provided with by the party that instructed them.

Thirdly, look at the process of reasoning that led to their conclusion. That should be explained in the report, but that is not always done. There can sometimes simply be a baldly asserted conclusion: 'Therefore in my opinion the claimant did not suffer any loss of pension benefits'. If it is not clear why that view is held from the report, the tactics of how to deal with that are not easy. If you address it in cross-examination, the other side can try to fix that in re-examination. If you do not, and just address it in submission, it can be argued that you did not challenge it. Overall therefore the better course is to challenge the assertion, suggest that it is simply an assertion, without any reasoned argument given in the report or letter, and suggest that it is wrong. If possible suggest why it is wrong.

If you have your own expert report, it helps to speak to your expert before the hearing. You should ask for their views about the other side's report, and why it is thought to be wrong, and where. You can then use that information to base your questions around. Ultimately, you will wish the judge to prefer your expert report to that of the other side. You need to give the judge the reason to do that. The basis for that is in your questions in cross-examination.

Remember too that the expert witness is there not to assist one side, but the court or tribunal. In a sense expert witnesses are intended to be neutral, giving evidence from their expert stance to help the judge decide matters correctly on a particularly technical or difficult point of evidence. The expert witness is not always appropriate. For example in a case of unfair dismissal, a party cannot call a retired employment judge and ask him or her for expert evidence on the question of fairness. That is for the judge in your hearing. Expert evidence is for points where expertise is required. It is therefore possible to object to the receipt of expert evidence from the other side if you consider that it is not appropriate in the circumstances of that case.

Last-minute preparations

It is often the case that in the lead up to the hearing, you will suddenly notice something that you have missed up until then. It is a form of heightened lucidity that seems only to happen when the pressure is on. It may be the adrenaline from knowing that the case is to be heard next day. It may be that that is enhanced by feelings of trepidation, if not fear.

First, do not be surprised if that happens, it is far from unusual. Secondly, see how you can work with this – if it is an entirely new point not in the claim, or the pleadings, think how you can get it to be a part of the case. Do you need to formally ask to amend the claim? That may be difficult at a late stage, and is almost certain to be opposed by the other side. Is it worth that additional time, and risk? Is it something that you can simply use in cross-examination for example, so that it does not need to be highlighted at all to the opposition?

You may well be nervous. That is normal. If you are not, that would be unusual. I was very often nervous before a hearing, even late in my career. I have seen the best QCs' hands visibly shake with nerves at the start of some high profile and important hearings. Nerves however sharpen the mind, and tend to reduce, if not disappear, when the hearing starts, as you are then focusing on what is going on. So if you find the butterflies in your stomach starting to take flight, try your best to ignore that and recognise that most of those involved, including the other side and witnesses are probably feeling much the same.

There is quite a lot published about what clothing to wear to impress, with sometimes detailed guidance about the colour of suit (dark blue is currently in vogue) and so on. My view is that you should wear what you are comfortable in wearing, recognising that this is like a very formal meeting. Do not go out as if you are about to go on a long walk in the country, or as if you are going clubbing in Ibiza. Wear something smart. If in doubt, some form of suit with a white shirt or blouse is a safe option, but there is no need to buy that.

Finally, remember that a case can settle at any time. Even if there has been no offer to settle the case until now, it is possible that that will change. Some parties deliberately leave making an offer until the last moment in the hope that that is when the other side feels most vulnerable. Other parties feel very confident initially, but just before the hearing suddenly see what the level of risk is, or become very nervous at the prospect of giving evidence, or do not wish the evidence to be public. Last minute settlements not only do happen, but happen quite regularly.

In light of that, be ready for any last minute proposals from the other side, but also reconsider your own position, see what if any discussions have already taken place, and consider if you are willing to compromise in any way. If you are, do not let pride get in the way of a settlement. Contact the other side, even if late on the night before, or on the morning of the hearing itself, and see whether they are prepared to have a discussion.

Covid-19

It is not known what the effect of the pandemic will be by the time you read this. It may still be significant, or it may have disappeared. At time of writing however it is significantly affecting the way cases are dealt with.

Whilst there can be some effects on each case, it makes only a small difference to the advice in this book. There are a few points to bear in mind, however:

1   Cases are liable to take longer to get to the stage of a final hearing, and that may give a greater incentive to see if a settlement can be reached.

2   There may be greater difficulties in having access to documents, witnesses or otherwise in some of the preparations. If you would like more time because of that, first approach the other side and ask them, and secondly raise it with the court or tribunal as soon as it becomes clear that it may be a factor.

3   There may be a possibility of having the case heard in a different manner from the usual route of a hearing in person, including by use of written arguments, telephone hearings or remote hearings on PCs, laptops, tablets and other devices. Consider whether that is possible in your case, but also if it is right for your case. It may be that one or other possibility would make the presentation of your side of the case better or worse. Think about what is best for you, then argue that that is what should happen. It may well not be your decision, but you can at least try to influence it.

4   If a witness is shielding, that may require particular care, both in taking details of what evidence they might give during preparations and when it comes to their giving evidence, which is likely to require either very careful measures, or doing so remotely. If the person is a reluctant witness, but someone who is vital in your view, that will be a real challenge. It is possible to seek a witness order, or equivalent, but the judge may be very reluctant to grant it in those circumstances unless the evidence is essential

for a fair hearing. Both why the witness is essential, and what steps are proposed for their safety, will need to be set out by you when making that application.

5   If someone, including you, falls ill, or possibly ill, at the last moment that again may cause a problem not easy to manage, but the first thing to do is tell the court or tribunal and the other party as soon as possible. There may be a need to seek a test, or to self-isolate, and that will prevent attending a building to give evidence but depending on how you feel you may be able to suggest attending remotely. It may however also be necessary to ask for the hearing to be adjourned and new dates fixed. If you have self-declared symptoms the other party may be suspicious about whether that is genuine. It may or may not be possible to obtain some form of GP certificate, but you could try to ask for one even over the phone. At least if you try you can refer to that. You could also ask a family member to write a letter confirming your symptoms for example.

6   If there is a hearing of evidence heard remotely that tends to take longer, and be rather more difficult to conduct. First there is a short time-lag between a question and the answer. Secondly the view of the person involved is more limited than at an in person hearing. Thirdly the view of the judge is very limited, and you may not be able to see much of what he or she is doing. As will be explained later, it can be important to check that the judge has heard the evidence, and written it down, by watching their pen. That may not be possible during such a hearing, so it is necessary to go particularly slowly and carefully. Fourthly, it can be tiring, concentrating on a small screen for what may be many hours. Breaks are often taken more frequently, but you can ask for one at any time, and if you feel yourself becoming tired do so. The worst that can happen is to be told that you should continue. As long as you don't do it too often, it is very unlikely that asking for a break will be received badly.

Chapter 7

Evidence at the hearing

Before you leave make sure that you have everything you need with you. Take all the documents you need including the pleadings and Bundle of Documents, any other documents such as earlier Orders issued you might want to raise or the other side might refer to, all your notes, copies of cases if you have them, a number of pens, enough paper to write notes on for the whole hearing, your laptop or other device if using that (check that it is fully charged and that you have a charger for it), money, your phone, a calculator if not on your phone, and anything else necessary. Then check it all again before you leave.

As a matter of practicability, check very carefully the time that the hearing is to start, where that is, and get there well beforehand. Often it is best to be there at least half an hour beforehand, if not an hour. If you are not sure of how long it may take to get there, give yourself enough leeway. Do not trust that trains, buses, taxis or other transport will get you there at the time advertised or expected. Putting it simply, you cannot afford to be late, even if the fault of that is not directly your own.

If there is a last minute emergency do your best to contact the other side and the court, either by email, phone, or otherwise to tell them. It may or may not be accepted by either the judge or the other side, so you also need to think of having written evidence to use later if needed. So if your child is suddenly taken ill, and in an ambulance on the way to hospital, try and get something in writing from the hospital to confirm that if you can, or ask your GP for it later. It is naturally very rare for such emergencies to take place, but they are not unknown.

Assuming that you arrive on time and without difficulty, you are then ready to commence the hearing. You have prepared the case as fully as you can, the documents are all lodged, there is no hope of any settlement or other resolution, you feel confident enough of success to want to go on, and the date of the final hearing has arrived. This is the time when advocacy assumes greatest prominence.

What is advocacy? In essential terms it is trying to persuade the judge that you should win. The focus at all times is therefore on the judge as the decision maker. The intent is to persuade him or her that you are right. That means, in essence, presenting the evidence you have chosen in the best way possible.

The hearing of the case, when the evidence is heard, has its own phases as follows:

(i)   Preliminaries

(ii)   Evidence – examination-in-chief

(iii)   Evidence – cross-examination

(iv)   Evidence – re-examination

(v)   Submissions

Preliminaries

Before the hearing starts fully, it is quite often that something is brought up either by the judge or the other side, or you may wish to raise something. That may be because a matter needs to be clarified, such as whether one particular claim is being pursued or given up, or a document might need to be produced late, and permission is needed for that, or a witness might be available only on one day and arrangements to hear that person out of the normal order might be required.

Often a judge will start by asking the parties if there are any preliminary issues. Normally the claimant will go first. If there are, say so. If not, say that there are not. There is no need to come up with something if you are just ready to proceed.

If the other side ask to do something, like lodge a production late, you do have an opportunity to comment on that, and to argue against it. Usually if there is a reasonable explanation it will be permitted, but not always. If it is allowed, you may wish to ask for time to consider it, or check if there are any documents to produce in response. In some cases that might even mean that the hearing is discharged, in effect postponed to another day.

If so, you can ask for an award of costs (or expenses as they are called in Scotland), and if there is fault on the part of the other side or their advisers that may well be granted. Generally speaking however there is a desire to proceed with a hearing once fixed, particularly where witnesses are present.

There may be other steps taken before the evidence starts. In court the evidence may be recorded by a shorthand writer, who is sworn in. There may be an interpreter required for someone for whom English is not their first language, and that person is sworn in. In some jurisdictions (and many cases in England and Wales) there can be opening statements given by each party to summarise their case in advance.

Subject to that however, the evidence is then heard. If you are going first, you should either have the witness in the room ready to start, or nearby in a witness room. Before the hearing starts, you should alert the witness to what happens, and where to go both to wait, and to give the evidence. Witnesses either take a religious oath, or a non-religious affirmation. They each have the same effect, and in simple terms are a promise to tell the truth. A clerk will usually ask either you or the witness which option is preferred.

The witness will then be sworn in, almost always by standing next to the table set aside for the witnesses, and where the documents are placed. Those documents are the only ones that a witness can generally refer to. Witnesses cannot therefore generally take their own notes with them. You are better to inform them of that before matters start, just to be sure.

After that, wait for the judge to tell you when to start. It may be a clear invitation to do that or just a nod of the head. You then ask your first question. In almost all tribunals you do that sitting down. In many court actions you stand when speaking, but not always does that apply. If in doubt, ask the clerk of the court.

Asking the questions

Having prepared the words to use for the questions in advance, you are organised for the hearing. That is one step short of doing the hearing however. The conduct of the hearing is far from easy. Witnesses do not always say what you think they will. Opponents do not always do what you think they will. Judges do not always do what you think they will. Things can go wrong, off the rails, or come at you out of the blue.

Go slow

There are some guidelines as to how to conduct the hearing, some of which are demonstrated by quotations. The first is this:

'If you go slowly, time will walk behind you, like a submissive ox' – Juan Ramon Jiminez

Those who are nervous, which is likely to mean you, tend to rush. They tend to speak quickly and in a higher pitch. Nerves constrict the vocal chords. That tends to mean less sound. Nerves also mean that your mind can go a bit to mush. You forget to do things. You miss what can be an important point. You become more easily distracted.

The first message therefore is to go very slowly. Take care about everything, and take the time to do things correctly. Asking questions in this context is not a conversation. It is eliciting evidence, which means getting the evidence you want in front of the judge. Sometimes the evidence is recorded by experts, such as shorthand writers. Sometimes it is recorded electronically. Sometimes it is noted by the judge. Whatever is the practice, most judges will write their own notes.

That means that you must go slowly enough for them to do that, to read documents being referred to, and to consider the evidence. So often, that is impossible because the questioner is going too fast. If that happens, evidence can either be missed, or its significance can be missed.

As a basic rule of thumb therefore, the speed you should speak at is no more than half the normal speed. Slower than that is probably better. If you are not sure about doing this, practice beforehand. You can record yourself both at your normal speed, and at half speed. Try and write down what you say each time, and see how easy or difficult it is. Check how your voice sounds, and whether you need to change the speed any further.

Before you start to ask questions about a document, check that everyone has both the document, and are referring to the correct page. Sometimes it takes longer than you think for that to happen. Your papers may be better organised than the witness's, or judge's, so if there is a need to wait until the judge finds the right page, simply say nothing until it is clear that she or he has found it.

If you have something like a plan, or photograph, or similar which you wish to have the witness comment on, start by asking about the document. When was it prepared or taken? Who did that? What does it show? Go through each element of it, perhaps using north, south, east and west or some other means of identifying parts. Do not assume that it means to the judge what it means to you. Educate the judge about its meaning, and importance.

Look up

Use your eyes to do more than just look at your notes. Think of this:

'I wasn't taught to paint. I was taught to look' – David Hockney

You need to be aware of what is happening around you. It is easy to keep your head in your notes, looking at the question coming up, or in the documents searching for the right part. That means that you miss both what the witness is doing, and what the judge is doing.

For the witness, you need to check for clues as to what they are thinking from their body language. If someone goes bright red, starts sweating profusely, starts fidgeting, spends a lot of time looking over to their representative, or friends behind them, or puts their head in their hands and starts to whimper, you need to recognise that. It is also important to make eye contact with them, particularly in cross-examination.

For the judge, you need to watch their pen. If they are still writing, you wait. If they are looking at the document being referred to, you wait. If they are staring into space, you wait, or ask them if it is appropriate to continue.

At the same time, you need to look at your notes, perhaps the document that is being addressed at that stage, and write your own notes. So this is not at all easy. It is a form of plate-spinning.

The best technique I have found is a scan. It is used by pilots, particularly when flying on instruments alone, so that they are not looking outside the cockpit either as it is dark, or as they are above or in cloud. The scan is a set pattern, looking at instruments in a particular order and checking them at each pass. In the hearing there are basically three things to keep looking at:

1   The witness.

2   The judge.

3   Your notes.

So you repeat that basic pattern, which is usually configured rather like a triangle. The judge tends to be more or less opposite you, the witness on one side and the notes immediately in front of you. Before each question, look up to the witness and judge. See what each is doing. Check that the judge is ready for each question.

Another important thing to remember is to make eye contact both with the witness and the judge. Try and read, if you can, what they are each thinking. It can be very difficult, but you may get a sense from a witness that they are not telling the truth, and direct eye contact can make it harder for people either to lie at all, or to do so convincingly.

If you make eye contact with the judge you may also get a sense of what she or he is thinking, whether you are going at the right pace or not, and whether your questions and the answers are making an impression or not. Judges will sometimes offer some assistance, and may say something to the effect that it is time to move on to the next point, or they may nod their head at a particular point. Pay attention to that. It is you who is conducting the case, but they will decide it, and generally it is best to act on comments about moving on. You are however entitled to keep trying if you are sure that it is vital to do so, and prepared to incur the displeasure of the person who decides the case. If the judge has nodded at a particular point, it can be a good idea to emphasise that evidence later in your submission (but do not say that the judge nodded in agreement, as that is going too far).

Listen

It may sound obvious, but you need to listen to the answer the witness gives. It is astonishing how often it is apparent that the questioner has not done that. The questioner has a list of questions, and asks them one after the other as has been written down, paying no attention to the answer. It was a guitarist who expressed it like this:

'Knowledge speaks. Wisdom listens' – Jimi Hendrix

Do not fall into the trap of just asking your question. Listen very carefully to the answer. Write it down, or at least a basic summary, or the key points given in answer. If the answer is not as expected, think. Should you ask another question? Should you repeat the question as it has not been answered? Is there a document that establishes that the answer is wrong?

Make a note of where you are in the questions if you need to go off on a tangent. That way you know where to get back to after that is done.

Taking notes is dealt with below, but it is important not just to take notes, but also to record what is important – you may forget later. So if the point is a good one, highlight it in some way, by underlining, or asterisks, or exclamation marks, or a red pen.

Take heed of what the judge says. If the judge tells the witness to answer the question, write that down so that you can refer to the need for that to be done in submission. If the judge is indicating that the answer is incredible: 'Are you seriously suggesting to me that ....' Write that down too.

If you are told to move on, it is generally best to do so. Not always so, however. You can sometimes need to stick to your guns on a vital point, but recognising that the risk is that you annoy the person who decides the case.

Do not give the answer

Once you have asked the question, wait for the answer. Do not rush to fill a void. Consider these words:

'The music is not in the notes, it is in the silence in between' – Mozart

Silence can be a weapon during questioning. There are times when leaving a period of silence can be powerful. It is possible to do that in the middle of the question you ask, for emphasis. That is particularly the case if you are asking a key question, for example one which you have built up to and encapsulates an important part of the case. Give it the space it needs to be heard, and considered.

If you ask a question and the witness does not immediately answer, do not rush in to fill it. For your own witnesses they may also leave a silent gap after you have asked a question, and it may just be that they need time to think. Give them what you consider to be a reasonable time for that before checking if they wish you to repeat the question.

In cross examination, the silence may be a witness trying to think of an answer that is not a simple 'yes', or making up a lie. You should leave that silence either to be filled at some point when the witness works out what to say, or wait until the judge intervenes. You have asked the question, and unless there was any objection or intervention by the judge, you are entitled to have an answer to it. The silence is eloquent, and can be something to refer to later on in your submission, so note that there was at the least a long silence, a delay, before the answer, or that there was no answer after that silence. The judge is however most likely to notice any unexpected silence, and it can be an indicator against the witness being credible.

Control of the voice

It is not always easy to do in practice, but remember that you need to be heard. That means asking questions in a voice loud enough to be heard by the witness, who may be reasonably close to you, but also the judge who may be further away. It is rather like being an actor, you need to project your voice so as to be heard at the back. This essentially means speaking more loudly than you do in a normal conversation.

Do not, however, shout. Do not speak so loudly that it appears that you are trying to intimidate the witness. At all times you must be appropriate, and professional. There can be a temptation to challenge, or to say something like: 'I don't believe that'. It is not your role to believe it. That is what the judge is there for. Just stay calm, and even if you are seething inside, hide it.

Some people speak in a single tone of voice, with no emphasis or modulation. Tone can be important. Variation first of all makes things more interesting. But secondly it means that you can add emphasis, and that can entirely change the meaning of the words used.

Some people naturally speak with variety of tone, pace and emphasis. If you do not, think about the delivery. Monotonous voices tend to be rather boring, and that lessens the effect. Variety is therefore important. Put emphasis where that is needed – and you can remind yourself by underlining a word in your notes, or have it in capitals.

In a phrase such as: 'What did you do to make your anger known?' the emphasis can be placed on any number of words: *you*, implying the witness as distinct from someone else; *do*, suggesting in effect that nothing was done by the witness personally, or that it is evidence of an act of some kind that you want from the witness, not their thoughts; *anger*, to emphasise that you want to highlight both that the witness was angry and what they did to make that manifest to the other person, and *known*, to be able to highlight later in submission that the other person must have been aware of the anger and the cause of it.

Modulation of the voice can also be very effective. It is the use of the pitch of the voice to indicate either surprise, or disbelief, or endorsement. It can be used to indicate what answer you seek, without being leading. A different example of the use of this is the reading of football results by the late James Alexander-Gordon, on BBC radio. For anyone not familiar with his delivery, it can be found online. From the modulation of his voice, you could tell the outcome from the first half of it. If he said 'Everton nil' in one tone of voice, you knew that it was a draw, as it tended to pitch up. If he said it in another pitch, with the nil lower in tone, you knew that they had lost. If he said 'Everton one' in a slightly higher pitch, but with somewhat greater emphasis, then you knew whoever they played had not scored.

Other tips

In speech, we often start sentences with the word 'And'. It is not a capital offence, but it tends to be annoying for the judge. The word is entirely unnecessary. Try to avoid it. Similarly, although on TV it may seem effective to be moving about in a dramatic way, in real life that tends to be distracting. Unless there is a good reason for it, stay in one place.

When I did advocacy training, one session was videoed. It was a dreadful experience but highly effective. I saw that I held a pen in my hand, and turned it round and round while I asked some of the questions. It was distracting. I never did it again. So try and keep reasonably still, and think about how you will be seen by the judge.

If you are going to use a gesture, which you are entitled to, think about how that will be perceived both by the judge and the witness. Ask yourself whether it will help you. Pointing at the witness in an aggressive way tends not to work very well. Shaking your head in disbelief can also not be received very well. What you think of the evidence is less important than what the judge thinks of it. Generally speaking keep reasonably still, and make the points you want to make about the evidence when it comes to the submission.

It is also important to keep in mind that this is not, despite the pattern of question and answer, a conversation. It is best to avoid a response such as 'OK' or 'good' or 'thank you' or the like. We use those words of endorsement or approval or encouragement in conversation of course, and it is quite often encountered in a hearing, but does not add anything and can detract from the evidence itself. Even worse is to say to your witness something like: 'Yes, I believe you' or to the witness for the other side: 'I don't believe that'. The assessment of the evidence is not for the questioner, but the judge, as stated above.

The final piece of advice is particularly for cross-examination. It can be very difficult indeed to decide whether to leave an answer alone, or follow it up. It can be almost impossible to know what the judge is thinking, and whether he or she is starting to believe, or disbelieve, that witness, and what if anything else to do. All you can do is be as fully prepared as you can, watch and listen to all that is happening, and then trust your instinct. If you have a sense that the answer was a poor one, and that you can make progress by exploring it further, then consider carefully doing that, and if so how. Think quickly or, if you can, ask for an adjournment. If you are near a natural break, note it down, so that you can use the break to think about what to ask.

This may seem contradictory, but another guideline is 'when in doubt, leave it out'. For issues you must cover, the key parts of the case including the evidence your side has given or is to give, you have no real choice. The guideline does not apply to that but to the margins, the areas where you have a discretion on what to do. You may decide that it is worth pursuing, but if having weighed up both possibilities you are just not sure, then the safer course tends to be not to do so.

Dealing with bad answers

Do not expect everything to go as planned. It tends not to. As it was once put -

> 'There aren't any embarrassing questions, just embarrassing answers' – Carl Rowan

It often happens that you ask a perfectly good question of your own witness, but the witness does not give an equally good answer. It may be very different from what you expected, or from what they had said to you or someone else earlier. There are a huge variety of reasons for that. Sometimes it is just because of the circumstances, the person is nervous, or confused, or finds it difficult to recall what happened. At other times it is because what they said earlier was wrong, and they are now on oath and have to tell the truth. Sometimes they are mistaken, and sometimes witnesses do not tell the truth.

How do you repair any damage that causes? It is not easy, but there are some ways to try to do that.

The first is to know the documents very well. You can then take the witness to whatever document helps you with that point. Before rushing in to it, you can ask about it – for example if the witness was at a meeting, and whether the record of that was correct. You can refer to an email, or letter, or anything else in the bundle of documents. Remember that if the witness is your own, you cannot lead them, unless they are to be argued to be hostile.

The second technique is to go to the pleadings particularly those of the other side. That can allow you to read out a section that contains something you think the witness will disagree with, and then use that as the springboard to go over the same point as their bad answer had covered.

The third is to go back in time and approach the issue again, but from a slightly different angle. You can go back to an earlier answer you liked, and build from there. It is a trick usually called 'loopback'. You say something like: 'Can I take you back to evidence you gave a little earlier. You said that you had not been present at the meeting between Linda and Elle on 4 April. Where were you that day?'

You do however have to be careful that by doing this you do not make the point worse by highlighting it. Trust your instinct as to whether you should be able to improve matters, of whether it is better just to leave that point alone and move forward.

Dealing with the witness who does not answer the question

Quite often, particularly with difficult questions, the witness will not give a direct answer to your question in cross-examination. They will act a little like a politician, and answer either the question they would have preferred to have been asked, or try to ramble on covering issues loosely and hope that no one notices. How do you deal with that?

There are a number of ways. One of the best is to say something like: 'I notice that you have not answered my question, let me repeat it.' And then repeat exactly the same question.

Another is to say to the judge: 'I notice, [Sir or Madam, or Your Lordship or Ladyship], that the witness has not answered the question, I wonder if I might ask you to direct that he/she does?'

Repeating unanswered questions does highlight the failure to give an answer. Famously Jeremy Paxman asked Michael Howard the same question 14 times in a television interview. That can make good television, with 14 different answers not directly responding to the question with a yes or no, but it tends to make rather poor evidence, and unless in unusual circumstances may lead the judge to lose a measure of interest.

As a very basic guide, I would advise asking the same question three times, and then saying something to the effect that as you have done so without an answer, you will move on. You need then to remember that, and mention it in the submission, as discussed later. It can be powerful evidence of a witness not being credible or reliable.

Keep track of time

Time can seem to flow differently when conducting a case. A children's writer put it rather well -

'How did it get so late so soon?' – Dr Seuss

Keep an eye on the clock. Time can run away with you when asking questions, or making arguments. It can both be a friend, and a foe.

There are normal working hours for each location, find out what they are. If lunch is taken between 1 and 2pm, and you are getting to the end of one section at 12.58pm, suggest that this might be a good time to stop for lunch. If you are getting towards the end but want more time for thought overnight, and it is say 10 minutes to the end of the day, you may wish to suggest that this would be a good time to stop for the day as you are about to start a new part of the questioning or words to that effect.

Keeping an eye on the clock can be important for other reasons. The general rule is that witnesses should be ready to give evidence when the judge is ready for them. It can cause practical and other difficulties if you estimate for a witness that they will be called on Tuesday at 2.30pm, but matters move more quickly and the previous witness finishes at 11.30am that day. Err very much on the side of caution, and have the witness wait if necessary. If there might be a problem, raise it as early as possible both with the other side and then with the judge. There is always a possibility that you will not get whatever leeway you want on timings. Rather than risk losing the case for such a matter of planning, try to make sure that the problem does not arise.

There sounds like a lot to do, watching the judge and witness, checking notes, keeping an eye on the clock, writing notes of evidence, thinking about what is said, looking at documents and so on. There is. It is a difficult task. That is one reason why taking it very slowly is a good idea. It gives a little more time to manage all these various issues, to keep all the various plates spinning.

Take notes

Throughout your questioning, you need to be taking at least basic notes of the answers. That is remarkably difficult. Just as a matter of practicability, you may be standing up, with the paperwork on a table, and your notes for the questions held in your hands. You are doing a lot at the same time and it is easy to be tempted to leave the notes until later. But there is really no way that you can remember everything that was said, and how it was said.

My own practice was to have my questions written on lined paper, and on the right hand side I drew a vertical line, about six inches from the right hand side of the paper. The questions were to the left of that line, and on the other side of it I would write either a note of the answer, or an observation. If the answer was as expected I would either add a tick, or a 'Y' for yes. If there was more to it, I would summarise the answer briefly. If the answer was important, I would write it out word for word, and use quotation marks to indicate that they were the words used. I would also make additional comments or markings where that would help. A good answer I would underline. A bad one I would add an exclamation mark to. If the answer was given with emotion, either tearfully or angrily for example, I would note that.

However you do it, have some kind of system, and a basic form of shorthand for some key matters.

Closing the evidence

At the end of the evidence, each side should say something to the effect that that is the evidence they wish to lead. If the other side do not do that, it is a good idea to check that with them and the judge. The reason for that is that you want the evidence to be concluded, locked down.

The basic rule is that both sides must come to the hearing and produce all evidence that is reasonably practicable to produce. It is very rare indeed for evidence to be allowed in later on. Unless it could not have been obtained, with reasonably thorough preparation, it is just too late. That is a double-edged sword, but you will have done all the preparation reasonably possible, so it is best that you ensure that the other side draw a line under their evidence.

Giving evidence as a litigant in person

Giving evidence without anyone asking questions is difficult, and can be tiring. If you find yourself becoming tired, or if you have wandered off track in rather a long piece of evidence because your mind is not concentrating well, ask for a break. Five minutes to clear your head will often be permitted, and allows a fresh start. If you are coming towards the end of your evidence and have a nagging feeling that you have not covered something again ask if you could either have a break, or a few minutes where you are to check. What you are not generally permitted to do is to go and check notes, but if you think that there is a point and wish to do that you can ask the judge for permission. The judge will usually ask the other party for comments, and it may be permitted or not but it is not likely that you will be criticised for asking.

When acting for yourself, you may not have anyone present to write down what is being asked of you when you are being cross-examined. If you can have someone attend to do that, so much the better. They will not be your representative, but can give you a note of what you said which you may need for later, particularly when making a submission.

If you are alone, you may ask the judge for permission to have some blank paper with you to write notes of what you are asked. There are two reasons for that. The first is to have a record of what you are asked, and what you say, which can be very difficult indeed to remember completely accurately. That can be relevant for submissions – for example you can check that you were not asked about one particular matter which you had given evidence about, and argue that that fact should be accepted because of it. The second is that you have an opportunity in re-examination to cover points raised in cross-examination. You can therefore note what points to make when that stage is reached. For example, you may be asked whether you attended a particular meeting, and then be referred to the note of that meeting. You may accept that you did attend and that the note is accurate. The questioner then moved on to other matters. You however want to give evidence about what happened immediately after that meeting in the corridor outside, when someone told you something, and can do that in re-examination. If you make a note about that point, you can then explain what happened then, what was said and so on, putting that evidence about the meeting in a wider context.

113

Re-examination

After the cross-examination of your own witness, and after any questions from the judge, you have a further opportunity to ask questions (or for the litigant in person to give further evidence) providing they arise from the questions of others. It is not an opportunity to ask something that has just occurred to you. What you should or should not ask can be a difficult judgement call. The answer may not have been what you wanted, but highlighting that by the question in re-examination may not be best. What is normally the lowest point for you is the cross-examination of your main witness. That is, in a sense, the point of cross-examination. There are few cases where there are not some points to score, or where a witness survives without a hair on their head affected in any way.

The decision must usually be made there and then, but there are some times where luck may give you some time, or where you may ask for, and be granted, a little time. Subject to that you must just make the decision.

What questions to ask arises from the points made in cross-examination. As soon therefore as there is both a question asked in cross-examination that you are worried by, and/or an answer that worries you, start thinking about what to do about it. Write down somewhere a note of this, and what the point is. Have a think about how to address it. Is there a document somewhere that might put the answer in perspective? Is there evidence from another witness that might help? Is there something that you can do to minimise the effect of the answer?

You need then to consider how to ask the question. Generally, questions in re-examination should not be leading ones. You can start by referring to the question asked, such as: 'You were asked in cross examination about whether you had raised any formal grievance'. That alerts both the witness and the judge to the question. You can then go on to address it: 'You said that you had not, but can I ask you to turn to page 50. What does that show?' With the answer being an email where an informal complaint was made.

For the litigant in person the same general process as was set out for examination-in-chief applies. Normally at this stage there are not too many points to make, but in some cases there can be many, and you may ask for permission to refer to your notes when giving your evidence. If that is not allowed, you just need to try and recall the points. One way to help with that is to know how many there are – say there are three, and put a one word description for each.

How can you tell if, or when, the opposition witness is lying?

The simple answer is that you cannot, at least not reliably. There are some urban myths about what people do which may indicate that they are lying, but many are simply wrong, and the rest are not reliable. Judges tend not to base the assessment on a gut instinct on who is telling the truth, but on what the evidence shows. That is covered later under submissions.

There are however some matters to consider when watching, and listening to, a witness. They may encourage you to keep going with challenges rather than move on to something else. They include:

- Being vague, not providing the kind of detail you would expect.

- Not answering the question immediately, including asking for it to be repeated.

- Distractions such as fidgeting, playing with hair, putting a hand over the mouth, putting fingers to lips and the like.

It used to be said that avoiding eye contact was a good indicator, but that is not always, if ever, right. In some cultures, avoiding eye contact is a sign of respect. It is therefore something to be very wary of indeed. At best what may be taken or thought of as clues to lying from body language are an indication of the possibility of lying, rather than proof of lying.

Testing has discovered that human beings are very bad at working out who is lying from watching and listening. Even those who are very well trained tend to get it right at best two times out of three, and most people would be about as accurate as the assessment they make if they tossed a coin.

The process in a court or tribunal is very different from an assessment of what people tell us in everyday life. The environment is an artificial one. There are stresses from being there, and from being put on oath or affirmation. Every word is being considered by, at the very least, the questioner and the judge, but often by others too, including any representative for the opponent of the questioner. What is said can be tested, both by further questions, and by comparing what is said to the documents, other evidence from witnesses who have, or will later, give evidence, and what was said earlier by that witness.

If an answer is vague, it can be probed further. Keep asking for more and more details. At this point, there is less risk in asking open questions in cross examination, but whether to do so, or to keep them closed, is a matter that needs to be considered and weighed in the balance. The vague answer might be that there was an earlier meeting when something else was agreed than you had understood to be the case. Rather than ask, for example: 'Who did you tell about this' you can ask: 'You have not mentioned this aspect before, have you?'' or: 'There is nothing in writing in the Bundle of Documents about this, is there?' or both. But it might be worth asking for details like:

- Where was the meeting you now say took place?

- What time?

- How did you get there?

- Who was present?

- Who saw you there?

- What time did it end?

- What written notes or records were taken at the time about it?

- What written notes or records were prepared afterwards about it?

- How did you pay for the travel to and from the meeting?

- Have you produced your bank account details to prove that?

- If not, why not.?

There are risks to this, which are that you may not be able to challenge the answers you get. So unless you feel very confident that you will get more out of those types of question than you risk, it may be better not to ask them at all.

If there is a sudden twist in a case, with entirely new evidence for which you have had no notice, you can also consider first objecting to it on that basis, and secondly if it is allowed, or you do not object, then asking for a short adjournment either to consider matters, particularly other documents, or to take instructions from your client.

If there is some particular element to what happened that you feel is important, remember to note it. You may wish to refer to that in submission later on. A large pause before an answer, or the witness obviously becoming flustered, or upset, during questioning are examples.

Do you always have to accuse the witness for the other side of lying?

Quite often representatives challenge everything someone says in evidence on the basis that all of it is a lie. It is as if they have seen that done on television or in films, and think that that is the best way to challenge the evidence. What works well on television however hardly ever works so well in the real world. Flamboyant and theatrical performances are best given by actors. In a court or tribunal, it pays to think carefully about what you need to challenge, why that is, and how to do it most effectively.

There are some people who lie for their own advantage. There are some who lie under pressure to try and get what they want. So there are some cases where it is necessary to argue that the person giving evidence, often the main witness for one side or the other, is lying.

More often however the person giving the evidence believes that they are telling the truth. Particularly for witnesses who do not have a financial or psychological stake in the outcome, they are often there to perform a kind of civic duty, not something they really want to do but either feel they should, or are compelled to do so by an instruction from someone such as their employer, or a witness order or similar.

For many witnesses therefore the issue is not so much whether they are lying, which is a matter of credibility, but whether they are likely to be right, in the sense of being accurate, which is a matter of reliability.

It can be important to work out in advance whether you are attacking the witness's credibility, or reliability or both. It can be important to consider whether you do so by looking only at their role in the case, or also the person more widely. For example, if the witness has a conviction for a crime of dishonesty that you are aware of, that can be put to that witness in cross-examination, particularly if it is fairly recent and even more so if it is related in some way to the facts of the case. If you are aware that the claimant is someone who has taken a series of claims against other employers, which have been dismissed on the basis that his evidence has been made up, that again is a good basis to mount a challenge on the person.

If however the witness is someone who has been at work without any incident of note, just going about their daily life in a normal way, who was involved in the process as part of their duties, for example as the person who investigated allegations, then mounting a direct attack on their credibility is unlikely to be easy, or productive. It can be far better to concentrate on the reliability of their evidence, and to give them a way out that does not lose face for them. So for example you can ask what training they had, if any, what information was or was not given to them at the start of the process, what help they had or did not have, how little time they were given to work with or factors such as that, before going through what was done and suggesting which parts of it were not right. It can be done in a low key way, without direct challenge, and far differently in tone from questions put to someone you believe is consciously and deliberately lying for their own financial advantage.

More often judges will make a decision basing in on reliability more than credibility. That is partly as it is so difficult to be sure who is lying, but also because evidence tends to be less than conclusive, there tend to be gaps in what the judge would like to have seen, or the question is a difficult one with a fine line between finding for one side or the other. What a judge usually uses as the basis for decision-making is something rooted in the evidence, not a gut feeling as to who was truthful or not, or accurate or not, so that the thought process can be based on something in the evidence, and if possible in the written evidence. That is why inconsistency in a document, or between two documents, or between a document and later evidence given orally, is so important. It is objective.

Think ahead therefore to the submission stage, and ask what you are likely to say about the evidence of the other side's witnesses individually, and why, then tailor your questions and style of asking them to that. There are comments under the submission chapter about the kind of factors that can be relevant to use and they are useful to consider at the stage of drafting the questions for cross-examination.

Objections

It can be necessary to object to a question put by the other side, or to a piece of evidence they seek to give. They may also object to a question that you ask.

The golden rule about objecting to a question is to do that early. If it is done after the evidence has been heard, the damage has been done. So if in any doubt, think about making the objection as soon as you feel that there is an issue with what is being asked.

There is a need to have a good basis to do so. What that is can depend on where you are, and in what context. The main issues are:

(i)   That it is a leading question in examination-in-chief.

(ii)   The lack of advance notice of this in the pleadings.

(iii)   The failure to put this point to the other side's witnesses in cross-examination.

(iv)   That it is irrelevant or otherwise improper.

(v)   That it is based on an assumption not warranted from the evidence heard.

(vi)   That it is ambiguous or otherwise confusing to the witness.

The normal way to do so is to say to the witness something like: 'Please don't answer that question' and then either outline the argument as to why or tell the judge that you wish to object and suggest that the witness leaves the room until the point is determined.

That becomes a little more difficult if the witness is a party litigant and just giving evidence. You then need to object to it as soon as you realise what is being said, and set out the argument (as the person is the party they have the right to be there to hear what you have to say, and to respond).

If the other side object to your question, think about the point that they make. If it is a leading question, you can offer to rephrase it, and the judge may suggest that. If you think that it is part of the pleading, even if not directly said in simple words there, explain your point. You may be able to argue that it was implied from the words used. If it is said to be irrelevant, you may be able to explain why you think it is relevant.

If the objection is upheld, you should just move on. Do not let that experience upset you. Objections happen in a large number of cases, and to the most experienced of advocates. Just go back to your notes, and ask the next question as if nothing untoward has happened.

Rules about witnesses

There are some strict rules about how to deal with witnesses during a hearing. Whilst they can vary, the basic ones tend to be these:

(i)   Be careful about what you tell one witness in advance of the hearing about what another witness has said. You do not wish to give the impression that you are trying to influence the evidence improperly.

(ii) Do not coach the witness, by telling them what to say. It is permissible and helpful to give general advice, such as to listen to the question and answer that, answer honestly, which can include: 'I don't know' or 'I can't remember' if that is the truth, and make sure that the answer is heard by the judge. You should never say something like: 'If you are asked why you did that, the best answer you can give is …'.

(iii) Once a witness has started his or her evidence, you should not discuss how it is going with them in any way during any break. The witness is in a form of isolation, and should not be influenced by you at all. Even seemingly innocent questions such as 'how am I doing' are best not answered, save by saying that you cannot answer that. Tell the witness what time to be back for the next session, or other details like where to get lunch, and also tell them not to discuss the evidence with anyone who is later to give evidence, on either side.

(iv) When the witness has finished giving evidence they can usually either sit at the back to watch the rest of the case, or leave. Sometimes it is best to ask the judge if the witness can leave. Those still in the court or tribunal can be recalled, and if you do not wish that to happen, it is better to suggest that they do not stay.

(v)   You should thank them for giving evidence later, and if they have expenses for attending, or lost wages, deal with that promptly.

(vi) The practice about witnesses hearing the evidence of others differs. In England and Wales, the practice is to allow witnesses to sit in to hear the evidence. In Scotland the practice is to have witnesses outside the court or tribunal, and called in one by one. If the person is the party, or the individual instructing the defence, then with permission that person can sit in throughout, even if they are also a witness. That can however sometimes affect how evidence is perceived, and there are times – particularly in cases where honesty if the main issue – where it is better to have them in the waiting room until they give evidence even if they would have been present.

(vii) There are other rules of ethics you should be aware of. If you are a lawyer there are many of them. If not, there are fewer, but they are fairly obvious ones. They include that you should never mislead the judge. Do not say that you have evidence on a point if you do not, and are only hopeful that it will turn up. If that is the position, say so. It may be that the representative of the other side has an ethical duty to assist you to some extent. That applies particularly when bringing to the attention of the judge an aspect of the law – such as a case, or statute – that is relevant to issues in the case. Do not assume that that is being done for some ulterior motive and is to harm you. It may be that it helps, and you can simply accept it.

The highs and lows

In every case there are times when the evidence goes well, and times when it does not. There are occasions when your questions work well, and others when they do not.

Equally, how you feel during a case as the person conducting it will change. It tends to look best during the examination-in-chief of the main witness. That is usually as the questions have been prepared in advance, and the witness should be giving helpful evidence because of that. But it can change both rapidly and substantially. The cross-examination of that witness can make the case seem far less certain, and less likely to succeed. But do not despair. That is normal. There is more evidence to come, and that feeling of it going less well, or very badly, or somewhere around that, does not tend to last.

The same happens to your opponent in reverse. He or she may be worried during examination-in-chief, but become more buoyed with their own cross-examination. It is almost an exact inverse curve relative to your own feelings. If we then take matters forward to the main witness for the opposition, they may well feel much the same as you did during cross-examination. The difference is that this time you are the cross-examiner, and they are the one feeling less hopeful.

Do not get too confident during your own questioning, or the evidence of your witnesses, and do not get too despondent during the evidence of the opponent, or their cross examination of your witnesses. What matters is not how you feel, but how the judge feels. The judge is not likely to have reached a final decision. That tends to be made, or at least confirmed, only after all of the evidence and hearing all of the submissions. Cases have been won, and lost, at the very last moment.

The process can be very difficult, and there are times when all can seem pretty much lost. You may feel that the judge from the questions asked has made up his or her mind against you. Do not assume that, however. What matters is the judges's assessment of all of the evidence, and even if there is a bad piece of evidence for you that may not lose you the case. It is I think best summed up in a quotation:

'If you are going through hell, keep going' – Winston Churchill

Throughout the whole time of the hearing however keep in mind that it is never too late to consider a settlement. Particularly for the respondent, if you see your evidence beginning to fall apart, if something unexpected happens that means your chances of success are becoming less, think about whether that means that you should still keep going or whether you try and have a discussion about settlement, on a without prejudice basis as discussed before. These are difficult tactical decisions, but cases have been resolved after some of the evidence has been heard. For some claimants, having told the court or tribunal their 'story' there can be almost a cathartic effect, in that they have had a chance to explain what happened and what the effect on them was, even for what may seem a purely financial claim for something like a claim for notice for breach of contract.

If the other side approach you about a settlement, do not just turn them away without thinking. Listen to what is on offer, and think about it. You may or may not be prepared to agree a settlement, but if the case is still to be concluded, if the other side has yet to give their evidence for example, then it may yet turn out badly.

Finally, whether there is a settlement or not, do not become complacent because the case has been going well so far. Cases have been won and lost by the very last question asked. I recall having one case where that happened. It was a case which I thought would be difficult to win, and half way through the evidence the person I was acting for recognised that and asked if we should give up. She had paid a lot of money to take the case this far, and I suggested that we complete it. I kept my best question to last, and when I asked it the witness for the other side had no answer. There was a long silence. That was the best evidence that we had in our case, and turned failure into success. So maintain your concentration right to the very last answer to the very last question.

Chapter 8

The submission

Phase one of the hearing, the evidence, is closed. Phase two begins. That is when there is a submission. Putting it simply, it is the time you can and should argue why you should win. The word 'submission' can be taken as meaning giving up, as in 'I submit'. In this context however it is the opposite. This is you trying very hard to win. It is your final chance to persuade. It is therefore very much part of advocacy, but deserves a chapter of its own.

Sometimes submissions are very brief, and on occasion people conducing their own case don't know what to say and stay silent. There is no requirement generally to make one, but it is an opportunity to influence the judge and you should take it if you can. Even a short and simple submission can be helpful. There are times when it can be powerful. I did a case once where the other side, in the form of a solicitor, said something to the effect that the judge had heard the evidence, and simply asked for a finding in favour of his client. I then produced a long written submission. That did not mean that my side won, but it increased the chances (in fact, my side did win).

You may notice something in the evidence not apparent to the judge. You may be able to highlight a part of the evidence that the judge had not thought significant. You may be able to put what was said by one witness in the context of a document, or other evidence, and argue why that witness is right, or wrong. You may be able to refer to the law, and why in your case it leads to the outcome you wish. Never think that it will not make a difference.

There is no need to prepare something in writing, but there are advantages to that. First, given what I have said before, you will have prepared an initial draft of it anyway, as part of the initial preparations. Secondly, it can be revised during the case, added to or completely re-written if it needs to be. Thirdly it allows you to look at the case a little more independently. Finally, it can help the judge by reducing the need for notes being taken.

If you do have a written submission, however, do not just hand it over. Speak to it, which means summarising it, and highlighting the key points. The reason for that is that although written communication is fine, verbal communication with emphasis, body language, pitch, tone and so on is more effective.

What should it say?

The structure is the same as I have set out, but the difference is first that the evidence has been heard, from both sides, and secondly more time has passed. It may be that you can focus on a particular part, or one claim and give up on another claim. I think that they key is to be clear on why you should win, and that was summed up, in a different context, in this:

'Three chords and the truth' – Harlan Howard

This phrase was coined by a songwriter called Harlan Howard in the 1950s which he used to describe Country music. He was a good songwriter. He wrote for example 'I fall to pieces' which was sung by Patsy Cline among others, and 'Busted' recorded by Johnny Cash. He was not being derogatory about country music, but describing it and endorsing it. The phrase essentially means that there can be great power in simplicity.

There are a very large number of examples of famous songs with three chords, but they include 'I walk the line' by Johnny Cash, songs built around the 12 blues like 'Crossroads' covered by Cream, and more recently 'Crazy in Love' by Beyonce. There are countless others. Songs with three chords can be very powerful and effective.

If I can extend the musical analogy, there are three chords normally found in the chord structure of tunes like these which are called a tonic, a dominant and a sub-dominant. The tonic is where it starts and ends, and is the base or foundation for the song. The dominant is usually an interval of a fifth from the tonic, which sounds good to the ear. The sub-dominant is usually an interval of a fourth from the tonic. It sounds different, and can be in a form of conflict with both the tonic and dominant. The order in which the chords appear can vary, but the best known example is 'Happy Birthday to you'. If it starts in the key of A that is the first chord, the tonic, the first change is to the chord of E for the first 'you' which is the dominant. For the second 'you' the chord goes back to A. When it changes to the name of the person whose birthday it is, the chord is D, which is the sub-dominant. It then returns to A.

The reason I have set out that explanation is that this kind of very simple structure is a good start in finalising the submission. The tonic chord in a submission is the foundation. It is the theme of the case, the essentials of it, the elevator pitch explaining why you win. The dominant is then the detailed explanation for that – which can be about the evidence heard, or the law, or both. It should sound right. It should seem to be the natural outcome of the case having heard the evidence. It looks at the case from the perspective of your side. The sub-dominant however is the opposite – it is your explanation of why the other side's case is wrong. The other side's case should sound wrong, discordant, unpleasant. Your argument should explain why the other side's position is contrary to common sense, or the weight of all of the evidence, or why one particular witness or part of the evidence should not be accepted (for example because of a prior inconsistent statement).

You can then return to the foundation, the tonic, and conclude by setting out exactly what you ask the judge to give you (which may either be the remedy if you are the claimant, or the dismissal of the claim if you are the respondent, for example).

Three chords and the truth does not mean keeping it very short. It means being focused both on what is important and in explaining clearly: (i) why it is you should get what you want; (ii) what is right with your case and (iii) what is wrong with the other side's case. It means trying to be persuasive on the key points in the case, in a simple but effective structure. The truth is what you want the judge to decide, and that is almost always a combination of why one side is right, and the other side wrong.

This depends in turn on what the case is about, what is in dispute and why that is. Is it simply a case of who is lying? Is it which side is giving more reliable evidence, meaning more likely to be right? Is it, on the other hand, what is to be made of documents? Is it in essence a question of the relevant legal provisions? Is the answer found in the lack of any written record of something, or a good answer to one particular question?

There is another old adage that 'facts win cases'. That is true more often than not. The law tends to give the structure to the dispute, a bit like fixing in place the goalposts, but where the ball is depends on what the witnesses, as the players, do with it.

This is where having good notes of the evidence is vital. If someone on the other side did not answer a question, or did so by avoiding it, or you asked it three times and never got an answer, say so. The judge may have forgotten. Make it clear what happened. You might say something like:

> 'The tribunal will remember that I asked Mr Jones on three occasions why he had not investigated the suggestion that another employee, Miss Knowles, had seen what happened. He avoided answering it each time. His evasion I suggest speaks volumes.

> 'The tribunal will recall that when asked whether he thought that holding the hearing on the day after the letter with the evidence was received by the claimant was reasonable, Mr Jones said "No, I now see that that did not give him enough time to prepare for it properly. If I had the time again I would have given him longer".'

If on the other hand someone on your side gave a very good answer, which is often one that was against their own interests, highlight that. Someone who accepts that they were wrong at one point, or that they could have done things better, or that something happened which showed them not in a good light, is often both a credible and reliable witness. For example you might say:

'When asked if he could have handled the hearing more effectively he said "On reflection and with the benefit of hindsight, yes" I suggest that that is a very candid and obviously honest answer, which does him great credit. The test however is not whether matters were handled perfectly, but reasonably and having regard to all of the evidence I suggest that it is clear that this was handled reasonably.'

If you called as witnesses everyone you thought relevant, but the other side did not call someone who was present and did not explain why, again make reference to that:

'The tribunal will recall that Mrs Evans was not called to give evidence by the respondent, despite the fact that she was present during the meeting where much of the dispute over what happened has focused. No explanation for that has been given. That is a very surprising position for the respondent to have chosen to take. I would invite the tribunal to draw the inference that the failure to call her was because she would support the claimant. If there is any other explanation for it, it has not been provided by the respondent in their evidence.'

Some other techniques can help. They build on the issues set out above about what may be important in the evidence. None are rules, and all have exceptions. For example, one is about common sense, but there are some situations which appear very odd at first glance that are, after considering all the evidence, the most likely to have happened. They are:

1   A document of any kind created at the time may well have the best evidence about what happened. Even informal documents such as handwritten notes, emails and so on can do that. Most often, that evidence can be the most reliable guide as to what had happened. You can refer to that, read out what the document says, and suggest that that is the most reliable evidence of what happened.

2   If a witness has no particular axe to grind, and gives evidence well, his or her evidence is not likely to be affected by partiality, and likely to be better than those who are more partial.

3   On the other hand, someone with a stake in the issue, either financial or personal (such as a family member, friend, work colleague etc) may give evidence that is affected by that relationship.

4   Consistency is a good indicator of a witness being credible and reliable, someone telling the same story right the way through a process and up

to the giving of evidence. You can point out where that happened, for example in an initial email, in an investigation meeting, a disciplinary meeting, an appeal hearing and then in the hearing before the judge.

5   Telling a different story at different times however is troubling, and someone whose story has changed may not be credible and reliable. The greater the extent of the inconsistency, and the less good any explanation for that, the more unreliable at least the evidence tends to be. You can emphasise what was said, at what point, and where the differences are.

6   The lack of a challenge to something at the time can also be telling. If that is documented, in particular, then the absence of any documented response, dispute, counter-allegation or the like can infer acceptance at least at that stage. If there is then a claim that what was alleged was untrue that becomes a form of inconsistency.

7   Someone saying on occasion 'I don't remember' can be entirely honest, but if it happens too often, particularly if on important points that you would expect to be remembered, that can raise doubts. Similarly, if the memory is selective, being very good on issues which help, but very poor or missing on challenging issues, that affects both if it is reliable, and if it is credible. Sometimes it is worth just counting up the number of times it was said, and saying something about that.

8   Common sense is still a guide. The more unusual, unexpected or contrary to normal something is said to be, the less likely it occurred.

9   If there are several witnesses saying one thing, and one person saying something entirely different, the chances are that the former group is accurate.

10   A Latin maxim I have found useful is this "Post hoc non ergo propter hoc" which roughly translates as 'Just because something happens after an event, does not mean that it happened because of it.' This can also be where the chronology comes in very useful. Was there any connection between the different events? Why was that? What is the evidence to establish it? What did the person who said something either helpful or damaging know when he or she did so?

11   Related to that is the importance of context. What was said can be explained away if the person did not know at that time what he or she later found out. The underlying meaning of words can change entirely given a different context. If the person said 'I was afraid' the context could be a fear of physical violence, or of losing a job which was such a perfect fit for them. If the person said 'I didn't trust her' that could either be because of what she had been told by another which is later shown to be wrong, or because of what she herself had seen that person do.

12   Burden (or onus) of proof is not used particularly often, but does sometimes help. Who has the burden of proof is generally the party that goes first, as discussed before in Chapter 6. If there is a claim of breach of contract, it is generally the claimant who requires to prove that, and thus has the burden of proof. But if the employer has terminated the employment summarily, without giving notice, the burden falls on the employer to prove that the employee had been guilty of repudiatory conduct that entitled them to terminate without notice. In employment cases, the employer has the burden of proving the reason for the dismissal, but not that it was fair, as there is no burden on the question of fairness. In discrimination cases on the other hand, the burden is initially on the claimant, but if a prima facie case is established, which means that there are facts from which discrimination could be inferred, or putting it simply it looks like there could well have been discrimination, the burden can shift to the employer to prove that there was no discrimination. The burden may be important in very tight cases, where the evidence is not clear and where the judge is having a difficulty in deciding which party has been successful. So if you do not have the burden, remind the judge of that.

13   Another adage, not always right, is that each case can be summarised in the answer to only one question. What is difficult is identifying that question. But it is a lot easier doing so after all the evidence has been heard, than at the start. So think about that – if you can only say one sentence to try and persuade the judge to find for you, what do you say?

14   Being clear and succinct in submissions is very helpful to the judge. The best arguments tend to be those that distil all the detail into short simple sentences, which persuasively explain why your side wins. The best advocates can spend hours, if not a day or more, in working out the language to use in one sentence that sums up the entire case, which they then use at either the start, or end, or both, of the submission. It can be very powerful when done well.

15   Particularly if you are representing someone else, avoid using the term 'I think', or 'I believe' or 'In my opinion'. What you think is frankly irrelevant. What matters is the evidence, and how that should be assessed by the judge. It is far more effective therefore to use standard terms such as 'I submit' or 'My argument is' or if you wish to distance yourself further saying 'The claimant's argument is'. It is also permissible, and sometimes highly effective to ask rhetorical questions, such as: 'You might like to consider what was in her mind when she [said or did something]', or: 'One can ask the question why the decision was taken so quickly if not affected by gender bias'.

Dealing with the law

The law can be found in a variety of places. It can be very difficult to know what to say about it for those not legally qualified, or experienced.

The most usual place to start is a statute – an Act of Parliament or Statutory Instrument. That can then be explained in case law, usually from an appeal court or tribunal. Case law is also referred to as 'authority'. It is a decision from a court of some kind. They are often published in case reports. There are many of these, and they are described by the name of the case, the year, the place where the case is reported, and the page the reports starts. The case referred to in the Appendix of *Burchell* follows that format, and the IRLR is a reference to Industrial Relations Law Reports. Not all cases are reported in this way, and other reports can be found online. That can be from the court itself, or from a service such as BAILII which covers a large number of cases in England and Wales. If a case has not been reported in a formal set of reports it can be referred to by the name, the year of the decision, the court, and the reference at that court which will usually include the year it was presented.

When referring to one of these authorities it is usually best to refer briefly to the facts involved, some of which can be summarised at the start of the report or case itself, and then highlight particular parts of the decision. Working out which ones to refer to is not easy but generally what you are looking for is an expression of the general principle that the case illustrates. An example of that is in the Appendix.

Other sources include, at least for the present at the stage this book was prepared, European instruments such as Directives, Treaties and others, together with case law from the Court of Justice of the European Union which explains them. In addition, there are common law principles, such as those relating to breach of contract. They come from the foundations of the law, and are also explained in case law.

Other sources still depend on the context. They can include guidance, from statutory bodies such as ACAS, the Equality and Human Rights Commission, or from statutory organisations such as the Health and Safety Executive, the Civil Aviation Authority, the Maritime and Coastguard Agency, and many others. There are publications from various government departments, many of which are found online. Some are set out in the source materials section at p xi.

There are also textbooks, some considered to be very authoritative, others more useful primarily as a source for obtaining the statutory provisions and case law that applies. Some can be found online, others are either in hardback format, or require to be paid for. Libraries may have some of them. Google and other search engines can also provide help.

Many decisions by tribunals and courts of all kinds are now online, and can be searched. That can be a useful place for guidance, as although the facts of the case may be different, the basic structure of the legal provisions and case law will usually be set out. It can also give an indication of the kind of issues that are important when a decision is taken. There is for example an online register of Employment Tribunal judgments.

As a very basic guide, the best structure for commenting on the law is to start at the highest level, and work down from there. That means for example considering the following order (at least for the standard case in the UK. For cases where there is a European element still relevant after the end of the transition period for Brexit it can be important to refer to the EU Directive or other instrument, and any case law of the Court of Justice of the European Union as well):

1   Acts of Parliament in the UK.

2   Statutory Instruments (rules, regulations or orders).

3   Case law related to those Acts and statutory instruments in the following order:

   (a)   Supreme Court (or House of Lords as it was formerly called).

   (b)   Court of Appeal or Inner House of the Court of Session in Scotland.

   (c)   Employment Appeal Tribunal/ High Court/Outer House of the Court of Session.

   (d)   District Court/ Sheriff Court/Employment Tribunal if relevant (though decisions at this level are less helpful as they are persuasive only).

   (e)   Any others (such as decisions from courts in other jurisdictions, and comments in textbooks).

4   For issues of contract there are both standard books which are regarded as authoritative, such as *Chitty on Contracts* in England and Wales or *Gloag: The Law of Contract* in Scotland, more recent books by academic writers mainly and case law that is referred to in those books.

The legal test that is to be applied to the facts tends to be what some submissions focus on, then an argument that the evidence does not meet that test. For some issues, the law is clear and settled. But for others, it may be controversial, with competing decisions saying either different things, or entirely opposite things. The test may be in some statute but not always so (for example breach of contract is not, but unfair dismissal is).

It can be important to identify which cases are helpful, and be clear why that is. The next stage is to identify the cases which are not helpful, and why, then to work out how you can argue around them, if you can. Do they cover different factual issues? Have they been commented on in other cases in a way that indicates that they might not be right? Are they now older ones, and from a time when context was very different? Are they binding or merely persuasive?

What is and is not binding is complex, but essentially a case is binding when it covers the same point as the one in your own case, and is from a higher court or tribunal. The employment tribunal is bound by the Employment Appeal Tribunal for example.

There are also times where there is no real guidance from case law, and the point is a novel one. Or it may be that it is difficult legally for some other reason, such as if an appeal court has issued two decisions that say more or less the opposite, as does happen. These can be the most difficult cases to make submissions about. The legal principles to apply may not be clear, or may not be easy to identify, or may not be easy to apply to the facts. In those cases, it can be helpful to go back to very basic principles of the law, such as that parties are in general bound by the contracts they freely enter into; that a party is liable if it is in breach of contract, and that damages should naturally and directly flow from the breach, and not be too remote from it.

Sometimes it is just a case of arguing for what is fair, but the absence of a particular legal provision of some kind to help you is most likely a red flag warning you that there is a lack of support for what you are saying. Unless the facts and circumstances are unique therefore it should normally give you cause to stop and consider.

At other times it can be sufficient to be very basic indeed. In an unfair dismissal claim, although it can be more effective to set out in detail what the legal tests are, and demonstrate how they have been applied in other cases, it can be enough just to say: 'That wasn't fair'. For the employer it may be enough to say: 'We did not deal with it perfectly but perfection is not required. We acted reasonably, and that is what the law requires'.

Indeed, when concluding a submission, it can help to be just that simple and straightforward. It can distil all of the law, consideration to all of the facts, into one single and straightforward proposition. Being clear, straightforward, and succinct can be powerful advocacy. It is easier said than done.

If you are to refer to legal authorities, have copies prepared for the judge, and if it is a panel of more than one, one for each member. Have those copies in the same order as you are going to refer to them in the submission so that it is easy to follow, and check whether the practice in that court or tribunal is to highlight in advance the section that you are to refer to, or not. If you are referring to a particular section that is not highlighted, be as clear as you can be: page 12, paragraph three, line six; or page 12 just above the upper hole punch; or page 12 just below letter C.

Listening to the other side

You may or may not go first when making the submission. It tends to depend on what the case is about, and the practice of where you are. Whether you go first or second, when the other side is making their submission stay absolutely silent.

Do not tut, huff, roll your eyes or display any other emotion, even if you are boiling with rage inside. If you go second, you can respond when you have that opportunity. If you go first, you may or may not be able to add to what you say.

If you do give your submission second, there is the option of changing to some extent what you have prepared. That may be important if the other side say something that you fundamentally disagree with, or if what they refer to is a part of the evidence and you wish to refer to another part that either contradicts, qualifies or explains what they have referred to. If you wish to have time to think about it, or to check notes of evidence, then it is possible to ask for that. You may or may not get it, but there is little if anything lost in the attempt. If you really want to and feel that that is important, ask the judge after the other side have finished if you can respond briefly to what has been said. You may or may not be permitted to do so, but again there is rarely anything lost by asking that. Then, be very brief.

There may then be a discussion about what happens next, such as whether to wait for a decision that day, or that it will be sent out later on. This is covered later.

Delivery

Do not just read the submission without looking up. Just as with the earlier stages, eye contact is important. You wish to engage with the judge. Be clear about what you are saying, and give the impression that you are entirely behind the argument you are making. Remember that at this stage too the judge will be writing the submission down, so unless you hand over a written submission, go slowly. As with asking questions of witnesses, watch the pen, and make sure that the points you make are being listened to, and understood.

Try not to speak in a monotone, but use modulation, just as in questioning witnesses.

Emphasise the important aspects, and stress what you consider to be the strongest aspects of the arguments you are making. You can use phrases such as: 'There is really no evidence to contradict that point' or: 'The evidence was contradicted by all the relevant written documentation. The witness was wrong on that point, and is not reliable because of that.'

Remember that the convention is not to refer to the judge as 'You', unless using it followed by 'Sir' or 'Madam'. Speak in the third person. If there is a panel of three, remember to maintain eye contact with all of them from time to time. Each has an influence on the decision, and each has the same vote. It may sound rather odd, but it can be better to say: 'The Tribunal may think ....' or 'The Panel will recall the evidence of Ms Smith on this point, when she said ...'.

My advice had been not to ask non-leading questions in cross-examination, because the witness may give an unhelpful answer, but doing so at the stage of submission is rather different. It may have been dangerous to ask the main witness for the other side: 'Why did you do that?' but it may be powerful advocacy to re-phrase it as a rhetorical question such as: 'Why would someone in his position have done that, if unaware of what had happened earlier?' If that is how it is to be handled, raise that issue looking directly at the judge. It may be a rhetorical question but you are asking it. It does not expect an answer, nor should you, but watch for any reaction. If you are lucky, there might be some form of nod of the head or other indicator of agreement. That is not however always what happens. The reaction can sometimes be the opposite.

Responding to questions from the judge

I have seen experienced lawyers put entirely off their stride by a single question from the judge. All the confidence from reading out their prepared submission seems to vanish. It was put this way by a boxer:

'Everyone has a plan until they get punched in the mouth' – Mike Tyson

There are times when the judge may interrupt you, indicating disapproval of what you have said on a particular point, or wait until you have finished, and then ask you one or more questions. Sometimes they are asked in a way that seems far from supportive, even directly challenging. That can be difficult to handle.

Litigation can be rather like that. In the heat of the moment, when a question is asked of you out of the blue, your brain can go absent without leave. That is no reason however not to have a plan. Quite the contrary, if you have a plan you are more likely to be able to handle the punches. Your plan might also enable you to second guess some of the questions you may be asked. There are always times however where the question is one to which you do not have an immediate and handy answer.

There are some suggestions on how to handle that. First, keep a cool head. Do not panic. Secondly, never assume that this means that you have lost. Quite often it is just the judge checking some details to ensure that you deserve to win. Thirdly, listen very carefully to the question. If you do not understand it, say so. The fault could be yours, but not necessarily so. It may just not have been very well formulated, or could be phrased more clearly. Fourthly, try your best to answer it then and there if you can, but if you have a real problem with it, ask for more time, even if only a minute or so to review your notes of evidence. You may wish to check other documents or just search your memory. You may or may not get what you ask for, but there is very rarely any down side in asking for that time. Finally, trust your judgement. Do the best that you can from the information you have.

Once you have finished covering the main arguments, it is generally best to finish by reminding the judge what it is you are asking for. Then, either simply stop or say what is often said by lawyers which is: 'Unless there is anything further I can assist with, that concludes my submission'.

Sometimes those who are not lawyers say something like thank you for listening or words to that effect, but I do not think that that is necessary. It is the judge's role to listen to and decide cases. No thanks are really due. And the result may or may not be what you seek.

Finishing up

The judge usually leaves first, which means that you are left with the other side in the room. That may include lawyers, witnesses, and others. How to handle matters with them depends on you, and the circumstances. There is an etiquette between lawyers, which I think is worth preserving. That involves shaking the hand of the other side, and either complimenting them on the job they did, or saying something more anodyne such as: 'I am glad that is over'.

There is however no necessity to do so, particularly for those who are not lawyers, and particularly if you have heard over several days that you are a liar, cheat, fantasist or similar. You can say nothing and leave very quickly, or say nothing, and slowly gather up your papers in the hope that the other side leaves first, if you wish.

What is a good idea however is to thank any witnesses you called to give evidence who are still there, and if they are not there to phone or email them to say thank you. It can also be helpful to speak to the administration where you are, usually a clerk, to ask how the decision is to be issued, how long that might take or similar.

Chapter 9

Outcome

Oral decisions

The outcome is usually called a judgment, or a decision. A written judgment or decision tends to be issued in writing later on, but not always so. Judges can issue decisions orally either immediately or after a delay that same day while they think about it. Judgments given at the time are called 'ex tempore' judgments. The judge will normally say after submissions whether or not that is to happen, and if it is you may be asked to wait, although sometimes you will be asked to come back later, at a set time, to hear it.

If you are hearing an ex tempore decision, then, as with submissions, do not react in any way. Keep silent, and write down what you hear. Wait to the very end, because what is said at the start may or may not indicate what the outcome is. Sometimes you hear words that either seem to say you have won, or lost, and there is then a 'But', and it all changes, right at the end.

If you have succeeded, sometimes the advocate says words of thanks, but that is not necessary for the same reasons as set out before and it tends to be best just to say nothing. There may be issues to follow up with, such as costs or expenses, which are covered later. Otherwise, just say nothing, but inwardly do a jig of delight. If you have lost, say nothing, and start thinking about what to do about it.

Written judgments and decisions

You will one day receive a letter, with the written decision inside. The wait may be long or short, it depends on factors such as the workload of the judge, the complexity of the case, and whether there needed to be meetings of the tribunal members to discuss the outcome. You should read it through very carefully, twice. Quite often in the excitement and stress of learning the outcome, points of detail are missed. So take care, and take time.

If you have won, check what the outcome is. If it includes payment of money, check that it is right, and that the calculations are correct. Make sure that it covers what you expected. There are times when you can raise any issue that may have been missed, or incorrectly calculated, by either an informal process or a formal one. It is rare, but not unknown.

Remember too that although you have won, the other side may be thinking of an appeal. So be a little cautious. Don't spend money not yet received.

Appeals

In litigation at least one side loses. It is a competition. Sometimes neither side wins, as there is an award, but far less than had been hoped for, and no one is particularly pleased. But I cannot think of a case where both sides win (although sometimes the loser claims that it was a success of some kind).

If you have lost, think about whether there is anything else you can do about it, and that generally means considering an appeal. Appeals are not easy. Most often they are taken on legal points alone, not on the facts. That is not always so, as sometimes an appeal on the facts is possible. It is something to check.

Appeals are an entirely different process and I shall only say a little about them. They are very difficult for a non-lawyer to conduct successfully, although some have done so. The reason for that is that the argument is about how the law is to be applied, or what the law is. It is rather like a more concentrated form of submission. What you need to do is show where the judge has got the law wrong.

If you are to appeal, check both when that is required by, and how it is done. There are again time limits that tend to apply and they can be applied brutally. Check also whether any step is needed before the appeal, such as asking the judge for permission (or leave) to do that. Again, that may be required within a time limit.

Appeals generally need an appeal document that sets out why the appeal is taken. If the judge got the law wrong that should be specified. If the law was wrongly applied, how that took place should be set out. If the assessment of the evidence was wrong, that generally needs to be on the basis that there was 'perversity', which means that no judge acting reasonably could have reached that conclusion. It is a very stringent test, difficult to achieve in practice, but possible to argue for and you should set out why the test is met in your case.

There can be documents required with the appeal, such as the decision itself, and other documents depending on what is involved. Check what is needed, and ensure that all that is required to be done is done.

Increasingly there is a process for appeals, where they are looked at initially to see if they have a reasonable argument within then. It is usually called a 'sift'. If you are told that the appeal does not survive that, there can be a process for challenging that, often at a further hearing before the appeal judge. Before you make that challenge, think what you will say, and how you are to persuade the judge that the initial view was wrong, Just repeating the same arguments as in the appeal itself will very likely not succeed, because the sift indicates that the appeal does not get off the ground. You need more. Think what you can give. If there is nothing, it may just be time to give up.

If you have won and the other side appeals, you generally need to send a document to the appeal tribunal or court to confirm that the appeal is opposed, or disputed. There are time limits to do that, and they must be adhered to. You can simply state that you rely on the decision in your favour, and that is the simplest response. There can be times however when you have lost one or more points in the case, and can take the opportunity to pursue an appeal of your own, usually called a cross-appeal. That means that although you argue that the decision was essentially right, you wish to challenge one or more parts of it, For example the judge may have found in your favour about the main issue, but held that you were partly responsible for what happened, and reduced the level of compensation because of that. If the respondent appeals the main issue, you may be able to appeal the point on compensation. But think about that carefully. There is a fine line to tread between arguing that the judge was right on one point and wrong on the other. Think carefully about whether the risk of a confused message is worth taking a chance on or whether it is better just to argue that the judge was right.

The appeal process is difficult, and asking for legal advice is worth considering. Sometimes there can be assistance at that level that is not available lower down, including by legal aid. At other times a lawyer may be prepared to act for you on either a speculative basis, or 'pro bono' meaning essentially for the good of the public at large.

Follow up issues

There may be matters that require further action on your part, or a reaction to what the other side are doing. That can include issues of costs. In some situations the party losing pays the costs incurred by the party winning, but that is not always the case, and sometimes they are not part of the system at all.

If you wish to seek expenses or costs, find out how to do that, and by when. Again time limits may apply. If you are facing a claim for expenses, check what is sought is correct, and see if you can challenge it either overall, or in part, or for some details. Even if you lost, not all of the other side's arguments or evidence may have been accepted. Do not just take the claim at face value, there can be a whole new dispute over what is sought, and why, and whether it is either correct or reasonable.

If the sums sought are large, it can be helpful to take advice, either from a lawyer or someone specialising in that, called a Law Accountant, Costs Draftsman or similar.

Administration

There may be steps to take to deal with, for example, papers that have been produced to the judge as part of evidence, which you need to collect and deal with once the time for appeal is passed. Things like medical records need to be treated with particular care. You may need to get them back from the court or tribunal, and return them to the hospital or doctor you got them from.

If you have an award, you may need to take steps to recover it. The other side may be ordered to pay, but fail to. How that is done depends on the detail, but it can involve first checking that the party, if a company, has not gone into administration or liquidation, and secondly asking for some form of formal document to enforce, then thirdly instructing an officer of some kind, such as a sheriff officer in Scotland or a bailiff in England, to take action to recover the sum due. If the other party is an individual that may involve applying for his or her bankruptcy. These steps can all involve expense, and some require action in court. You do need to check that the cost of that is worth spending, and that there is a reasonable chance of getting the money.

There are other times when you can apply for payment to another party. In employment cases, there is a body called the Insolvency Service which deals with some claims against insolvent employers. There may also be a liquidator you can make a claim to, for example.

What you are awarded may also be something that is taxable. It is worth checking that, and if unsure either taking advice from an accountant or similar expert, or disclosing it to the Revenue.

Media interest

Most decisions are public, and either available to the press or published on the internet. Media organisations, or social media generally, can be involved. You may even be asked for comment.

There are times when it is fine to do so, and times when that can be dangerous and come back to haunt you later. If you have won, saying that you are pleased normally has low, if any, risk, but remember that there can always be an appeal by the other side. As a basic rule of thumb, it tends to be best to say nothing. If you do say something, be temperate. Do not lambast the judge for incompetence, or worse, and do not say that the liars have won or words to that effect. There can be consequences for improper comments, with very little if any upside, and very serious potential downsides. Keep your own counsel, and if you must speak about the result do so to family and friends who you trust to keep your comments private.

Reflection

If you are a lawyer or other representative this may be the first of very many cases. Whether you have won or lost, it is great experience in your career. It is entirely different from what may have been learned in university, or in training sessions. Having now seen what the judge thought, consider what lessons you can learn. That applies whether the result is success or failure.

If you have failed, don't panic. That does not mean that this is the wrong job for you. It does not mean that the next case will go the same way. All representatives involved in litigation to any real extent lose cases. The very best, whoever they are, lose cases. The representative who never loses a case probably doesn't take on cases unless they are certain winners, and that is not being good at the job.

Learning from mistakes

One of the most famous quotations ever is this:

'That's one small step for man, one giant leap for mankind' – Neil Armstrong

Neil Armstrong was an outstanding astronaut and pilot. He had shown in many previous instances a very cool head under immense pressure. He was chosen to be the first man on the moon because of the incredible depth of his competence at his job. He underwent long and detailed training for each element of what was to come. When he made his remarks on his first step onto the surface of the moon he made a mistake. The line should have included the word 'a' before the word 'man'. Missing it out technically changed the meaning, but everyone knew what he meant, and given the circumstances the slip was entirely understandable and forgivable. The point is however that even the most trained, experienced and brilliant person got something wrong at a crucial point. All of us make mistakes, and that often happens when we are under pressure. Conducting litigation is an environment where there is a lot of pressure.

Losing, however painful the experience, has the seeds of a great lesson. You tend to forget wins more quickly than you do losses. With a loss you can think about it for years after, with the question you didn't ask, or asked in the wrong way, the piece of evidence that tripped you up, the clever argument the other side put forward that you hadn't thought of, and had no answer to. Learn from it, and use those lessons in future. Next time you can be the one who came up with the argument that wins the case.

All representatives make mistakes, or do not do things as well as they could. Learn from that. It is why the more effective lawyers tend, as a rule of thumb, to be the more experienced ones. The experience they have is often bitter, but makes them better next time.

If you win, do not be complacent. It may well have been helped by your advocacy, but not necessarily so. It may have been success despite you, not because of you. Think, exactly in the same way as if you had lost what you could have done better.

Where you are acting for yourself, learning lessons is more difficult. This may well be your only experience of litigation. You do not have a chance to put into effect the lessons learned. You may feel a great sense of injustice, or that it was all your own fault, or otherwise. It is however a life experience. You will have learned valuable lessons. You will have gained experience and techniques, an understanding of how human beings behave, and things like that, which will stand you in good stead either in work, or just in life.

It may seem odd to say this after a lengthy series of tips about the best way to conduct a case, but many cases are won and lost simply by what happened. That is water under the bridge. You can try and heat that water up a little, or cool it down, or channel it, or colour it, but some things are beyond change.

Don't therefore beat yourself up if you lose. These things happen. Both sides go into a case expecting to win, and one doesn't. The reasons for that can be many and varied. They can include luck. They can include what a witness said when asked a particular question by the other side which you could do nothing about. They can include what a judge thought of a person when giving evidence, forming an impression that was not the same as yours. It is not a perfect system, and applying the law can lead to some harsh outcomes.

Advocacy does not itself win cases; it helps. But sometimes you just have to take the loss on the chin, and move on. Rarely is it the end of the world, even though it feels like that in the rawness of the moment.

Chapter 10

Conclusion

The conduct of litigation is highly complicated, and requires the simultaneous exercise of a number of difficult skills. It is rather like giving a performance of a play as the lead actor, writing new lines of script, dealing with hecklers from the audience, whilst at the same time flying a plane.

The system used in the UK, and many other jurisdictions, is adversarial. It is a fight between the parties, who look after themselves subject to the rules. The thinking behind that is that by having that competition between the parties it is likely that the most just outcome can be achieved. That is distinct from the inquisitorial systems, where it is the role of the judge to find out what happened, and decide the result from that, and where parties may play a lesser role. The adversarial system does mean that those who can afford legal representation might be able to gain an advantage, but there are an almost innumerable number of examples where that advantage did not translate into success. Cases can be, and are, won by litigants in person and representatives with no legal experience against a legal team led by a QC.

As I have said before there is risk in all litigation. That is why seeing if there might be some form of negotiated settlement is worth exploring at all phases of the case. Sometimes it is the pressure of the morning of the hearing that is the key to unlocking the positions each side had taken.

If the case does proceed, you do the very best that you can after preparing for it as well as you can, and that is all that you can ask of yourself.

I wish you luck.

Appendix

To try and give a practical illustration of the conduct of a case, I have built on some of the basic facts of what is probably the most frequently cited employment law case, called *British Home Stores Limited v Burchell* [1978] IRLR 379. The case was one of unfair dismissal only, but for illustrative purposes in this exercise the employee Miss Beechcroft will claim breach of contract as well as unfair dismissal, and the employer will counterclaim for breach of contract for what it claimed as losses incurred by her dishonesty. The case is fictitious.

The case will start with a statement from Miss Beechcroft, and separately a statement from the investigator for the store. Obviously in a real case one side would not see the statement for the other at the early stage, and in many cases would never do so, but they may do so later if witness statements are exchanged as part of the preparations for the hearing.

There are then documents obtained in the investigation, notes of the investigation interview with her, the disciplinary hearing, the letter of dismissal, her appeal, and the decision on the appeal. The documents would then be in a Bundle, which start with her Claim, the employers' Response Form, which includes the counterclaim and her response to that, and end with documents as to remedy, and a Statement of Agreed Facts. It does not include all that might have been produced, such as a plan to show where the various departments were within the store, photographs of some of them, photographs of the two kinds of sunglasses which are referred to so on. It has been assumed that the person who conducted the investigation has left the company to go travelling abroad and is not available to give evidence.

What is then produced are the draft notes for questioning in the Tribunal by each side, and the two draft submissions prepared for the end of the hearing. They have been kept fairly short. In a real case they may be much longer.

Finally, there is an indication of the decision that might have been made, rather more for illustration of what can happen than an attempt at giving a real result.

This is all an exercise which is trying to demonstrate some of the issues and techniques commented upon in the book. The hope is that it may put a little flesh on the bones of that, and make putting it into practice easier.

1 Statement of Linda Beechcroft

I, Miss Linda Beechcroft write this statement on 1 August 2019.

I worked at the VHS department store in High Street, Lontown, for over five years. I started on 2 February 2014. I was a shop assistant. I worked 37 hours per week. I am 25 years of age my date of birth being 25 January 1994.

The shop had a form of staff discount scheme, with rules around how that worked. I was shown the rules when I started, but now cannot remember them in detail. I was also given a contract of employment which I signed, and some disciplinary rules which I did not.

I was summarily dismissed on 24 June 2019 and the allegation was of dishonesty. There were three facts that were used against me and said to have led to the belief that I had been dishonest. Originally there were four but one was discounted. The three matters were:

1. A claim that there was a departure from the standard method of signing for internal purchases, in that the sales assistant who signed a docket for the purchase by the employee should work in or near to the department for the goods purchased so as to be familiar with the goods and with the prices payable for them. An investigation was said to have disclosed a pattern of signing for staff purchases involving a group of four members of staff who did not work in the departments for the purchases very often. I was said to be one of them.

    This is not however the case. I worked in the Lighting Department. I was not part of any group of four people. I just carried out my work. There were a few times when I signed for goods purchased by other staff members, who came to me from time to time to ask me to do that, and I just did. I did not see anything wrong with that. I was trusting them as colleagues.

2. One of the four, who has only been referred to as Mrs L, was spoken to and accused of being a part of the group which had been using the departure from the procedure as a cover for purchasing goods at less than the appropriate cost even with staff discount. She admitted that something like this had taken place, and she said that I was one of the others involved in the group.

    I think that this is probably Lorraine Lamont. She and I never got on. She worked in the cosmetics department. She and I fell out about six months ago really badly. I thought that she was disrespectful towards my mother when she came into the store. She called her something like 'dowdy', and swore when she did so. Later on that day, she posted something on Facebook, which I saw as at that stage I was a friend. It said 'You won't believe the person who came in today, asking for lipstick and hair dye like she was 18. She must be 60!' I was sure that she was referring to my mother, who is 51. I think that she was lying about me being involved to try and get back at me by getting me into trouble. I challenged her about it, and we have hardly spoken since then.

3.	There was a record of a purchase of sunglasses by Mrs L. There was a more expensive type costing £220 and a cheaper type costing £35. It seems that Mrs L had bought the more expensive pair on the basis of the price for the cheaper pair and had done so a docket which had been signed by me. I was shown this docket, and it did look very much like my signature. I don't remember doing that, and frankly am surprised I did given the background of our disagreement but I probably just signed it without looking to get rid of her. I was asked about this in the meetings, and agreed that I knew of the prices of the two types of sunglasses was very different, with an expansive brand called Mior and a cheap one called Chippy, and accepted that I signed the docket.

This all came up when I was called into a meeting on 1 June 2019, without warning. I was seen by Angela Adams, who told me at the end of it that I was being suspended on allegations of dishonesty to do with staff discounts. I was sent home.

Angela told me at the meeting that she was investigating allegations of dishonesty, and showed me the dockets I had signed, ones others had signed, prices, and a spreadsheet, and asked for explanations. I gave them as best I could. I didn't think much would come of it really.

I was then written to with an invitation to the disciplinary hearing. That was a letter dated 3 June, and had Angela's report with it. It also confirmed my suspension. The meeting took place on 8 June. It was held by Francis Faulds, who is the deputy store manager. Someone from HR was there taking minutes. He told me after it that I had been dismissed with immediate effect. On 9 June 2019 he wrote to me saying that I was dismissed.

I obviously appealed that, which I set out in my letter of 14 June. An appeal hearing was arranged for 28 June 2019. It was held by Gillian Grant, who is the Store Manager. In the appeal I showed her a text from Lorraine, which I thought made it clear she was out to get me. I did not think at the time that she thought it important. On 3 July 2019 she wrote to me to reject the appeal.

I then started Early Conciliation but ACAS told me that the company would not make me any offer.

I have decided to claim unfair dismissal. I believe that I was unfairly dismissed. I do not wish to try and get my job back as I do not feel I can work there again. I wish to seek compensation.

My contract also entitled me to three months' notice after four years work, and so I claim for three months' pay.

I was paid £30,000 per year. My normal take home pay was about £1,800 per month. I had a pension, which had employer contributions of £200 per month. There were no other benefits. I was off work for six months, and then found a part time job earning £1,000 per month net working 22 hours per week. It is the best I could find. I applied for over 20 jobs, some by post and some online, and had 5 interviews. I think that the dismissal has stopped me getting them.

I am still trying to find full time work, but that is more and more difficult as the High Street is suffering with the growth in online sales, as has been widely documented. I think that it will take me at least another six months to find full time employment and be paid the same as I had got from VHS.

2 Report by Angela Adams

I, Angela Adams an HR assistant at the VHS store in High Street, Lontown, give this report into the investigation I carried out in relation to misuse of the staff discount scheme.

There is a policy for staff discount which everyone gets on induction. I attach a copy (item 1). Under the scheme, staff can buy the store's products at half price. The process requires sign off on a docket by someone in the department where the item is on display. There is then a receipt given as for any customer, but it has 'SD' on it to show the discount.

The Company had a tip off which came to a whistleblowing reporting line, from someone who remained anonymous, that was then passed on to the HR department, that a group of staff were misusing the scheme. There were four people involved, we were told. One of them was Linda Beechcroft (LB). The others were Lorraine Lamont (LL), Mary Travers (MT) and Neil Upminster (NU). It was said that they operated a scam by taking goods of a higher value, but pretending it was something similar, at a lower price, and getting the discount on that lower amount so that they paid less than they should.

I was asked to investigate the allegations. I obtained a copy of all staff discounts in the first quarter being the three month period which ended on 31 March 2019. I then prepared a spreadsheet with names of the employee who obtained the discount, the name of the approving manager, the amount of the item, and a description of it. From that I prepared an extract with the relevant items for the four in the group (which is item 2). I could see a pattern emerging. There were employees who had had approvals given by others in the group of four I mention, and in almost all cases the approval was not from someone working in the correct department.

LB had made two purchases herself. One was of a golf club, approved by NU. It was at the correct price. The other was perfume, which NU also approved but he does not work in the perfume department, he works in sports. The price LB paid was lower than it ought to have been. It should have been on a gross price of £100, and that was on the staff discount docket that was signed by NU giving his approval, but the price paid was £40. There was therefore an underpayment of one half of the difference, being £40.

For LL, she had made two purchases initially. One was a hairdryer. This was in electrical goods, and had been signed off by NU. The second was again for perfume, from the perfumes department, signed off on this occasion by MT. Neither NU nor MT work in those departments. NU works in the sports department as I have said, and MT in female fashion. This was therefore a breach of the policy on both occasions. The sum for the hairdryer was £45, which meant that it would normally cost £90, and for the perfume £24, so the normal cost was £48. I have not been able to verify whether on both occasions the right price was paid for the item. The docket and price ticket for the perfume purchase which LB approved is attached (items 3 and 4).

There was then a further purchase I found, which LB had approved for LL, for sunglasses. There were two types, one costing far more than the other. She purchased the higher cost ones, priced at £220 but the staff discount was given for the lower priced ones, priced at £35 which meant that she got them at far less than their proper price with the discount. The loss to the company on this one items was nearly £100.

The docket for that purchase and the price ticket for it are attached (items 5 and 6). The docket to approve the staff discount with the wrong price on it was signed by LB, and she did not work in the department selling them, which was female fashion. She worked in the lighting department. She should therefore not have approved that purchase at all, and of course should not have done so at the lower and wrong price.

There was a similar pattern for the other members of the group. I decided to challenge each of them about it. I did that at a series of meetings held with them on 1 June 2019. Given the allegations I did not consider it appropriate to give them advance notice of the meeting. They were not accompanied, but this was an investigation meeting and they did not have the right to be accompanied.

The first person I spoke to was LL. She worked in the cosmetics department. I showed her the spreadsheet. She immediately went very red, and started to get upset. She kept saying sorry. I asked her to explain. She said that there had been discussions over coffee, and that it would give them a bit of extra money to be able to buy goods cheaply. So that was done a few times, without any check that the right department employee approved it. She said that after a month or so, as it was clear that the checks were so limited, she decided to try and get expensive sunglasses for the price of a cheaper make. She got a pair valued at £220. She then got the price ticket for a cheaper brand, which was £35. She took the higher value sunglasses with the lower price ticket to LB, who signed the docket. She had therefore got a pair of sunglasses that with discount should have been £110 but she paid £17.50. The loss was £92.50 on that one item, as I explained to her.

She said that it had happened only once, and she had worked two hours extra one day to make up for it, and had not claimed for those hours. She did not mention buying the hairdryer or perfume.

I said that that appeared to me to be theft. She asked me not to call the police, said that she would co-operate. I asked her who the other members of this group were. She said LB, MT and NU. She then told me that she resigned. She put it in writing in front of me and left within about ten minutes. Later on, more recently, I tried to contact her and ask for a fuller statement, but she did not reply to my messages, and I have not been able to have her do so.

I then immediately, that same day, went to NU, whose department which was sports was nearby. I asked to speak to him. He at that very moment got a text as I heard his phone ring. He looked at it and went white. I will never forget how suddenly he did. I showed him the spreadsheet. He said nothing. I asked him for an explanation and he said 'No comment'. He then got up, said 'I resign' and walked out quickly. I also tried later to get a fuller statement from him, but he has not replied to my messages either.

I then went over to MT, who worked in female fashion. She had also I think got a text as she was watching for me when I came over to her department. She said 'I know what this is about'. We went into a room near her workplace, and she said 'Look, I know I have been stupid, but will you accept my resignation.' I asked her to explain first what had happened, but she said 'I really can't discuss things, I have two children to look after, I am sorry for what's happened, and will leave now'. She then got up and left. She hand delivered a resignation letter that evening. It was accepted. She too has not replied to my messages and I have not been able to take a fuller statement from her.

I then went to speak to LB. Her department was the furthest away. It was obvious that she knew what was coming, but she was more combative. I showed her the spreadsheet, and she said 'I don't understand this.' I tried to explain, but all she said was 'I have done nothing wrong'. I showed her the docket and ticket for the sunglasses that LL had bought (items 3 and 4). She confirmed that it looked like her signature on it. I asked her if she knew the policy for that, and that approvals had to come from the same department as the item. She said she did, but that no one applies that, and that staff are trusted. I thought at the time that that was a very strange reply. I believed that she was not being honest with me.

I asked her about the purchase of perfume she had made, and showed her the docket and ticket for them. She said that she could not remember purchasing that, and could not see that there had been anything wrong. I refer to the docket and price ticket below.

I then said that she was to be suspended on full pay pending an investigation further. She said 'I am innocent'. I told her that she had to leave the store, and hand in her keys, and she did. I wrote to her that evening to confirm the suspension, that it was not a disciplinary sanction and did not involve any prejudgment, and that she would remain on full pay.

I have appended to this statement the dockets that LB signed for the hairdryer and the sunglasses, and the two prices for the sunglasses LL purchased. I have attached the extract spreadsheet I refer to, showing purchases LB made, or where she was the approver. It shows the cost to the company by this groups of staff improperly signing dockets for others within the group, or gaining improper access to items herself not following the policy, totalling over £1,000.

I have not been able to find the dockets and receipts for the perfume LB purchased, which were on my desk after I met her being the ones I had shown her at our meeting. They have vanished from there. I do not know why that is. They probably were removed by someone. I do not know who. It is entirely possible that that was done deliberately. I can however confirm that I saw them and that the information on the spreadsheet is all correct. I also confirm that I showed them to Linda at our meeting, and she did not deny that that was her purchase or that the correct price was higher than the one she did pay, even allowing for the staff discount. I attach the price tag for the perfume that LB bought (item 7).

I concluded that there had been evidence of dishonesty, and in light of the fact that Linda has not resigned that a disciplinary hearing should be held to address the allegations.

Angela Adams
2 June 2019

3 Staff Discount Policy

This policy sets out a non-contractual benefit that the company provides to its staff.

1.   Staff may purchase goods from the store in which they work at 50% of the marked price at which they are sold to customers.

2.   In order to apply for the discount, the staff member should fill out a docket as set out below.

3.   The docket should be approved by a member of staff working at the department where the goods being purchased under this policy are offered for sale.

4.   When the purchase is being made, the person on the till should be told that it is a staff discount purchase, be shown the docket, and then that person will use the SD button on the till so that the receipt is stamped with those initials to confirm it is a staff discount purchase.

5.   Statutory rights for the purchaser are not affected, but in the event of any claim arising in relation to the goods sold, and a refund or payment, that shall not exceed the discounted price that the staff member paid.

6.   These arrangements will be reviewed periodically. Misuse of them may amount to gross misconduct and lead to dismissal.

4 Dockets

1

Name	Item	Approver	Price
Lorraine Lamont	Elix Hairdryer	N Upminster	£90

2

Name	Item	Approver	Price
Lorraine Lamont	Rivenchy perfume	M Travis	£48

3

Name	Item	Approver	Price
Lorraine Lamont	Chippy Sunglasses	L Beechcroft	£35

5 Price tickets

1.

   Item – Elix hairdryer

   Price £45 SD

   Date – 3 Jan

2

   Item – Rivenchy perfume

   Price £25 SD

   Date – 6 Feb

3.

   Item – Chippy Sunglasses

   Price – £17.50 SD

   Date – 22 Mar

6 Price tags

1.   **Item – Mior sunglasses**

   Price – £220

2.   **Item – Chippy sunglasses**

   Price – £35

3.   **Item – Heaven scent perfume**

   Price – £100

7 Extract from spreadsheet

Date	Name	Approver	Full price	Description, department
6 Jan	LL	LB	£90	Hairdryer, elec goods
13 Jan	MT	LL	£95	Silk scarf, female fashion
3 Feb	LL	LB	£80	Perfume, perfume
4 Feb	LB	NU	£75	Golf club, sports
15 Mar	NU	LB	£110	Table lamp, lighting
18 Mar	NU	MT	£240	DVD player, elec goods
22 Mar	LL	LB	£220	Sunglasses, female fash
22 Mar	LB	NU	£100	Perfume, perfume
23 Mar	NU	LB	£225	Jacket, male fashion
Total			£1,265	

8 Letter to Linda Beechcroft

3 June 2019

Dear Linda

You are required to attend a disciplinary hearing at our office in High Street, Lontwon on 8 June 2019 at 11am. I attach a copy of the investigation report I have prepared and the documents referred to there.

It is alleged that you have been guilty of dishonesty in misuse of the staff discount system, as set out more fully there. No decision will be taken until after the meeting but I must warn you that if the allegations are established, that may amount to gross misconduct, and one outcome may be your summary dismissal.

You have the right to be accompanied by a fellow employee, or trade union representative, at the meeting. You may produce documents, or call witnesses which you must arrange yourself. If you have any question about the meeting or these arrangements please contact me immediately.

In the meantime I confirm that you are suspended on full pay. This is not a disciplinary sanction and does not imply guilt. You should not attend for work or speak to any employee, customer or supplier except with my prior written approval.

Yours sincerely
Angela Adams
HR Assistant

9 Notes of disciplinary hearing on 8 June 2019

Present:

Francis Faulds (FF)

Linda Beechcroft (LB)

Karen Kay (Note taker)

FF started the meeting by reminding LB that this was a disciplinary meeting, and that KK would take a note of it. LB was happy to continue. She was reminded of her right to be accompanied but said that she had not been able to have anyone attend with her.

FF asked LB if she had read the letter calling her to the meeting, the disciplinary policy, the staff discount policy, and the investigation report. She confirmed that she had.

She asked LB about the purchases of two items by her one of which had not been approved by someone in the department selling them. LB confirmed that she had made the purchases. She said that she thought that the approvals had been in accordance with the policy. She was asked why Neil Upminster (NU) had approved the purchase of perfume, when he did not work in that department, and she said that he might have done to cover for someone on holiday or off ill. She was then asked if she had anything else to add about those two items, and said no.

She was asked about the price paid for the perfume. She said that she thought that she had paid the right price. She confirmed that AA had shown her the docket and ticket during the investigation meeting, and she had not commented at that time.

FF asked about the purchase of sunglasses by Lorraine Lamont (LL). She said that she had no recollection of that. She was shown the staff discount docket signed by LB. She confirmed that that was her signature. She was shown the ticket for the sunglasses, and accepted that that was for the higher priced item, not the lower priced item from the docket. She was asked to give an explanation. She said that she could not remember the transaction, but can only have made a mistake. She had worked in a busy department, and there were times when customers were waiting. She had never acted in a dishonest way, and was very upset that she was accused of that. She had worked for the company for over five years, and had never had any question raised about her performance, and the allegations had made her feel sick.

At this point she became emotional and upset, and FF decided to have a five minute break.

When the meeting resumed, FF asked LB if she wished to make any further comment. She said that she had seen the statement about what LL had said, and that it wasn't true. She and LL had fallen out previously. It was just a lie.

She added that LL may have come to her with the sunglasses when she was busy in her own department, looking after customers which needed to be given priority, and then may have taken advantage of that.

FF asked if there was anything else that she wished him to take into account. She said no. FF then said that he would consider everything and issue a decision in writing.

10 Letter of dismissal

9 June 2019

Dear Linda

I refer to our meeting yesterday, and now attach the minutes of that. Please check them and confirm whether you wish to propose any changes.

I considered all that you said, and looked at all of the documentation. Having done so, and considered all of the evidence, I confirmed after the meeting that I had come to the belief that you did act dishonestly in your use of the staff discount scheme, both for a purchase that you made yourself, and in your facilitation of purchases by other staff for items which were not properly paid for.

I have taken into account that there were at least three occasions on which you breached the policy, once when you made a purchase of perfume at the wrong, and lower than appropriate, price, once when Mr Upminster did, and finally when Ms Lamont purchased sunglasses at a price far below the appropriate sum, at the lower price with discount. That was supported by the evidence from Lorraine Lamont that you had been part of a group involved in a scheme that had the effect of defrauding the company. I also took into account that the tip off named you as a member of the group involved in the dishonest scheme, and that other members of that group who had been named did not dispute that and resigned immediately. I did not have before me the dockets and receipts for your purchase of perfume, but they had been seen by Angela when she prepared the spreadsheet, an extract of which I did have, which she raised with you when she met you on 1 June 2019 and which you did not challenge. You did not challenge matters at the disciplinary hearing.

I consider that this is all evidence of your involvement in that scheme, which defrauded the company.

I have taken account of your length of service and good record up to now, but I have concluded that dismissal is the correct penalty. The company takes such dishonesty seriously. It completely undermines trust and confidence in our staff. It threatens the continuation of a staff discount policy where it is misused.

You are therefore dismissed with immediate effect. Your employment ends today, 9 June 2019. You will be paid wages up to that date, any accrued holiday pay that you are entitled to, and any expenses outstanding, but the company reserves the right to take action against you for the losses that it has incurred by your dishonesty. Your P45 will follow separately, and you will also have sent to you details about your pension options.

You have the right of appeal against the decision, and if so please reply within five working days setting out your reasons.

Yours sincerely
Francis Faulds
Deputy Store Manager

11 Letter of appeal

14 June 2019

Dear Francis

I write to appeal your unjust decision to dismiss me. I have not been dishonest. At worst I made a genuine mistake. I have been a loyal and trustworthy employee, and the evidence used against me included false claims by someone out to harm me.

I strenuously deny the allegations made, and look forward to having details of the appeal hearing.

Yours sincerely

12 Notes of appeal hearing held on 28 June 2019

Present

Gillian Grant (GG)

Karen Kay (Note taker)

Linda Beechcroft (LB)

GG opened the meeting by asking LB to elaborate on her points for the appeal.

LB said that she had been unjustly accused. She had explained what had happened at the disciplinary hearing and could not imagine how she had not been believed. She had purchased perfume, and had asked another member of staff to approve that. She did not remember the detail but knew from the form that it was Neil Upminster. He could have been working at the perfume counter when it was sold, covering for someone off ill or on holiday. She assumed that that meant that the approval was appropriate. It had so far as she was aware been bought at the right price. The docket and ticket had not been produced. The purchase of the golf club was in accordance with the policy.

She was not part of any group which was misusing the staff discount scheme. If there had been, the police would have been called. They were not.

Ms Lamont (LL) had originally been one of her friends, but they had fallen out over a personal matter. Ever since, she had been out to do her down. She had stopped speaking to her at work, and in effect sent her to coventry. She encouraged others to treat her similarly. She was a nasty piece of work, and may well have been dishonest herself but that did not mean that LB was.

GG asked what had been the cause of that falling out. LB said that LL had been very disrespectful about her mother when she had been in the store, saying in a post that she was over 60 when she was 51, and implying that she was mutton dressed as lamb. After that post, LB had spoken to her to challenge her about it, and LB had refused to say anything except 'Sticks and stones'. LB then showed GG a message on her mobile phone, from LL to her on 18 January 2019. It said 'You will regret this. What goes around comes around'. LB said that that had been sent after she had challenged LL. She did not know what was meant at the time, but now does. LL was trying to get revenge by blaming her for what happened, and getting her dismissed.

LB said that she could not remember her approving the purchase of sunglasses by LL. She thought that LL may have targeted her when she was busy in her own department with customers. LB confirmed that she had not worked in female fashion. She said that she probably just signed the form when LL asked her, without any particular check, as she did not have the time to do any more and did not wish to cause any scene with her in the shop in front of customers.

LB asked GG to review the case independently, and said that if she did it would be obvious that LB was not guilty of any dishonesty, just of not applying the staff discount scheme precisely. She had not been trained on the scheme, it had just been issued to her when she started. Until the investigation she had not been aware that it would be enforced so rigorously. If she had been aware of that she would have been more careful to ask where each person worked before seeking approval for a purchase, and would have scrutinised very carefully what was being purchased against the staff discount form she was being asked to approve herself. She did not think it fair that she had been singled out for this treatment, and thought that many other staff will have acted exactly in the same way as she did. It would not be consistent to treat others one way, and her another way.

GG asked if LB wanted to say any more, and LB said that she did not. GG asked her if the minutes of the disciplinary hearing were accurate, and LB confirmed that as far as she could remember they were. GG thanked her for attending, and confirmed that she would issue a decision later in writing.

13 Letter of decision on appeal

3 July 2019

Dear Linda

Appeal against dismissal

Thank you for attending the meeting with me on 28 June 201i9 to discuss the appeal. I have considered very carefully all that you said. I have also spoken further with Angela Adams about some of the issues that you raised. Angela informed me that there was no evidence she found from her investigation that any other staff had not accurately followed the staff discount scheme. She also said that when new members of staff start with the company there is an induction process where the staff discount scheme is introduced, and explained.

She said that Neil Upminster who had approved your purchase of perfume worked in another department, sports, and it was very unlikely indeed that he would have been near the perfume department at the time you purchased them. She found no evidence of his ever working in that department.

The evidence is clear that on three occasions you acted in breach of the staff discount policy. When you purchased that perfume you did not have the correct approval. When you approved another purchase you did not work in the department to do so. Crucially however you approved a purchase of sunglasses at under value by Ms Lamont, when you did not work in the department to do so. Not only is that a third breach of policy, but there is clear evidence of the amount of the discount being on the lower and wrong price, not that for the sunglasses involved.

I accepted what Angela told me about the documents she had seen which then disappeared from her desk. She showed those to you at the investigation meeting, and you did not at that stage dispute them.

You showed me a text from Lorraine Lamont, but I do not consider that that has any relevance. It was very vague indeed. It proves nothing, I believe, and it certainly does not establish that she was motivated to try to set you up as you now claim.

I have also taken account of the allegation made in the tip-off that four people, one of which was you, were involved in dishonest activity described as a scam, and that one of them, Ms Lamont, alleged that you were involved. Taking account of all that was before me, I believe that you have been involved in dishonesty.

I consider that there is evidence of a pattern of behaviour from which it is reasonable to believe that you were involved in attempts to defraud the company by deliberate misuse of the staff discount scheme, and I am satisfied that it was the correct decision to dismiss you from the company's employment because of that.

I therefore refuse your appeal. That concludes the internal disciplinary process.

Yours sincerely
Gillian Grant
Store Manager

14 Claim Form – paper apart (giving reasons for claim)

I was dismissed for allegedly defrauding the company by misuse of the staff discount scheme. I was not dishonest. I did not make any financial gain. I was unjustly accused by a colleague out to discredit me after we had had a personal disagreement. No reasonable employer would have dismissed an employee with good service in the circumstances. The decision was unfair.

I appealed the decision to dismiss me. The appeal sought further information. I was not given an opportunity to comment on the outcome of that.

I was unfairly dismissed. No reasonable employer would have believed that I had been guilty of dishonesty. It was outside the band of reasonable responses to dismiss me. I had five years of service, with no disciplinary record of any kind.

The decision to dismiss me summarily was a breach of contract. I seek notice pay for the period of three months that was due to me under my contract of employment.

15 Response Form – paper apart (giving reasons for defending claim)

The claimant was dismissed as the respondent believed that she had been guilty of fraudulent misuse of the staff discount scheme. The reason for dismissal was her conduct. Conduct is a potentially fair reason for dismissal.

The dismissal was procedurally and substantively fair. There was a belief in dishonesty, which was based on a reasonable investigation. The claimant had purchased perfume under the staff discount scheme which was not authorised by an appropriate person under it. She approved purchases of goods by other staff when it was not appropriate for her to do so. The purchase of one item, a pair of sunglasses, was approved by her at a price substantially less than the appropriate price. The evidence as a whole, including evidence from one person that the claimant was involved in a dishonest scheme, was sufficient for a reasonable employer to believe that the claimant was involved in that scheme.

The decision to dismiss was within the range of penalties open to a reasonable employer. It was not unfair.

In the event that there was any procedural failure, there would have been a fair dismissal with a different procedure and no award should be made.

Separately, the claimant contributed to her dismissal to the extent of 100%, and no basic award or compensatory award should be made as each should be reduced to nil.

The claimant was summarily dismissed in accordance with the terms of the contract of employment. There was no breach of it. The claimant was guilty of repudiatory conduct and the respondent was entitled to accept that repudiation and terminate the contract.

Separately, the respondent makes an employer's contract claim against the claimant for its losses occasioned by her own breach of contract. It was an implied term of the contract that the claimant would apply the staff discount scheme honestly. She did not. She defrauded the company by her own purchase of items, and by facilitation the purchase of items by others which she purported

Appendix

to approve. The respondent reasonably estimates its losses at £1,000. It is making further enquiries into the dishonesty of the claimant and the extent of losses and reserves the right to increase that sum on receipt of additional evidence.

16 Schedule of Loss

EMPLOYMENT TRIBUNAL, LONTOWN
Case No: 123456/2019

Ms Linda Beechcroft, Claimant

v

VHS Ltd, Respondent

SCHEDULE OF LOSS

Claimant's net monthly wage – £1,800

Pension (10%)	£180
Staff discount	£20
Total income per month	£2,00
Equivalent per week -	£461.54

Age at dismissal – 25
Length of service – 5 years

(a)   Unfair dismissal

Basic award
£461.54 v 5 =   £2,307.70

Compensatory award

(a) Past loss
    Weeks from dismissal to Final Hearing –
    36 × £461.54 =   £16,615.44
(b) Future loss
    Capped at a further16 weeks ×   £461.54 = £7,384.64
(c) Loss of statutory rights -   £500
    Total -   £24,500.08
    Total award for unfair dismissal   **£26,807.78**

Breach of contract

Net monthly income £2,000 (set out above)
Damages for notice period = £2,000 × 3 months =   **£6,000**
TOTAL   **£32,807.78**

Note

The claimant applied for over twenty positions in retail stores following the dismissal. She received five letters of rejection which are attached. She continues to search for employment, including by searching online websites, attending at the Job Centre and reading newspapers.

She has received benefits since the dismissal, and continues to do so.

17 Statement of Agreed Facts

EMPLOYMENT TRIBUNAL, LONTOWN
Case No: 123456/2019

Ms Linda Beechcroft, Claimant

v

VHS Ltd, Respondent

STATEMENT OF AGREED FACTS

1. The claimant's contract of employment with the respondent contained the following provision:

    '13 Termination

    After four years of continuous service you shall be entitled to notice of termination of three months, unless the contract is terminated on account of any repudiatory conduct by you, in which case it may be terminated summarily (without notice, and without any accrued but untaken holiday pay beyond that to which you are entitled under the Working Time Regulations 1998)'

2. The respondent operated a non-contractual disciplinary policy which had the following provisions:

    'If any allegations are made against an employee they shall be investigated fully and fairly. No disciplinary action shall be taken without the employee having a full opportunity to respond to the allegations, including leading any evidence…….

    If there is an allegation of gross misconduct, or other circumstances where suspension would be reasonable, the employee may be suspended with pay or, in exceptional circumstances where there is strong prima facie evidence of dishonesty, without pay, pending completion of the investigation. Any suspension does not constitute a disciplinary penalty and does not imply guilt……..

    No decision on any disciplinary allegation shall be made until there has been a full and fair investigation, and the employee has a reasonable opportunity to respond to the allegations made, including if he or she wishes leading evidence. The employee may also be accompanied at any disciplinary hearing by a fellow employee or appropriate trade union representative.

An employee whose conduct is considered to amount to gross misconduct may be summarily dismissed. The list of gross misconduct offences includes, but is not limited to............dishonesty.

Any written warning, or dismissal, may be the subject of an appeal by the employee. The appeal shall be heard by an independent manager at a higher level than the person who decided on the initial penalty. On hearing the appeal, the disciplinary sanction can be quashed, varied or confirmed.'

18 Bundle of documents

EMPLOYMENT TRIBUNAL, LONTOWN
Case No: 123456/2019

Ms Linda Beechcroft, Claimant
V
SHV Ltd, Respondent

INDEX

Page number

19 First draft submission for claimant

(a)   Unfair dismissal

Has employer proved conduct as reason?

Section 98(4) of the Employment Rights Act 1996 – test is of reasonableness having regard to size and resources. Respondent is major retailer with huge resources.

No proper training in use of scheme
No evidence of dishonest intent
No investigation of explanation regarding LB
No witness statements from others
Not all dockets and receipts used for spreadsheet
Not considered with open mind.
Not reasonable belief in guilt
For appeal – no chance to comment on additional information obtained.
NU could have provided cover. No attempt to investigate that further
Simple mistakes were made, but everyone does that. There was no investigation into that. The decision was inconsistent with the treatment of others.

(b)   Breach of contract

There was a breach of contract. LB was not guilty of dishonesty. The test is the balance of probabilities. Onus on respondent. There is no real evidence.

(c)   Remedy

LB was paid £300 net per week. She has tried to get another job but without success. She has been off work for six months, and likely to be off for about another six months. Pay included pension worth 12% of salary, and the staff discount scheme which on average was worth another £30 per month.

LB should have a basic award for unfair dismissal, and a compensatory award of the maximum of one year's pay.

She should also have an award for three month's notice for breach of contract.

Schedule of loss accurate. [Check that we have all vouching]

Issues

1.   What was the reason for dismissal?

2.   If potentially fair was it so under s.98(4) and in particular –

   (i)   Was there belief in guilt?

159

(ii)   Had there been a reasonable investigation?

(iii) Was the belief reasonably held?

(iv)   Were the procedures followed fair having regard to the ACAS Code of Practice?

(v)   Was the penalty of dismissal within the range of reasonable responses?

20 First draft submission for respondent

(a)   Unfair dismissal

For employer to prove reason.

The reason was conduct – potentially fair – sections 98(1) and (2) Employment Rights Act 1996 (ERA).

Fairness – s 98(4) ERA

Burchell test

No onus of proof on either party

ACAS Code of Practice

There was an investigation, disciplinary hearing and appeal. Fair procedure was followed.

Range of reasonable responses test – Iceland Frozen Foods. Not for Tribunal to substitute its decision for that of employer.

Ample evidence to establish reasonable belief – breach of policy in three respects, two issues of wrong price used, perfume and sunglasses, LB involved both as buyer and approver, LL statement to AA, anonymous tip, others resigned.

Spreadsheet was prepared, some documents not available in suspicious circumstances, but put to LB at interview.

There was a reasonable investigation and a belief that was reasonable in all the circumstances. Note that LB said very little at the time. Focus is on what was before FF.

Penalty was within range of reasonable responses

In any event, Polkey deduction as dismissal inevitable – 100%

Contribution by claimant – 100%

Note – we have onus of proof on contribution

(b)   Breach of contract

Evidence of guilt on balance of probabilities – same evidence as for unfair dismissal.

Counterclaim for losses – £1,000 at present. [Should we investigate further?]

(c) Remedy

Net earnings £1,800 per month, plus pension of 12%. Nothing for staff discount as it was abused.

No sufficient attempt at mitigation. Loss should only be for four weeks [note – our emphasis]

For breach of contract – no mitigation and again only four weeks at most should be awarded

Employer's contract claim – loss from underpayment by using wrong prices. Little loss at present, but more likely if we investigate more fully. Seek say £500.

(d) Costs/expenses

Pursuit of this claim, and defending the counterclaim, is wholly unreasonable. Should we seek our costs (legal expenses) – suggest £10.000?

21 Chronology

(i)   Started 2 February 2104

(ii)   1 June 2019 tip off

(iii)   Investigation meetings that day

(iv)   Claimant suspended 1 June 2019

(v)   By 2 June 2019 perfume documentation missing

(vi)   2 June 2019 investigation report

(vii)   3 June 2019 letter calling disciplinary hearing

(viii) 8 June 2019 disciplinary hearing

(ix)   9 June 2019 letter of dismissal

(x)   14 June 2019 letter of appeal

(xi)   28 June 2019 appeal hearing, claimant produced text dated 18 January 2019

(xii)   3 July 2019 letter of appeal outcome

22 Questions for FF in examination-in-chief

1.   What is your name?[1]

2.   Where do you work?

3.   How long have you worked there?

4.   What is your role?

5.   What does that involve?

6.   What experience do you have of conducting disciplinary hearings?

7.   What was your relationship with the claimant Linda Burchell?

8.   How often did you come into contact with her?

9.   What is document 3?

10.   [Invite EJ to read][2]

11.   How was that communicated to employees?

12.   What was said about it at induction?

13.   What does it provide for in relation to the benefit that can be secured by the employee?

14.   How does the process in relation to that benefit work?

15.   Where is the female fashion department?

16.   Where is the electrical goods department?

17.   Where is the lighting department?

18.   Where is the cosmetics department?

19.   Where is the sports department?

20.   Which department did the claimant work in?

21.   Which department did MT work in?

22.   Which department did LS work in?

23.   Which department did NU work in?

24.   Can I now take you to some more of the documents in the bundle?[3]

25.   What is document 4 [for each of the documents have the witness explain what it is, and read out the relevant parts]?

---

1   Start with basics. It helps the witness settle in.
2   Reminder to you.
3   Use of a signpost.

26. What is document 5?

27. What is document 6?

28. What is document 7?

29. What is document 8?

30. What is document 9?

31. Please turn to the minutes of the meeting you held, document 10.

32. How accurate a record of that meeting is the minute?

33. What did LB say about each of the allegations against her? [read relevant sections]

34. What was your opinion of her answers?

35. What belief did you hold in relation to the allegations against LB?[4]

36. Please explain to the Judge what evidence was before you that led you to hold that belief.

37. After the meeting what did you do?

38. What did you consider the outcome should be?

39. Please explain to the Judge why that was.

40. What was your assessment of the seriousness of the finding of dishonesty?

41. Why did you decide on the penalty of dismissal?

42. To what extent did you take account of the claimant's responses?

43. To what extent did you take account of her length of service?

44. To what extent did you take account of her lack of any disciplinary record?

45. To what extent did you consider alternative outcomes other than dismissal?

46. What was the reason for the dismissal?

47. The claimant may allege that there had not been a reasonable investigation. What is your response to that?

48. It will I think be suggested that your decision was unfair. What is your response to that allegation?[5]

49. Can I refer you to the claimant's schedule of loss? [invite Judge to read]

---

4   This is the key question. Depending on the answer you may need to break the allegations down into individual issues.

5   It is not always necessary to ask this, but it does give the witness a chance to set out her position first, before the cross examination.

50.　We understand from it that the claimant has not yet found new employment. What is your view of the attempts that she has made to find new work?

51.　What do you consider would be a reasonable period of time to secure a new position in the circumstances?

52.　What level of pay would that position provide?

53.　How many jobs were there for someone in the claimant's role from the time of her dismissal to now?

54.　What is the extent of the current jobs market for those in her role?

55.　What evidence did you see that the claimant had not operated the staff discount scheme for her own purchases in a way that was appropriate under the scheme?

56.　What value do you consider to be reasonable to put on the scheme in light of that?

57.　Separately, Angela Adams conducted the investigation. What is her current status as an employee of the respondent?

58.　Why has she not been called as a witness in these proceedings?

59.　Finally, there is a claim for breach of contract.[6]

60.　Why did you terminate the contract with immediate effect?

61.　What was your assessment of the effect of dishonesty on the contract of employment?

62.　What effect did you consider that had on the trust and confidence you had in her as an employee?[7]

23 Questions for FF in cross-examination

1.　There is no written record made at the time of the tip-off is there?[8]

2.　There is no written record of when that was received?

3.　When the claimant attended the meeting before you, she said that she had not been dishonest?

6　Set out differently as the test in law is different.

7　Try if you can to finish on a strong point. This may not be the strongest point, but it is a logical place to end, and should be with a reasonably good answer.

8　Start strongly in cross examination, but with a question that the witness can only answer in a way favourable to your arguments.

4.   When she purchased the hairdryer, she paid the correct amount?[9]

5.   It was approved by someone in the electrical goods department?

6.   The purchase was in accordance with the exact terms of the policy?

7.   There is no evidence that the hairdryer purchased by LL and approved by LB was at an incorrect price is there?

7.   The second purchase LB made was perfume?

8.   The docket and price ticket for that were never before you

9.   It is possible that the approval was when NU worked in the perfume department temporarily?

10.   It is not a matter you ever properly investigated?

17.   Linda worked in the lighting part of the store didn't she?

18.   It is a busy department?

19.   The priority is to give attention to customers?[10]

20.   There can be a need to do work quickly because of that?

21.   If a staff discount form is presented to someone in that department, and there is a customer being served or waiting nearby, it is reasonable to process that quickly?

22.   It is inevitable that many staff discount forms were signed for by someone not from that department?

23.   Other staff must have done so as well as Linda?

24.   It is not dishonest?

25.   It is a technical failure to follow the rules of a scheme on which Linda was not formally trained?

26.   The person here who was dishonest was Lorraine Lamont?

27.   She benefitted from purchasing sunglasses at a lower cost than they should have been?

28.   She was the one who gained from that dishonesty?

29.   Linda had no personal gain from it at all?

30.   The disciplinary policy requires there to be a full and fair investigation?[11]

---

9   Focusing on the evidence that helps the claimant.
10   In preparing the question, think what follow up there might be if the answer was no.
11   It is also possible here to read out the terms of the policy itself, even if already looked at in examination in chief.

30. You did not enter the investigation with an open mind?

31. You did not conduct a full investigation?

32. You made no attempt to find evidence that might assist Linda?

33. You were proceeding on an assumption that she was guilty only because of what Lorraine had said?

34. Lorraine had fallen out with Linda?

35. Lorraine had a motive to lie because of that?

38. Yet you believed her, even though she was dishonest?

39. That is not reasonable?

40. No reasonable employer would have believed that Linda was guilty of dishonesty?

41. You jumped to a conclusion from what was in the report by Angela Adams?

42. You did not pay any attention to what Linda said at the disciplinary hearing?

43. If you had done, you would not have dismissed her?

44. The hearing was on 9 June 2019?

45. Your letter of dismissal was dated the same day?[12]

46. You did not consider matters properly at all?

40. The staff discount scheme is a benefit for employees?

41. £30 per month is a reasonable estimate of the value of that benefit?

42. You are still working?

43. You have not had to try and find new employment?

44. You are in no position to say how easy or difficult it was for Linda to seek new employment?

45. She has provided the 20 letters she sent and received to seek a new position?

46. There are very few jobs available now?

47. You have not produced any document to show a single vacancy have you?

---

12 Stick to facts. It is tempting to ask questions that draw conclusions, but that is best avoided as it lessens control over the witness.

46. It is reasonable to expect that it will take another six months to find a position?

47. Can I ask you about the claim for breach of contract? There is no evidence of her dishonesty is there?

48. Angela Adams has not given evidence?

49. Nor has Lorraine Lamont?

50. The truth is that you acted on the basis of suspicion from an anonymous tip off, from someone not identified, when what was said was never written down at the time?

51. You sought to rely on the purchase by Linda of perfume, but the documents about that are not before this Tribunal, and were not seen by you?

51. It was not reasonable to rely on something that the company itself had lost, was it?

52. The company has breached the contract of employment by not paying notice?

53. The truth is that Linda has not been dishonest?[13]

24 Questions for GG in examination-in-chief

1. What is your name?

2. Where do you work?

3. How long have you worked there?

4. What is your role?

5. What does that involve?

6. What experience do you have in disciplinary matters?

6. When were you first asked about the appeal against dismissal by Ms Burchell?

7. What information was provided to you?

8. What documents did you have [go through documents 3–12]?

9. Please turn to document 13?

---

13 End strongly.

10. To what extent are these minutes a reasonably accurate record of the meeting?

11. [Invite EJ to read]

11. What did you do after the meeting?

12. Who did you speak to?

13. What did she tell you?

14. What is the practice when an employee is undergoing induction?

15. What is said to them about the staff discount policy?

16. What view did you form about what AA told you?

12. What did you decide to do in light of the information you had?

13. Why did you consider that Ms Burchell had been dishonest?

14. Why did you consider that dismissal had been the correct penalty for that?

15. Please turn to document 14 – what is that?

16. [Invite EJ to read]

16. We have heard that Ms Burchell has not yet obtained employment. What is your evidence about that?

17. What time do you consider is reasonable to have expected her to obtain a new position?

18. Why is that?

19. How is the jobs market for those in her position?

20. What level of pay would she expect to receive?

25 Questions for GG in cross-examination

1. You were aware of the disciplinary policy requiring a full and fair investigation into allegations?

2. You must have noted that the decision was made on the same day as the hearing?

3. When the claimant attended the meeting before you, she said that she had not been dishonest?

4. When you made your own enquiries, you did not take the trouble to put them into writing did you?

5. At no stage did you give Linda an opportunity to comment on them?

6. That was not reasonable?

7. When she purchased the hairdryer, she paid the correct amount and had the correct approval?

8. That was exactly in accordance with the policy?

9. The purchase of perfume by Linda does not have the docket or ticket?

10. You did not see them?

11. Someone could work in a department temporarily to cover for someone else, couldn't they?

12. It is not something that you investigated?

13. Linda worked in the lighting department of the store didn't she?

18. It is a busy department?

19. The priority is to give attention to customers?

20. There can be a need to do work quickly because of that?

21. If a staff discount form is presented to someone in that department, and there is a customer being served or waiting nearby, it is reasonable to process that quickly?

22. It is inevitable that many staff discount forms were signed for by those not in the correct department?

23. Other staff must have done so as well as Linda?

24. It is not dishonest?

25. It is a technical failure to follow the rules of the scheme?

26. The person here who was dishonest was Lorraine Lamont?

27. She benefited from purchasing sunglasses at a lower cost than they should have been?

28. She gained from that dishonesty?

29. Not Linda?

30. Yet you believed LL's comment that Linda was involved despite that?

31. That was not reasonable?

32. Nor was it reasonable to rely on an anonymous tip off not even written down?

33. Nor was it reasonable to rely on the purchase of perfume where the docket and ticket are not able to be checked?

34. Lorraine had fallen out with Linda?

35. That gives her a motive to lie?

36. It was supported by the text that she showed you?

37. Any reasonable person would take that into account?

38. The only reasonable conclusion is that there was no basis to believe that Linda was guilty of dishonesty?

40. The staff discount scheme is a benefit for employees?

41. £8 per month is a reasonable estimate of the value of that benefit?

42. You are still working?

43. You have not had to try and find new employment?

44. You are in no position to say how easy or difficult it was for Linda to seek new employment?

45. She has provided the 20 letters she sent and received to seek a new position?

46. It is reasonable to expect that it will take another six months to find a position?

48. The company has breached the contract of employment by not giving her notice?

26 Questions for claimant in examination-in-chief

1. What is your name?

2. What is your address?

3. What is your date of birth?

4. When did you start working for the respondent?

5. What was your role?

6. Who did you report to?

7. What is document 3 (staff discount scheme)?

8. What if any training did you have on that staff discount scheme?

9.   How rarely was that mentioned by management in meetings?[14]

10.   When did you first learn of any concern over your use of it?

11.   What is document 5 (docket re golf club)?

12.   Who made that purchase?

13.   Who approved it?

14.   What department did he work in?

15.   To what extent is that purchase in breach of the staff discount policy?

16.   What is document 7 (docket re perfume)?

17.   Who purchased it?

18.   What do you recall of how that happened?

19.   When was the purchase made?

20.   To what extent did you see the docket and price at the investigation meeting?

21.   To what extent at the time did you consider that there was any failure to comply with the staff discount policy?

22.   Who is Lorraine Lamont?

23.   What was your relationship with her?

24.   When were you on good terms with her?

25.   When did that change?

26.   Why was that?

27.   How did that affect your relationship?

28.   What did she do?

29.   What effect did that have on you at that time?

30.   Can you go to the appeal minutes document 13?[15]

31.   What record is there of a text message being referred to in those minutes?

32.   Who sent the text message?

33.   What were the circumstances of that being received by you?

---

14   The usual phrase in everyday speech is 'how often' but 'rarely' emphasises the point you are trying to make.

15   A form of signpost.

34.   What did you do in response, if anything?

35.   What is document 8 (form for sunglasses)?

36.   Who approved that?

37.   In what circumstances did you do so?

38.   What do you recall of that matter now?

39.   What did you know about the item being purchased?

40.   What was in your mind at that stage?

41.   How busy was your department?

42.   What was the main priority for you when working there?

43.   What was said to you by managers about that?

44.   What was your reaction when you learned of the allegation that you had been dishonest?

45.   What happened at the investigation meeting?

46.   How short was it?

47.   You were later called to a disciplinary meeting. What documents did you have for that?

48.   What documents did you have about the alleged purchase of perfume?

49.   How short was that meeting?

50.   To what extent do you consider that your comments were taken into account?

51.   Why do you think that?

52.   What had your length of service been?

53.   What had been your record up to that point?

54.   What was your reaction when you read the dismissal letter document 10?[16]

55.   What is document 11 (appeal letter)?

56.   Look at document 12 (minutes of appeal). What discussion was there about there being more evidence to consider?

---

16 Only ask this question if you have checked in advance that the answer helps, ie that she will say that she was upset, or felt it unfair, not something to the effect that she was not surprised.

57.   To what extent did you consider that your comments were taken into account at that meeting?

58.   How short was that meeting?

59.   What was your reaction when you received document 13 (letter of appeal rejection)?

60.   If you had been given an opportunity to comment on the additional evidence referred to there in paragraph 3, what would you have said?

61.   What evidence in writing might exist in relation to what is said there?

62.   What efforts do you know the respondent made to find that evidence?

63.   What net pay did you receive from the respondent?

64.   What was the pension benefit that you received?

65.   What was the value of the staff discount scheme to you, on average?

66.   Can I now turn to the position after the dismissal. What attempts did you make to find alternative employment?[17]

67.   What is found in document 15 (letters of application to other companies)?

68.   What is your current employment situation?

69.   When did you start that job?

70.   How much are you paid?

71.   What does the attachments to document 14 show (current pay slips)?

72.   What do you consider is likely to be the period of time to find new and better paid employment?

73.   Please turn to document 14 itself. What is this (Schedule of Loss)?

74.   For the compensatory award, you are seeking the maximum of a year's pay. Why is that?

75.   For breach of contract, what income did you receive in the three months after dismissal?

76.   How has the monthly pay in the schedule of loss been calculated?

77.   To what extent do you believe that other staff acted as you did in approving or making purchases under the staff discount scheme?

78.   The respondent makes a counter claim. You purchased perfume. What price did you pay for that?

---

17   This is moving to proving losses, and attempts at mitigation.

79.   What do you say about whether that is the correct price or not?

80.   The respondent alleges that you were dishonest, and part of a scam to defraud them. What is your response to that?[18]

27 Questions for claimant in cross-examination

1.   Please turn to document 3, which is the staff discount scheme. You were provided with this document when you joined the company, isn't that correct?[19]

2.   You were also told about how it worked at induction?

3.   You did not ask any manager or HR for advice about it at any stage did you?

4.   The terms of the scheme are simple?

5.   On page 29 does it not state that approval is required from a member of staff of the department for the item being purchased?

6.   On page 30 does it not state that deliberate misuse of the scheme is gross misconduct and is liable to lead to summary dismissal?

7.   When you purchased perfume on 31 March the approval was by NU?

8.   He worked in the sports department?

9.   You knew that?

10.   You knew as you had purchased a golf club with him as the approver a little earlier?

11.   Perfume is not sold in the sports department?

12.   It is sold in the perfume department?

13.   You should have sought approval from someone in the perfume department?

14.   You did not?[20]

---

18 Trying to finish strongly.
19 Starting on the policy that is the foundation for the claim of gross misconduct.
20 These questions state the obvious but doing so helps to establish control.

15. Someone in the perfume department would be aware of the correct price for an item sold there?

16. Someone in the sports department would not know the correct price for an item sold in the perfume department?

17. Angela Adams showed you the docket for the purchase of perfume, and that had NU as approver didn't it?

18. Angela Adams also showed you the price ticket for the perfume you bought, at £100, and the price you paid with staff discount of £20 didn't she?

19. You did not try to dispute that at that stage did you?

20. You purchased the perfume at the wrong price, lower than was due?

21. In the extract from the spreadsheet document 4 there is an accurate summary of purchases by you and others in the alleged group of four staff?

22. It is an accurate document?

23. The documents for the perfume purchase were on AAs desk, she said in her investigation, but removed by someone. Did you remove them?

24. She spoke to the three other members of staff implicated?

25. One of them, LL said that you were involved?

26. The only reason she said that is because it is true?

27. The report refers to the approval by you of sunglasses bought by LL under the staff discount scheme?

28. The price for those was £220 but the price actually paid was with staff discount on the lower price of £35?

29. £17.50 was paid when it should have been £110?

30. That cost the company a loss of £92.50?

31. You approved that?

32. Your signature appears as approver on the document?

33. The true price is on document 4?

34. You did not work in female fashion?

35. You could not properly approve that purchase of sunglasses?

36. You did so, however, as part of the scam you were involved in?

37. You were dishonest in approving that purchase?

38. You knew that it was for the wrong price?

39. Each of the four of you implicated in the scam approved under-priced items for the other?

40. That is how your scam worked?

41. That is what the tip off said?

42. You said in your evidence earlier today that NU worked in the perfume department for a period to cover for another member of staff?[21]

43. Please turn to the minute of the disciplinary hearing document 10?[22]

44. You were aware that this was an important meeting?

45. You knew that it was to investigate allegations made against you?

46. You were telling the truth at that meeting?

47. You knew that you needed to give a complete explanation of what had happened?

48. This is an accurate record of the discussions isn't it?

49. You accepted that in the appeal hearing, is that not so?[23]

50. That is clear from the final paragraph of the appeal minute, document 12?

51. Nowhere in this minute did you say that NU worked in the perfume department for a period to cover for another member of staff, did you?

52. Nowhere do you comment on the purchase of the perfume by you?

53. You have only made this allegation in the hearing today?

54. You did not even make it in your Claim Form did you (document 1)?

55. You have made it up to try and bolster your claim?

56. The only argument you have put forward for the allegation by LL that you were part of the group not being correct is that you had fallen out with her?

57. You did not raise any formal or informal complaint or grievance about that at the time did you?

58. The minute records that you said almost nothing about that in the disciplinary hearing?

---

21 The prior inconsistent statement process of REP starting – this is repeating the earlier evidence to be challenged.

22 The explain phase.

23 In a sense you hope that the answer to the previous question was no, so that this point has added force, but this is starting the put phase.

59. Lorraine Lamont left the company's employment the same day as the issue was raised with her didn't she?

60. The other two members of the group NU and MT did so too?

61. They were all part of the group of four staff named in the anonymous tip off?

62. You were the other member named in that tip off?

63. It was reasonable for FF and GG to believe that you were guilty of dishonesty?

64. Your dishonesty was reasonably regarded as gross misconduct wasn't it?

65. You have not made reasonable attempts to get new employment?

66. You have been employed in the retail sector where there are lots of jobs

67. Companies in the sector have a high turnover of staff?

68. If you had sought a new job properly it would have started within four weeks?

69. You have deliberately not tried hard enough to find new work in order to maximise your claim before this Tribunal?

70. The only benefit you derived from the staff discount scheme was by abusing it?

71. You were dishonest in the way you applied the staff discount scheme for the transactions we have discussed?

72. You have been dishonest in the evidence to the Tribunal?

73. You defrauded the company?

74. You breached the contract you had with the company by doing so?

75. The company has lost sums because of that?

76. £500 is a reasonable estimate of the loss caused by your involvement in this dishonest scheme?[24]

28 Draft Final submission by respondent

This is a claim for unfair dismissal and breach of contract. The respondent has made a counter claim. I will invite the Tribunal to dismiss the Claim, and to make

---

24 Finishing on the counterclaim.

an award of £500 in favour of the respondent for its counterclaim. It was clearly within the band of reasonable responses for the claimant to be dismissed.[25]

I suggest that both witnesses for the respondent gave clear and candid evidence. They had no reason to do other than that. AA could not be present as she has left the respondent's employment and is travelling abroad.[26]

The law that applies to the case is not likely to be disputed. The respondent must prove the reason for dismissal. That is clearly conduct. Conduct is potentially a fair reason for dismissal under section 98(2) of the Employment Rights Act 1996. The test of fairness is then addressed under section 98(4).

The case law is clear that there is a range of reasonable responses open to the employer, and the Tribunal must not substitute its decision for that of the employer – *Iceland Frozen Foods Ltd v Jones*. The range also applies to all aspects of the procedure – *Sainsburys plc v Hitt*.

The first question is whether the respondent had a belief in the guilt of the claimant, and quite clearly it did. The second and third questions are related, and are whether there was a reasonable investigation, and whether the respondent had a reasonable belief as to guilt.

The evidence against the claimant was compelling.[27] She had herself breached the terms of the staff discount policy. It is very simple. It is very clear. It was given to her when she started and explained at induction. It is not the kind of policy that requires formal training, and no question about it was raised by the claimant at the time.

The tip off was adequately referred to in the written investigation report. By its nature it is not necessarily something that would be written down, and there is no requirement to do so. What Ms Adams did in her investigation was well within the band of reasonable responses.

It is clear that the claimant breached the terms of the staff discount policy in her purchase of perfume. I ask the tribunal to accept that the claimant was shown the docket and price ticket by AA at the investigation meeting. Those documents were not before the Tribunal as in very suspicious circumstances the evidence was, but by whom is not known. It was however referred to in the investigation meeting. The detail of the docket and price ticket was not challenged at the disciplinary hearing, where very little was said about that purchase. That is very surprising if the claimant did not accept the details about that in the investigation. The lack of comment speaks volumes. It is not even a point mentioned in the Claim Form. What the claimant has now done is to raise an entirely new point, that NU worked in the perfume department temporarily. But that too has not been raised before. It suggests a lie made up to try and cover up what had happened.

---

25 Setting out what you want.
26 Setting up the foundation of the argument, the tonic chord.
27 This is the basis of the argument why there was a fair dismissal. In a sense it is the dominant chord.

She and a group of three others used the system to their financial advantage. They approved purchases by each other when not entitled to, and in at the very least one case an item was purchased not using the correct price. That was the tip-off that was made, and of those against whom allegations were made three accepted that they were true, and left. That supports the truth of what was alleged.

The purchase of sunglasses which the claimant authorised is also highly significant. It is her signature on the staff discount form. She should not have done so. She did not work in the department. The docket she signed shows the lower price, for a cheaper brand. The actual purchase was for a far more expensive pair, and a different brand. That was an obvious and clear breach of the terms of the policy. There can hardly be more convincing evidence of her involvement in dishonesty than that.

That alone would have been sufficient to found a reasonable investigation and reasonable belief in guilt, but it was supported by two pieces of evidence I have already mentioned. There was the anonymous tip off. The evidence has demonstrated that what was claimed in it was correct. There was also the purchase by the claimant of perfume approved wrongly by NU.

There was in addition support for the belief in guilt from the comment by Lorraine Lamont when asked about the matter in the investigation interview. She accepted that there was a group, and named the three others. Two of them immediately left. The third person is the claimant. The evidence from LL supports the belief in guilt.

Taking the evidence as a whole as it was before the disciplining officer there is I submit more than sufficient evidence to establish a reasonable belief in the guilt of the claimant. The claimant said really very little of substance at the disciplinary hearing. She made no mention of some of the issues she now attempts to rely on.

The focus is on what was before the employer at the time of dismissal, and in the case of *Small* the court said:

'It is all too easy, even for an experienced ET, to slip into the substitution mindset. In conduct cases the claimant often comes to the ET with more evidence and with an understandable determination to clear his name and to prove to the ET that he is innocent of the charges made against him by his employer. He has lost his job in circumstances that may make it difficult for him to get another job. He may well gain the sympathy of the ET so that it is carried along the acquittal route and away from the real question – whether the employer acted fairly and reasonably in all the circumstances at the time of the dismissal.'

There was then an appeal by the claimant. That was handled entirely appropriately, and the very fact that further enquiries were made is evidence of it being conducted openly and fairly. The evidence supported the original findings.

The delay in the period up to this hearing has given the claimant an opportunity, now and having thought long and hard about it, to come up with an entirely new argument.

The claimant on the other hand has lied both to her employers, and the Tribunal (28). She has a motive to do that, as she is seeking an award from the Tribunal. Her dishonesty runs as a thread through the evidence at the time, up to the point of this hearing. The text she referred is ambiguous at the very least, and the kind of thing that might be said in any text message. It does not nearly amount to evidence that required a reasonable employer to believe only the claimant.

The claimant's lack of candour, her limited comments at the hearings that were held, and the new evidence she puts forward for the first time at this Tribunal, are clear indicators that she is neither credible nor reliable. That was most clearly demonstrated by her allegation about Mr Upminster working in her department, something not raised in the disciplinary process, nor even in the Claim Form. She made it up. She was dishonest, her evidence to the Tribunal is dishonest and the respondent was acting entirely reasonably in coming to the belief that they did.[28]

The penalty of dismissal is quite obviously one within the range of reasonable responses given that. There can be no serious argument to the contrary.

If there was any procedural flaw in the decision to dismiss, and I suggest that there was not, then the appeal cured that. The evidence was looked at carefully and independently. The claimant had an opportunity to comment on any matter that she wished to. Her new evidence was considered, but was nowhere near sufficient to lead to another conclusion. That was a decision well within the band of reasonable responses. I refer to *Taylor v OCS*.

There has been no breach of the ACAS Code of Practice.

I therefore submit that the claimant was not unfairly dismissed.

If the tribunal were not to be with me on that point, then I suggest that had there been a different procedure there would have been a fair dismissal, under reference to *AE Dayton Services Ltd v Polkey*.

Separately I suggest that the claimant contributed to her dismissal by 100%, and that no award should be made in light of that. I refer to sections 122(2) and 123 (7) of the 1996 Act.

If any award is to be considered, I suggest that the claimant has not mitigated her loss under section. She has not found a new post despite being experienced in retail, and despite the high turnover of staff that applies as spoken to by the respondent's witnesses. It would be reasonable to conclude that a new post, paying at least the same level of pay, should have been secured within four weeks.

In so far as the claim of breach of contract is concerned, I submit that it has been proved on the balance of probabilities that the claimant did act dishonestly.

---

28 This is the sub-dominant chord – why the claimant's position is wrong.

The evidence against her is the same as that I rely on above. The written record of the claimant approving the purchase of sunglasses at undervalue is compelling evidence. The claimant's own evidence is simply not credible for the reasons I have given. On the balance of probability she was part of a group that collectively acted to defraud the company. The precise amount by which she benefitted cannot be known with any accuracy, but the clear evidence was of participation in a scheme with others, and losses of at the very least £500 are likely to have been sustained. I therefore ask the Tribunal to award that amount by way of counterclaim.

In conclusion, I would invite the Tribunal to dismiss the claimant's Claim, and to make an award to the respondent for its own employer's contract claim. I ask the Tribunal that I be permitted to address it separately on costs {expenses in Scotland] after the Tribunal's decision has been issued.

Unless there is any matter on which I can assist the Tribunal, that concludes my submission.

Note – full citations to be given when making submission

29 Draft Final submission by claimant

I ask the Tribunal to find that there was an unfair dismissal, and a breach of contract by the respondent.[29]

The test for unfair dismissal is set out in section 98(4). In assessing reasonableness, all of the circumstances must be taken into account, as well as the size and resources of the respondent.

Despite the huge size and resources of the company this was a cursory investigation at best.[30] That is despite the terms of its own disciplinary policy requiring a full and fair investigation, and the terms of the ACAS Code of Practice.

The claimant was innocent of any wrong doing[31]. She explained what happened and why it did, and not believing her was entirely wrong. She did not act dishonestly. She did the best she could at a busy store. There was a lack of training, and it was obvious that there may be times when the staff discount policy might not operate as the words of the policy indicated, but that does not mean that there was any dishonesty.

The investigation and disciplinary process was conducted very unfairly.[32] The anonymous tip off said to have been received was not committed to writing, and

---

29 Setting out what you want.
30 The best argument put forward at the start, in a sense the tonic chord.
31 The basis of the argument for the claimant, and the dominant chord.
32 Starting the explanation of what is wrong with what the respondent did – the sub-dominant chord.

is not before either this tribunal, or before either FF or GG. The documentation concerning the purchase of perfume is not before this tribunal, or before FF or GG. Witness statements were not taken from the other persons spoken to initially. Three of those spoken to left very quickly. No proper attempt apparently was made to contact them again. The investigation was not a full and fair one. There was no attempt to find evidence to exculpate. It was only seeking to find the evidence to support allegations made.

The evidence of Lorraine Lamont, who certainly had been dishonest when purchasing sunglasses at undervalue, was believed. No reasonable employer would believe someone who acts in the dishonest manner that she clearly did. The evidence she gave to the investigation must be tainted by her own admitted dishonesty.

The evidence from LL implicating LB should therefore have been entirely discounted. So far as the two purchases by the claimant herself are concerned, one was approved by someone working in the correct department and the correct price was used. The other could easily have been made in the same situation, as the claimant suggested. The claimant did not have a fair opportunity to respond to it. A reasonable employer would not rely on that purchase of perfume in forming its belief in those circumstances.

What does that leave? Only one form, signed admittedly by the claimant, for when Ms Lamont in effect conned her way into buying more expensive sunglasses at a lower price. That was her dishonesty. It was not the dishonesty of the claimant. Again taking matters at their very worst for the claimant, she had not noticed the different price. But that is a mistake that is so easy to make in a busy department, where the priority is for the customers.

There was not therefore a reasonable investigation. The belief in dishonesty was not reasonably based. It was the result I suggest of a desire to act on allegations as if they must have been true. There was simply an assumption that the claimant had been part of a group abusing the staff discount scheme, and the evidence is clear that she did not. That is all in the context of no formal training on the scheme, and where it was liable to be treated in rather a loose way by staff in practice. Customers came first, for good reason, and it would not always be practicable to have someone in one department only approve a purchase. People did move around from time to time, as would be expected.

The conclusion can only be that there was not nearly sufficient evidence for a reasonable employer to believe that the claimant had been guilty of gross misconduct, and there was an inadequate investigation, disciplinary hearing, and appeal. By the appeal stage the claimant had produced further evidence to show why LL was implicating the claimant, but that was not considered sufficiently, and minds had been made up. The appeal cannot have cured the obvious unfairness of the dismissal. Collectively the failures were very substantial indeed. This cannot have been a fair dismissal.

So far as the claim for breach of contract is concerned, the position is even more clear. It is for the respondent to prove the breach by the claimant that is repudiatory such as to entitle summary termination. That is assessed on the balance of probabilities. It requires credible evidence. Insufficient evidence has been led to do so. In fact, there is no real evidence at all, rather a mixture of hearsay, supposition and guesswork. This is not a question of belief, but of proof. The simple fact is that there is no proof.

I therefore invite the tribunal to find that there was a wrongful dismissal in breach of contract.

Given the lack of adequate evidence I also suggest that no reasonable employer would have dismissed the claimant. Her involvement was minor at worst, and more an error than any direct action by her. She was not accused of negligence, but deliberately being dishonest.

I turn to the issue of remedy. There is no basis for any reduction to compensation. There was no possibility of a fair dismissal at any stage, regardless of procedure. Had there been a proper procedure, the inevitable outcome would have been the dismissal of the allegation that was made, which was of dishonesty.

There is no contribution, as there was no dishonesty. The claimant has never been alleged to have acted negligently or similarly in her operation of the staff discount scheme. She may have been deceived by LL, but she cannot be held at fault for not noticing what was happening given the circumstances.

The sums sought are accurately set out in the Schedule of Loss. They should include the benefit of the staff discount scheme, and the argument by the respondent about that shows the lengths to which they will go to try and do down the claimant. It is indicative of a mindset against her which has nothing to do with the evidence.

The level of compensation I suggest should be the statutory maximum of one year's pay. She has tried to find a new role, without success. It is likely to take at least another six months to do so. She has taken reasonable steps to mitigate her loss, and I would invite the Tribunal to disregard the evidence to the contrary from two witnesses who can hardly be described either as independent, or experienced in the finding of new employment. Although they claim that there are lots of vacancies, not one piece of written evidence of that has been produced.

In conclusion[33] I invite the Tribunal to find that the claimant was unfairly dismissed, and award the full basic and compensatory awards due to her, together with pay of three months as damages for the breach of contract, all as set out in the Schedule of Loss.

---

33 Repeating what has been asked for, going back to the tonic chord.

Appendix

30 Indicative decision of Tribunal

EMPLOYMENT TRIBUNAL, LONTOWN

Case No: 123456/2019
Final Hearing held at Lontown on 28 September 2019
Employment Judge J Smith

Ms Linda Beechcroft,	**Claimant**
1 High Street	<u>**Represented by**</u>
Anster	**Mrs A Beechcroft,**
AN10 IAA	**Mother**
Against	
VHS Limited	**Respondent**
I Paris Way	<u>**Represented by**</u>
Lontown	**Ms Ann Law**
LN2 2BB	**Trainee Solicitor**

JUDGMENT

1.	The respondent's summary termination of the contract of employment with the claimant was in breach of contract, and the claimant is awarded the sum of SIX THOUSAND POUNDS (£6,000.00) in damages against the respondent.

2.	The claimant's claim for unfair dismissal does not succeed and is dismissed.

3.	The respondent's counterclaim is dismissed.

REASONS

Introduction

1.	The claimant claimed that she had been unfairly and wrongfully dismissed by the respondent. The respondent denied doing so, and alleged that the claimant had herself been in breach of contract, and pursued a counterclaim.

2.	The claimant was represented by her mother. The respondent was represented by Ms Law. Neither had conducted an Employment Tribunal

Claim before, and both are to be commended for the manner in which they did so.

Evidence

3. Evidence was given for the respondents by Mr Faulds and Ms Good. Evidence was given by the claimant herself. The parties spoke to a Bundle of Documents which had been prepared in accordance with the Orders given in case management. It included a Statement of Agreed Facts.

Facts

4. The Tribunal found the following facts to have been established.

5. The claimant is Ms Linda Beechcroft.

6. She was employed as a sales assistant by the respondents from 2 February 2014.

7. The respondent is a major retailer with stores across the United Kingdom. It has about 12,000 staff.

8. The terms of her contract of employment included a provision on notice that entitled her to notice of three months after service of at least four years, unless the claimant was guilty of repudiatory conduct in which case the respondent was entitled to terminate the contract without giving notice.

9. The respondent had a disciplinary policy which included under the list of gross misconduct offences for which there could be summary dismissal 'dishonesty'. It required there to be a full and fair investigation of any allegations made.

10. The claimant worked at its store situated at 1 High Street, Lontown.

11. The store was situated on five floors.

12. The claimant worked in the lighting department.

13. The respondent operated a staff discount scheme, whereby staff could purchase items at one half of the price at which it was sold to the public. That was subject to conditions the material one of which was that any purchase required written approval by another member of staff working in the department that sold the item. Breach of the policy could amount to gross misconduct.

14. When the claimant joined the respondent she underwent induction at which there was a discussion on how the staff discount scheme operated.

15. Thereafter the claimant made no formal enquiry into that scheme with any of her managers or with HR.

16. At a time not given in evidence the claimant had a disagreement with Ms Lorraine Lamont, another sales assistant of the respondent.

17. Ms Lamont worked in the cosmetics department of the respondent, which was situated on the third floor.

18. On 1 June 2019 an anonymous tip off was received by the respondent on a whistleblowing hotline. It alleged that four members of staff were involved in an operation to defraud the respondent using the staff discount scheme to do so, being Ms Lamont, two other members of staff Mr Upminster and Mrs Travers, and the claimant.

19. Angela Adams of the respondent undertook an investigation into that on that day. She interviewed each of the four members of staff against whom allegations were made, including the claimant. The record of her doing so in her investigation report dated 2 June 2019 is a reasonably accurate record of her meeting with the claimant.

20. In the investigation Ms Lamont admitted that there had been a group involved, of which the claimant was a part. She accepted that she had purchased sunglasses at undervalue, but claimed to have worked overtime without pay in recompense. She resigned during the investigation meeting. Mr Upminster and Mrs Travers also resigned at their investigatory meetings, and did not deny the allegations made specifically.

21. The investigation undertaken by Ms Adams included the preparation of a spreadsheet identifying claims for discount made by those four members of staff.

22. It also included obtaining three staff discount forms which the claimant had signed.

23. One such form was dated 3 January 2019 by the claimant and related to the purchase of a hairdryer by her for the discounted sum of £45. It was purchased at the correct price and in accordance with the staff discount policy.

24. The second form was related to the purchase of perfume by the claimant for the discounted sum of £20. It was approved by Mr Upminster, who did not work in the perfume department and was not authorised under the

staff discount policy to approve that purchase. That form and related price ticket disappeared from Ms Adams desk on or around 2 June 2019.

25. The third form was for the purchase of sunglasses by Ms Lamont for the price of £35 without discount, being the price for the Chippy brand of sunglasses. Ms Lamont did not purchase that brand of sunglasses.

26. The receipt for the sale of the Mior brand of sunglasses Ms Lamont did purchase stated a sale price for it of £220, being the price without discount.

27. The price paid for the sunglasses was therefore underpaid by £92.50

28. The docket for the approval of the sunglasses by Ms Lamont at that undervalue had been approved by the claimant.

29. The sunglasses were sold from the female fashion department.

30. The claimant did not work in the female fashion department.

31. She did not have authority to approve the sale of the sunglasses under the scheme.

32. The claimant was suspended at the investigation meeting held with her, and on 3 June 2019 summoned by letter of that date to a disciplinary hearing. The letter had attached the investigation report by Ms Adams, and the attachments there set out. It warned the claimant that the outcome could be her summary dismissal if the allegations were upheld.

33. The claimant attended a disciplinary hearing with Mr Faulds on 8 June 2019. The minute of that meeting is a reasonably accurate record of it.

34. Mr Faulds dismissed the claimant summarily following that meeting. He set out his reasons for doing so in letter dated 9 June 2019.

35. The claimant appealed that decision by letter dated 14 June 2019.

36. The appeal was heard by Ms G Good, and the minute of their meeting dated 28 June 2019 is a reasonably accurate record of it.

37. Ms Good spoke to Ms Adams after the meeting, and thereafter confirmed by letter dated 3 July 2019 that the claimant's appeal was rejected.

38. The claimant's net pay with the respondent was £300 per week. She had employers' contribution to pension of £30 per week and a benefit from the staff discount scheme of £8 per week.

39. The claimant took reasonable steps to mitigate her loss after dismissal. She has not yet found employment, and it is likely to take her a further six months do do so. When she does, she will likely be paid no less than she had earned with the respondent.

Respondent's submission

40.   The following is a basic summary of the argument made. Ms Law argued that the reason for dismissal was conduct, that it was potentially fair, and that it was in the circumstances fair. She argued that there had been a belief in misconduct, based on a reasonable investigation and that it was reasonably held. She argued that there was a penalty imposed that was within the range of reasonable responses. If there was any unfairness, she said that that had been cured by the later appeal. She invited me to consider matters as they were known to the respondent at the time.

41.   She argued that the evidence was sufficient to show that it was likely that the claimant had been involved in dishonesty and that was a breach of contract. She invited me to dismiss the Claim, and make an award for the employer's contract claim.

Claimant's submission

42.   The following is also a basic summary of the submission made for the claimant. Mrs Beechcroft argued that her daughter had been unfairly dismissed. There had been no fair and adequate investigation, and the belief which she accepted was held was not reasonably held. Any reasonable employer would have conducted a fuller investigation, and that would have led to the conclusion that the claimant was not guilty of any offence.

43.   There had been evidence that there was a dispute with one of those involved in the matter, and that was sufficient to establish a motive for unjust accusations to be made.

44.   The whole basis of the dismissal was wrong, and that meant that the dismissal was unfair. The respondent had not proved on the balance of probability that the claimant had been in breach of contract. It was not a question of belief but of proof, and there was none.

45.   The claimant should therefore be awarded the basic award, and the maximum compensatory award for her. She had not contributed to dismissal, and had mitigated her loss.

46.   There was also a claim for one month's pay for notice for breach of contract, and the employer's contract claim was to be dismissed.

The law

(i) The reason

47.   It is for the Respondents to prove the reason for a dismissal under section 98 of the Employment Rights Act 1996 ('ERA'). The burden is on the employer.

48.   In *Abernethy v Mott Hay and Anderson* [1974] ICR 323, the following guidance was given by Lord Justice Cairns:

> 'A reason for the dismissal of an employee is a set of facts known to the employer, or it may be of beliefs held by him, which cause him to dismiss the employee.'

49.   These words were approved by the House of Lords in *W Devis & Sons Ltd v Atkins* [1977] AC 931. *In Beatt v Croydon Health Services NHS Trust* [2017] IRLR 748, Lord Justice Underhill observed that Lord Justice Cairns' precise wording was directed to the particular issue before that court, and it may not be perfectly apt in every case. However, he stated that the essential point is that the 'reason' for a dismissal connotes the factor or factors operating on the mind of the decision-maker which caused him or her to take that decision.

50.   If the reason proved by the employer is not one that is potentially fair under section 98(2) of the Act, the dismissal is unfair in law.

(ii) Fairness

51.   If the reason for dismissal is one that is potentially fair, the issue of whether it is fair or not is determined under section 98(4) of the Act and

> 'depends on whether in the circumstances.....the employer acted reasonably or unreasonably in treating [that reason] as a sufficient reason for dismissing the employee, and shall be determined in accordance with equity and the substantial merits of the case.'

52.   There is no onus on either party to prove fairness or unfairness under the terms of section 98(4). The onus under that part of the section is neutral.

53.   That section was examined by the Supreme Court in *Reilly v Sandwell Metropolitan Borough Council* [2018] UKSC 16. In particular the Supreme Court considered whether the test laid down in *BHS v Burchell* [1978] IRLR 379 remained applicable. Lord Wilson considered that no harm had been done to the application of the test in section 98(4) by the principles in that case, although it had not concerned that provision.

He concluded that the test was consistent with the statutory provision. Lady Hale concluded that that case was not the one to review that line of authority, and that Tribunals remained bound by it.

54.   The *Burchell* test remains authoritative guidance for cases of dismissal on the ground of conduct in circumstances such as the present. It has three elements

(i)   Did the respondent have in fact a belief as to conduct?

(ii)   Was that belief reasonable?

(iii)   Was it based on a reasonable investigation?

55.   It is supplemented by *Iceland Frozen Foods Ltd v Jones* [1982] ICR 432 which included the following summary:

'in judging the reasonableness of the employer's conduct an Industrial Tribunal must not substitute its decision as to what the right course to adopt for that of the employer;

'in many (though not all) cases there is a band of reasonable responses to the employee's conduct *within which one employer might reasonably take one view, another quite re*asonably take another;

'the function of the Industrial Tribunal, as an industrial jury, is to determine whether in the particular circumstances of each case the decision to dismiss the employee fell within the band of reasonable responses which a reasonable employer might have adopted. If the dismissal falls within the band the dismissal is fair: if the dismissal falls outside the band it is unfair.'

56.   The manner in which the Employment Tribunal should approach the determination of the fairness or otherwise of a dismissal under s 98(4) was considered and summarised by the Court of Appeal in *Tayeh v Barchester Healthcare* Ltd [2013] IRLR 387.

57.   Lord Bridge in *Polkey v AE Dayton* Services [1988] ICR 142, a House of Lords decision, said this after referring to the employer establishing potentially fair reasons for dismissal, including that of misconduct:

'in the case of misconduct, the employer will normally not act reasonably unless he investigates the complaint of misconduct fully and fairly and hears whatever the employee wishes to say in his defence or in explanation or mitigation.'

58.   The focus is on the evidence before the employer at the time of the decision to dismiss, rather than on the evidence before the Tribunal. In *London*

Ambulance Service v Small [2009] IRLR 563 Lord Justice Mummery in the Court of Appeal said this;

> 'It is all too easy, even for an experienced ET, to slip into the substitution mindset. In conduct cases the claimant often comes to the ET with more evidence and with an understandable determination to clear his name and to prove to the ET that he is innocent of the charges made against him by his employer. He has lost his job in circumstances that may make it difficult for him to get another job. He may well gain the sympathy of the ET so that it is carried along the acquittal route and away from the real question – whether the employer acted fairly and reasonably in all the circumstances at the time of the dismissal.'

59.   The band of reasonable responses has also been held in *Sainsburys plc v Hitt* [2003] IRLR 223 to apply to all aspects of the disciplinary procedure.

60.   The event of an appeal being heard, that can lead to a finding of a fair dismissal despite any earlier unfairness – *Taylor v OCS Group Ltd* [2006] IRLR 613.

61.   The Tribunal is required to have regard to the terms of the ACAS Code of Practice on Disciplinary and Grievance Procedures. It gives guidance on the procedure to follow when an employee is suspected of misconduct.

62.   A claim for breach of contract is determined according to the civil standard of the balance of probabilities. Where there is an entitlement to notice and the argument is that there has been a repudiatory breach of contract on the part of the employee that entitled the employer to treat that as entitling them to end it summarily, the onus of proving that there was a breach and that it was repudiatory falls on the employer.

Observations on the evidence

63.   I was satisfied that both Mr Francis and Ms Good were credible and reliable witnesses. They were candid in their answers, and accepted where appropriate points put to them in cross examination.

64.   For most of her evidence the claimant gave that evidence in a clear and appropriate manner, but there was one question which she did not answer directly, in relation to what was not in the Claim Form. That did cause me to doubt some aspects of the evidence she gave at the time, but on balance I have concluded that her evidence is generally to be accepted.

Discussion

65.   I was satisfied that the respondent had proved that the reason for the dismissal was conduct, and this was not in reality in dispute.

66.   The second question was the fairness or otherwise of the dismissal, and that falls to be considered against the test in *Burchell.* I was satisfied that the respondent did in fact have the belief in misconduct. The next question is whether that belief was reasonably held, and whether it was based on a reasonable investigation.

67.   This requires to be judged in light of what was before the employer at the time, and what steps a reasonable employer might have taken in such circumstances. As the *Jones* case makes clear, it is not for me to substitute my view for that of the employer. I do not consider what I would have done, but whether what the employer did falls within the range of responses open to a reasonable employer.

68.   It is certainly true that matters might have been handled rather better. There could have been further attempts to obtain evidence, but overall I consider that what was done did fall within the band of reasonable responses. Three members of staff against whom allegations made left employment abruptly. The evidence was not entirely compelling, but there was sufficient to entitle a reasonable employer to believe that the claimant had been involved in the staff discount scheme in a way not permitted by it, and that there had been an involvement by her in the misuse of it by another. The fact that an employee implicated her in the scheme to defraud the respondent is one factor. It is not conclusive, but it is relevant. That other employees implicated resigned in response, and were those implicated in the tip off, does not provide direct evidence against the claimant, but might lead a reasonable employer to believe in the accuracy of the overall allegation.

69.   The evidence against the claimant was that before Mr Faulds, and included her purchase of perfume, which Ms Adams had commented on in her report. That report explained that the docket and price ticket had been on her desk, but then removed. The person who did so has not been identified. Whilst Ms Adams did not give evidence I heard that she was travelling the world having resigned from the respondent. What was I considered important was the absence of any material comment about the perfume purchase by the claimant at the disciplinary hearing, although it had been mentioned in the investigation report. In particular there was no suggestion that Mr Upminster had been working temporarily in the perfume department. There was no other evidence to suggest that he had done so save that given by the claimant herself. That failure to challenge

what Ms Adams said in the report on that was I considered a relevant factor for a reasonable employer to have in mind.

70. Finally, there was the purchase of sunglasses at gross undervalue with the claimant's signature on the docket. Clearly that might have been in error on her part, or the claimant might have been targeted for the approval without her knowledge, but the question for me is whether the respondent was entitled to have regard to it as evidence that was part of the belief in dishonesty. I concluded that they were.

71. Whilst the evidence is far from the standard of proof beyond reasonable doubt it does not need to be either that, or (for this purpose at least) on a balance of probabilities. I consider that there is just enough that a reasonable employer might have dismissed. The procedure was overall a fair one, and there was I consider no breach of the ACAS Code of Practice. The penalty of dismissal was within the band of reasonable responses given the belief in what had occurred.

72. I also consider that the appeal was undertaken independently, and that there was nothing said in it that would question to a material extent the decision to dismiss. Again what I might have done is not relevant. The appeal officer was I consider entitled to come to the view that the additional evidence put forward, particularly the text message, was not sufficiently clear to exonerate the claimant.

73. I therefore have concluded that the dismissal was not unfair.

74. I turn to the claim for breach of contract. This is not assessed against the standard of belief, but whether or not the respondent has proved on a balance of probabilities that the claimant was in breach of contract which amounts to repudiation, in particular breach of an implied term of contract to act honestly. I have concluded that the evidence is not sufficient to do so.

75. The claimant was shown the documentation about her purchase of perfume at the investigation meeting. Those documents were then lost, or removed, but there is no evidence of the claimant having done so, indeed that would have been highly difficult as she was suspended at the time.

76. The evidence of the claimant not following the precise terms of the staff discount scheme is not irrelevant but does not itself prove her dishonesty. The spreadsheet produced by Ms Adams does not prove itself, nor does her claim in the report that the perfume purchase was at undervalue and not properly authorised. It is a form of hearsay evidence at best, which the claimant has not been able to respond to and challenge. I do not consider that of themselves these parts of the evidence amount to a great deal as proof that on the balance of probabilities the claimant was part of a fraudulent scheme as has been alleged.

77. The most telling evidence against the claimant is two-fold. The first element is the implication of her by her colleague, Ms Lamont. But that implication came from someone who was on their own admission being dishonest, and has not given evidence before me. I am not satisfied that it is sufficiently reliable evidence for this purpose. That concern is exacerbated by the terms of the text from her, which whilst vague and from an earlier point in time does indicate an animus against the claimant to an extent at least.

78. The second aspect is that the claimant approved the purchase of a much higher cost pair of sunglasses at a lower price. That was clearly wrong, and a breach of the procedure. But the claimant's explanation for it was one I regarded as credible. In a busy department I can entirely understand why it may not be clear which price was the correct one. Not without hesitation, I have considered that the claimant's explanation for her signature appearing on that docket is to be accepted on the basis she gave in evidence.

79. Taking all of the evidence as a whole, I have not been persuaded that the respondent has discharged the onus of proof upon it. There is certainly suspicion, and I consider as I have held above sufficient for a reasonable employer to hold the belief that there was dishonesty, but I do not consider that there is sufficient to hold that the respondent has proved that the claimant was, on the balance of probabilities, dishonest. To dismiss her without notice is accordingly in breach of contract.

80. The claim for damages is for the period of three months of notice provided for in the contract. I consider that the evidence is that the claimant did mitigate her loss for that period at the least. The loss I consider should include the value of the staff discount scheme. The loss sustained has been proved by the claimant.

81. The respondent having been found in breach of contract is not able to pursue its own claim for breach.

Conclusion

82. I have found that the claimant was wrongfully dismissed in breach of contract, and I have awarded her damages for her loss of three month's earnings.

83. I have dismissed the claim for unfair dismissal.

84. I have also dismissed the respondent's contract claim.

Index